Zanzibar Under Colonial Rule

EASTERN AFRICAN STUDIES

Zanzibar
Under Colonial Rule

Edited by

Abdul Sheriff
Professor of History
University of Dar es Salaam

&

Ed Ferguson
Associate Professor of History
Oregon State University

James Currey
LONDON

Heinemann Kenya
NAIROBI

Historical Association of Tanzania
DAR ES SALAAM

Ohio University Press
ATHENS

James Currey Ltd
54b Thornhill Square
Islington
London N1 1BE, England

Heinemann Kenya
Kijabe Street, PO Box 45314
Nairobi, Kenya

Historical Association of Tanzania
PO Box 35050, University of Dar es Salaam
Dar es Salaam, Tanzania

Ohio University Press
Scott Quadrangle
Athens, Ohio 45701, USA

Map by Almac

British Library Cataloguing in Publication Data

Zanzibar under colonial rule. - (Eastern Africa studies).
1. Tanzania. Zanzibar. Political events, history
I. Sheriff, Abdul   II. Ferguson, Ed   III. Series
967.81

ISBN 0-85255-080-4 (Paper)
ISBN 0-85255-081-2 (Cloth)

Library of Congress Cataloging-in-Publication Data

Zanzibar under colonial rule / edited by Abdul Sheriff & Ed Ferguson.
p.   cm. -- (Eastern African studies)
Includes bibliographical references (p.   ) and index.
ISBN 0-8214-0995-6 (cloth). -- ISBN 0-8214-0996-4 (pbk.)
1. Zanzibar--History. 2. Social conflict--Zanzibar. I. Sheriff,
Abdul. II. Ferguson, Ed.   III. Series: Eastern African studies
(London, England)
DT449.Z27Z36   1991   90-25407
                                                  CIP

ISBN 0-8214-0996-4 (Ohio U.P. Paper)
ISBN 0-8214-0995-6 (Ohio U.P. Cloth)

Typeset in 10/11pt Baskerville by Opus 43, Cumbria
Printed and Bound in Great Britain by Villiers Publications, London N6

Contents

Contributors

A. M. Babu — Former General Secretary of the Zanzibar Nationalist Party, leader of the Umma Party, and a Minister in the Union government for many years. Now a free-lance journalist in London.

Zinnat Bader (Ph.D., University of London) — Senior Lecturer in the Department of Sociology at the University of Nairobi.

B. D. Bowles (Ph.D., Makerere University) — Taught history at the University of Dar es Salaam, 1970—1976. Presently on the staff at the College of St. Mark and St. John, Plymouth, England.

Jacques Depelchin (Ph.D., Stanford University) — Taught history at the University of Dar es Salaam, 1975—1979, and Eduardo Mondlane University (Mozambique), 1980—1986. Now teaching in California.

Ed Ferguson (Ph.D., University of California, Los Angeles) — Taught history at the University of Dar es Salaam, 1973—1979, and Oregon State University, 1979—1991.

George Hadjivayanis (M.A., University of Dar es Salaam) — A member of the Department of Agriculture, Education and Extension at Sokoine University of Agriculture. Working on a Ph.D. degree from the University of Paris I, Pantheon-Sorbonne.

J. R. Mlahagwa (Ph.D., University of Dar es Salaam) — Senior Lecturer in History at the University of Dar es Salaam.

Abdul Sheriff (Ph.D., University of London) — Professor of History at the University of Dar es Salaam, where he has taught since 1969 and has served as Head of the Department of History.

A. J. Temu (Ph.D., University of Alberta) — Currently Professor and Head, Department of History, University of Swaziland, and formerly Head of Departments of History at the University of Dar es Salaam, and Ahmadu Bello University (Nigeria).

Illustrations

Illustrations

Acknowledgements for illustrations

Peabody Museum, Salem, for plates 1, 3, 4, 5, 24; Capital Art Studio, Zanzibar, for plates 2, 6, 19, 27, 31; the Zanzibar Archives for plates 9, 25, 33. The frontispiece and plate 30 come from *A Guide to Zanzibar*, Government Printer, Zanzibar, 1952. Plates 11 and 32 come from E. Younghusband, *Glimpses of East Africa and Zanzibar*, London, J. Long, 1910. Plates 20 and 21 come from *The Spice Mill*, December 1925, pp. 2543 and 2549. Plate 14 comes from *Independent Zanzibar*, Zanzibar, 1963, p. 29. The rest come from A. Sheriff's collection.

Preface

In the 1970s, as part of its effort to provide a series of interpretative textbooks on the history of East Africa, the Historical Association of Tanzania (HAT) organised a number of conferences for history teachers. The credit for initiating these gatherings on Tanzania (1974), Kenya (1975) and Zanzibar (1976) goes to Professor A.J. Temu, then Head of the History Department at the University of Dar es Salaam, and Chairperson of HAT.

The papers presented at the first conference were published as *Tanzania Under Colonial Rule* (1980), but the dispersal of academics from the University in the late 1970s hindered the preparation of papers for subsequent volumes. When the task of revising the Zanzibar manuscripts was completed in 1987, foreign exchange problems prevented immediate publication. That obstacle has now been overcome through a generous grant from the Royal Norwegian Ministry of Development Co-operation, to whom HAT and the editors would like to express their gratitude for making possible the publication of this book and its distribution in Tanzania. Earlier versions of Chapter 2 appeared in *African Economic History*, 18 (1989); Chapter 4 in *Maji-Maji*, No. 28 (November 1976); and Chapter 8 in *African Events*, March/April 1988.

We are deeply appreciative of the seminal role the University of Dar es Salaam has played in this project from its inception. Most of the contributors were teaching members of the University who were readily given leave of absence to do research in Zanzibar. The University Research and Publications Committee provided funds for the research and the Institute of Education, in collaboration with the Ministry of Education, financed the 1976 conference in Morogoro at which many secondary school teachers made valuable comments on the first drafts of the chapters.

Our thanks go to Fatma Maghimbi and Julia Bruce for typing the manuscripts.

Abdul Sheriff & Ed Ferguson

ix

Abdul Sheriff, Ed Ferguson, the Historical Association of Tanzania
and James Currey Publishers acknowledge the help of
the Royal Norwegian Ministry of Development Co-operation
in making an edition of this book available
in Tanzania

Introduction

A Materialist Approach to Zanzibar's History

ABDUL SHERIFF

Zanzibar, which consists of the islands of Unguja and Pemba, may be considered only a dot in the Indian Ocean. With an area of about 1,000 square miles and a population of half a million, it is indeed a small place. However, it is a territory with a long history which has evoked romantic notions far beyond its shores; more importantly, it has occupied a prominent place in the history of eastern Africa. There was a popular saying in Zanzibar during the nineteenth century that

> When one pipes in Zanzibar
> They dance on the lakes.[1]

But the tune that was being played was not one of political control, for the Sultan's sway did not extend beyond the narrow coastal belt even at the height of his power. Zanzibar did control the external trade of a large part of the region, but it must be remembered that, in the pre-capitalist period before the imposition of colonial rule, production of commodities for export to the outside world formed only a small proportion of the total production of East African societies. As a result of its political and economic pre-eminence at the coast, however, Zanzibar did develop as a seat of learning and a centre of Swahili culture, a fountainhead of Kiswahili and Islam from which the language and the religion were disseminated over a vast region of middle Africa. This is the enduring cultural contribution of Zanzibar to the history not only of East Africa but of humankind in general.

These aspects of the apparently more glorious pre-colonial history of Zanzibar have received a fair share of historical attention.[2] There is, however, a more urgent need to study the recent

1

history to understand that rare phenomenon in the process of African decolonisation, a revolution that broke out within a month of the achievement of political independence from British colonial rule in December 1963. The revolution laid bare in a few turbulent days the deep social contradictions engendered by Zanzibar's long history, colonial as well as pre-colonial. It provides an ideal case study of the process of class formation and class conflict, and of the essentially reactionary role of colonialism in hindering the maturation of social contradictions and so distorting the course of social change and development.

These were some of the considerations which led the Historical Association of Tanzania (HAT) and the History Department of the University of Dar es Salaam to commission an integrated series of historical studies of colonial Zanzibar for presentation to the annual HAT conference at Morogoro, Tanzania, in 1976. Unlike earlier HAT conferences on colonial Tanganyika (1974) and Kenya (1975), which largely aimed at providing a new interpretation based on existing secondary works, the Zanzibar project involved original research since so little work had been done on the colonial period.[3] However, the time and funds available to the researchers were limited, and the resources of the Zanzibar Archives for the colonial period were then incomplete.[4] What is being offered here, therefore, is the beginning or foretaste of a new generation of interpretative studies rather than a definitive history of colonial Zanzibar.

While the contributors have been able to uncover new evidence, what they consider more critical is their use of the method of historical materialism to produce the studies in this book. As Karl Marx pointed out, history cannot be reduced to the collection of 'self-explanatory' facts. To start with, facts are not 'given'; they are perceptions according to the specific philosophy of the observer, the recorder or the historian who select what each considers significant. It is therefore necessary for a historian to peel away the pulp built up by the interpretations of past observers and recorders in order to uncover the kernel of truth. This requires an understanding of the stated, or unstated, theoretical frameworks of those recorders. The task of the historian is then to interpret those truths, and this can be done consistently only through an explicit theory of social development.

Such a theory is not given, either. It evolves out of an analysis of concrete social realities. In analysing capitalist society, for example, Marx began by uncovering the fundamental nature of its most typical and very tangible product, a commodity. He showed that a commodity is not merely a physical entity but a product of complex social relations of production within a society at a particular level of its development. An iron hoe and a combine harvester are both agricultural implements; a spear and an atomic bomb are both tools of destruction; but they are products of vastly different social systems.

To understand a particular product or analyse a social system it is necessary to understand how production is organised since the production of the material means of subsistence is the fundamental prerequisite of all social existence. Production involves, in the first place, a relationship between humans and the natural environment adapted to their needs through labour and appropriated as their livelihood. Through this activity humans develop their skills and technology, in short the productive forces. Moreover, they interact not only with nature but with one another. They produce by cooperating, through division of labour and by entering into definite relations of production. The existing stage in the division of labour determines the relation between classes in society as regards ownership of the means of production and appropriation of the surplus. The two relationships – with nature and between humans – are not distinct and separate, but dialectically interrelated, so that every essential change in one brings about changes in the other. This articulated combination of the two aspects of social existence is called a mode of production in Marxist methodology. Of the two it is the relations of production that dominate in the combination: thus Marx defines epochs in human history not in terms of technological developments, such as the Stone Age or the Iron Age, important though these are, but in terms of dominant social relations, such as primitive communism, slavery, feudalism, capitalism and socialism.[5]

A mode of production, however, is a theoretical abstraction: it is a tool for analysis of a concrete social formation at a specific time in its historical development. In a formation that is constantly developing, or is in transition from one mode to another, elements of several modes may coexist. In Zanzibar during the period under consideration elements of communal and slave modes existed within an emerging colonial capitalist mode. Thus, while it is possible to speak about the Zanzibari social formation, it would be nonsensical to speak of a Zanzibari mode of production. The following chapters analyse the transition in Zanzibar from a slave mode to that of colonial capitalism as the social formation came under the sway of world-wide capitalism. The first object is to analyse the political economy of Zanzibar from 1873, when the abolition of the slave trade began to transform the production system, to 1963. This provides the basis for detailed examinations of

3

Introduction

the process of class formation in Part Two. A.M. Babu's chapter, a participant's view of the 1964 Revolution, explores the emerging social structure at a revealing moment of crisis and transformation.

Zanzibar in the nineteenth century was the seat of a vast commercial empire. Its economy was based partly on the production of cloves and coconuts on the islands themselves, using slave labour, and partly on the eastern African transit trade for which Zanzibar was almost the sole entrepôt.[6] In the opening chapter, Depelchin examines the transition from a slave mode of production dominated by merchant capital to a capitalist mode which nevertheless contained pre-capitalist elements. In abolishing slavery, he argues, the British had to ensure that colonial production was not impaired. They had to facilitate the flow of labour to the clove plantations. The former slaves and peasants became semi-proletarianised 'free' labour, while the former slave owners were transformed into capitalist farmers. But the latter rapidly fell into the clutches of moneylenders and merchants, and were reduced to little more than managers of their plantations. Only the intervention of the colonial state prevented the landlords from going under.

In Chapter Two, Ferguson studies the rise of colonial capitalism from 1915 to 1945. Unlike labourers under metropolitan capitalism, who are landless proletarians, the labour force in Zanzibar was not totally dispossessed of its land. Here it is illustrated how capitalists exploited labourers in the colonial setting through payment of a piece wage for work in the clove and copra sectors of the export economy. The overall analysis demonstrates how exploitation took place through the creation of surplus value by labour and its appropriation by capital in the Protectorate between the two world wars.

Amidst the deepening crisis of colonialism after World War II, as Bowles shows in Chapter Three, the ideology of nationalism could not mature. Every class had at one time or another come up against the might of the colonial state and been left with a grievance: the merchants in the 1930s when their grip on the economy was broken; the workers when their strikes in the 1940s were crushed; the peasants who recognised colonialism as the cause of their impoverishment and saw their leaders imprisoned after the cattle riots of 1951; and the landlords who saw their state dismantled at the end of the nineteenth century, realising belatedly that the colonial state and the Clove Growers' Association were not their protectors but instruments of colonial exploitation. These various conflicts had exposed a potential for class alliances, such as that between the workers and the peasants during the 1948 General Strike; and a broad nationalist alliance between the peasants, the landlords and the urban petty bourgeoisie towards the end of the colonial period. Nevertheless the deep social fissures, complicated by ethnic differences, prevented the emergence of a unified nationalist party. As Bowles puts it, the anti-colonial movement was overshadowed by class struggles just as independence itself was later to be eclipsed by revolution.

Following these three studies in the historical development of Zanzibar's political economy from 1870 to 1963, Sheriff's analysis of the Zanzibari peasantry in Chapter Four is the first of the detailed studies in class formation. Peasants were 'incomparably the cheapest instrument' for colonial agriculture, but the position of landlords and merchants, entrenched through their dominance in the nineteenth century, prevented the colonial authorities from concentrating their attention on the peasants. Lacking official support, peasants nevertheless began to emerge as a force in production after the abolition of slavery, initially as a reservoir of 'free' seasonal labour, and then also as small-scale producers. Under the impact of capitalism the peasantry, formerly homogeneous, began to break up into different strata. A small segment of 'rich' peasants emerged who were socially and politically influential, but they were prevented from becoming capitalist farmers by colonial super-exploitation. The self-sufficient 'middle' peasants were unstable and became impoverished; they were sinking to join the large mass of 'poor' peasantry that was becoming semi-proletarian. This created a class that was more volatile politically. When it split along class lines during the political struggles leading to independence the social contradictions became more clear-cut.

Mlahagwa and Temu show in Chapter Five that landlords performed an essential function in maintaining production and facilitating colonial administration. It is argued that the main-tenance of pre-capitalist relations of production was essential under imperialism to permit super-exploitation of the producers and production of cheap raw materials. The British, therefore, were prepared to rescue the landlords from the stranglehold of the moneylenders and merchants in the 1930s. But the commitment of the colonial state to the landlords was not absolute, particularly when that class appeared incapable of sustaining production. Realising this, the landlords had to organise themselves at both economic and political levels to prevent their demise, a futile attempt to reverse the course of history.

The commercial dimension of Zanzibar's economy is analysed by Bader in Chapter Six. She shows that while the social formation may have been coming under the domination of merchant capital during the nineteenth century, the merchants themselves were being subordinated and converted into agents of industrial capital. British dominance was expressed more decisively at the political level, turning both the Busaidi dynasty and the merchant class into allies and tools of British imperialism. When the landlords appeared to be faltering after the abolition of the slave trade and slavery, the merchants vied for primacy at the local level, particularly with the declaration of Zanzibar as a 'free port'. After the partition of the mainland, however, Zanzibar's entrepôt role diminished. The appropriation of the surplus by merchants and moneylenders appeared increasingly burdensome and a fetter to colonial production, particularly during the Depression. Forced to choose between a class which appropriated the surplus in the sphere of circulation and the landlords who organised production, the British had little difficulty in making their choice. They resolved to clip the wings of merchant capital. With their backs to the wall the merchants could only resort to their ultimate weapon – a boycott of Zanzibar cloves with the support of their Indian counterparts. This partially succeeded because of the dependence of Zanzibar's colonial economy on the world economy. The merchants won a reprieve, and a more modest share of the colonial cake.

The development of a working class in Zanzibar is examined by Hadjivayanis and Ferguson in Chapter Seven. Its size and revolutionary potential was limited by the nature of the colonial economy. The export-oriented agricultural economy produced a heterogeneous proletariat. A large proportion consisted of the semi-proletarianised poor peasants who seasonally went to pick cloves. Many of the permanently urbanised workers were concentrated in the service industries, as houseboys, casual construction workers, transport and dock workers. Industries developed very late and employed a minute portion of the working class. Among the workers the most advanced section consisted of the more skilled dockworkers who organised strikes in the 1940s. The colonial state moved quickly to establish its control over the trade unions and divert them towards economic demands exclusively. With the intensification of political struggles for independence the workers, numerically and ideologically weak, were rapidly harnessed to political parties largely led by different sections of the petty bourgeoisie. The workers were guided, it is argued, instead of being the vanguard of the political struggles.

In the next chapter Babu provides his analysis of the 1964 Revolution for the first time. As a former General Secretary of the Zanzibar Nationalist Party and a leader of the Umma Party, his is an account by one of the leading participants in the struggle. He

6

brings together the various threads of the struggle commencing with the 'Anthrax Revolt' or *Vita vya Ngombe* (Cattle Riot) of 1951, and surveys the changing balance of class forces within the political parties that culminated in the violent overthrow of the month-old independent government of Zanzibar in January 1964. Babu argues that although the revolution was 'a lumpen-proletarian affair', it was transformed into a revolutionary insurrection which heralded a new era in African politics.

One last word about the ethnic factor which has hitherto mesmerised social scientists and historians dealing with Zanzibar. Many of them have tended to adopt the racist ideology used by the colonial rulers to obscure class contradictions and misdirect class struggle. As Flint writes, 'the population was labelled by race, and race denoted function'.[7] Challenged by the Marxist method and the need for class analysis, some eclectic historians have taken a short cut by boldly asserting that Zanzibar society was 'divided into a number of exclusive classes differentiated mainly by race'.[8] But chapters in this volume demonstrate that classes cut across racial boundaries and political alignments. Bowles rightly argues in his chapter that ethnic identities are images people have of themselves or of others, and to use these skin-deep identities to analyse history is 'to write the history of images'.

Notes

1. L.W. Hollingsworth, *Zanzibar Under the Foreign Office, 1890–1913*, London, Macmillan, 1953, p. 6.
2. Such as R. Coupland, *East Africa and Its Invaders*, Oxford, Clarendon Press, 1938; R. Coupland, *The Exploitation of East Africa*, London, Faber and Faber, 1939; J. Gray, *History of Zanzibar*, London, Oxford University Press, 1962; and C.S. Nicholls, *The Swahili Coast*, London, Allen and Unwin, 1971.
3. The proceedings of the 1974 conference, edited for the Historical Association of Tanzania by M.H.Y. Kaniki, were published as *Tanzania Under Colonial Rule*, London, Longman, 1980.
4. A large proportion of government records were then scattered in various ministries, often in a very poor state of preservation. Most of these have since been transferred to the archives and catalogued.
5. For further discussion of the Marxist method and concepts see Bade Onimode, *An Introduction to Marxist Political Economy*, London, Zed Books, Ltd, 1985. For original texts see H. Selsam *et al.* (eds), *Dynamics of Social Change*, New York, International Publishers, 1970.
6. See A. Sheriff, *Slaves, Spices and Ivory in Zanzibar: Economic Integration of East*

Africa into the World Economy, London, James Currey, 1987.
7. J.F. Flint, 'Zanzibar, 1890–1950', in V. Harlow and E.M. Chilver, *History of East Africa*, Vol. II, Oxford, Clarendon Press, 1965, p. 651.
8. G.A. Akinola, 'The Sultanate of Zanzibar, 1870–1890', Ph.D. dissertation, University of London, 1973, pp. 42–43.

Part One

Political Economy
of Zanzibar

Zanzibar Stone Town

One

The Transition from Slavery
1873–1914

JACQUES DEPELCHIN

Introduction

The history of Zanzibar in the nineteenth century is essentially a history of the transition of a social formation in which a pre-capitalist mode of production gave way to the capitalist mode of production which nevertheless continued to contain pre-capitalist elements. It is a history of economic, political and ideological subjugation to expanding imperialism represented by British consuls and traders. The period under study, 1873–1914, is therefore only the culmination of the process of imperialist expansion beyond its geographical area of origin in capitalist Europe.

In studying this history, it is not enough to chronicle the various events which have occurred over time and fill in the gaps with a text. As Marx pointed out, history would not be a science if it were reduced to recording events as they happened. It is not sufficient to collect a series of facts and then assume that they will be self-explanatory. The historian must investigate what lies behind the events. That task will be carried out in this chapter within the theoretical and conceptual framework of historical materialism. This methodology will enable us to explain the history of Zanzibar at three levels. First, we investigate the economic level at which we observe:

1. The transformation of a slave-based economy into one based on the use of free labour;
2. The transition from a merchant-dominated formation to one dominated by productive capital;
3. A process of peasantisation and proletarianisation where self-

11

sustaining agriculturalists were forced to produce cash crops for sale; or they went to work for a wage, as labour itself was being transformed into a commodity.

Second, we detail this economic process by studying the social relations of production which reveal:

1. Exploitation of the slaves by slave owners;
2. Entry of merchant capital and, through usury, the erosion of the land-owning class;
3. Antagonism between fractions of capital: European-based merchant capital against merchant capital tied to India.

Third, in politics, we analyse class alliances at the level of the state between the Sultan and the ever-growing arm of British capital represented by that country's consular officials.

A note of clarification is in order on the use of terms like 'Indian' capital, 'European' capital and 'Arab' plantation owners. D. Nabudere has argued that the use of these ethnic qualifiers is the result of 'intellectual eclecticism'.[1] The criticism exemplifies what could be called an abstractionist view of history, because it argues that ultimately all determinations are linked to finance capital located in the capitalist metropoles. It also illustrates a view of capital which denies any possibility of internal contradictions between fractions of capital whether distinguished on a geographical or a sectoral basis. The most serious weakness of Nabudere's argument for the overall dominance of finance capital is the *a priori* exclusion of historical specificity. Once it is established that finance capital operates in a particular social formation, actual historical development is ignored. The consequences are bound to be disastrous for understanding the nature and history of class struggles in that particular social formation. This being said, it should be clear that when terms like Indian, Arab or European are used to qualify a particular social class, they should in no way be seen as the determining element.

This clarification is instructive in view of a widespread misconception that exists among non-Marxist African historians. In G.A. Akinola's Ph.D. thesis one reads of 'Zanzibar [and] East African coastal society which was divided into a number of exclusive classes differentiated mainly by race; Arabs, European merchants, indigenous populations'.[2] It is true that on the surface, ethnic groups seem to coincide with class divisions: Arabs as planters and slavers; Indians as merchants, financiers and traders; Wahadimu as independent cultivators; Africans from the mainland as slaves; and Europeans as traders and government agents. But there is a danger in equating ethnic origins with class positions in Zanzibar society. What is determinant in relations of production is the class position

12

Plate 1 The ivory trade of Zanzibar at the end of the nineteenth century. Indian merchants, their backgrounds as varied as their style of dress, in attendance at the German Customs House. In the earlier century, ivory and slaves had dominated the Zanzibar economy.

the class position and not the ethnic origin. The danger resides in substituting ethnic solidarity for class solidarity. Obviously there are cultural and historical elements which will tend to draw, for example, the Indians or the Arabs together, but even when this takes place, it does so along class lines. When the Protectorate officials were proposing the importation of Indian 'coolies', it is clear that those poor immigrants were not to mix socially, politically or even culturally with the successful Indian traders. Furthermore, among the Arab planters quite a good number were pauperised by the prohibition of the slave trade and, later, the abolition of the legal status of slavery. Their former status must have influenced their arrogant attitude towards the ex-slaves and local Hadimu, but in terms of relations of production they were closer to the latter than to the richer Arab landlords. This point cannot be stressed too strongly in view of the widespread tendency in the study of East African history to use convenient but imprecise ethnic categories of explanation in place of class analysis.

Plate 2   An Arabian dhow unloading dried shark. The dark complexions of some of the crew may indicate slave origin. Arabian traders and colonisers came to Zanzibar from Muscat and Oman.

Zanzibar before 1873

The history of transition in Zanzibar is complex. Prior to the nineteenth century, it was dominated by Arab colonisers and traders dealing in ivory and slaves. The Sultan and the Arab population came to Zanzibar from Muscat and Oman.[3] That was determined by the interests of the ruling class of the Omani coast. From our limited knowledge of Middle Eastern social formations, it is reasonable to argue that the dominant mode of production there was feudalism, but it did not preclude the use of slave labour. Theoretically, there is nothing contradictory in the feudal mode of production maintaining or fostering slave relations of production.

Yet it would be an error to extrapolate from this and say that Zanzibar was characterised by a feudal mode of production in the nineteenth century. The reason is the very position of Zanzibar in the path of European capitalist expansion. The introduction of cloves in the early 1800s, and the subsequent development of a plantation system, deeply affected relations of production on the island. The slaves that were taken from the continent were no

14

longer solely a trade item for the island merchants; they became a source of productive labour on plantations. The combination of slavery and a plantation economy meant that the ruling class had moved from supporting itself through trading activities alone — which is unproductive of surplus value — to control of a servile plantation labour force productive of surplus value. The economic survival of the slave owners came to depend on the supply of cheap labour in the form of captives raided or purchased from the mainland for the production of cloves in Zanzibar.

The transition to this new mode of production was set in motion by the growing activity of Great Britain in the Indian Ocean resulting from the development of merchant capital. The influence which Great Britain and other European powers began to exercise in Zanzibar was paralleled by the Sultan's loss of political and economic autonomy. This process had begun long before 1873, perhaps with the signing of a series of 'Amity and Commerce' treaties with the United States of America (1833), Great Britain (1839), and France (1844), giving them 'most favoured nation' privileges. All of these treaties were accompanied by the placing of consulates in Zanzibar Town for the protection of commercial interests in East Africa and in the Indian Ocean.[4] The process quickened in 1873 with the signing of a treaty prohibiting the slave trade within the Sultan's dominions.[5] The suppression of the slave trade was followed in 1897 by the abolition of the legal status of slavery in Zanzibar and Pemba. The problems provoked by that legislation constitute the most important economic and political issue in the history of Zanzibar during the period under study.

The signing of the 'Amity and Commerce' treaties closely followed the introduction of cloves, the growth of a lucrative slave trade, and the use of slave labour. The slaves introduced a contradictory element in the relations that were developing between the capitalist metropoles and the Zanzibar ruling class, for it occurred precisely at that time when the dominant capitalist classes in the United States and Europe were advocating the abolition of slavery because it hampered the pace of capital accumulation.[6] Locally, this discrepancy between the economic systems of Zanzibar and the capitalist metropoles led to constant debate on the merits of eliminating slavery on the islands.

Abolition would have had a significant impact on the labour supply and threatened the economic survival of the plantation owners during the transition from slave to free labour. The commercial petty bourgeoisie faced difficulties because of the inability of planters to manage the surplus extracted from labourers so as to repay mortgages and loans. Yet the varying fortunes of the

15

Plate 3   The old palace, Beit al-Sahil, before it was bombarded in 1896 to ensure the Sultan's fullest compliance with Britain's imperial designs in its 'Protectorate'. On the right is the Beit al-Hukm and the tower.

Arab planters and the merchant petty bourgeoisie had very little impact on the state except in so far as it had to resolve political and economic problems arising from its role as the instrument of a dominant class not based on the island.

From pre-capitalism to imperialism

The Zanzibari political economy was part of the Omani formation in the early nineteenth century. However, the growing independence of the Omani Arabs from their original homeland went hand in hand with – one is tempted to say, was provoked by – the parallel penetration of European and North American capital in the Indian Ocean region. From the 1870s onwards, the Zanzibari social formation was characterised by a hybrid state of which the Sultan was the nominal head. His real power was increasingly limited and controlled by the European consuls who often worked as directors or representatives of well-known trading firms such as Smith Mackenzie & Co., Boustead Brothers and Hansing & Co.[7] This economic dominance was buttressed by military force.

In the gradual dissolution of the Sultan's power 1873 was a key date. Up to then, he had more or less preserved the economic base of his political power, which was the revenues from slave labour

Plate 4   The Beit al-Hukm palace during a Friday review of the troops. It was destroyed in the 1896 bombardment.

and the slave trade. The first blow to this economic base was struck by the 1873 treaty abolishing the slave trade; the second came with the abolition of the legal status of slavery in 1897. The first treaty inaugurated the era in which the Sultan became the bourgeoisie's overseas link with the dominant local classes. The British offered him what amounted to a salaried position as compensation. Even if the Sultan had wanted to resist British encroachment by force, that alternative had been completely dashed by the 1872 hurricane which destroyed whatever was left of the Sultan's navy.

Of even greater significance was the quarter century gap separating the 1873 treaty and the 1897 proclamation. The period between the two measures illustrates very concretely the economic problems engendered by the transition from slave relations of production. While the change was an economic necessity, politically it had to be carried out with great care because the embryonic colonial state could not mature politically and ideologically without the class of landlords, previously a ruling class whose power rested on unrestricted access to slave labour.

17

Plate 5   An inside view of a consular house at the end of the nineteenth century.

Before examining this transition process, it is necessary to discuss some well-established assumptions about Zanzibar history.

It has been held that Zanzibar's economic importance stemmed from its trading activities. It is true that the island developed into an entrepôt for goods destined for and coming from the interior of the continent. However, it should not be forgotten that the growing interest of imperialist powers in Zanzibar coincided closely with the introduction of clove plantations on the island. The economic base of the island was not in trade, but in the cultivation of cloves. Trading is by nature an unproductive activity in that it does not produce surplus value.[8] Furthermore, a full and correct assessment of trading and its importance to the island requires the context of imperialist expansion of the capitalist metropoles. Any historical analysis of the Zanzibar social formation that does not take into account the dynamics of imperialist domination is bound to give a distorted, subjective and idealised picture of the relations of production there.

The necessity of approaching Zanzibar history in this wider context cannot be overstressed in view of the proliferation of so-called comparative studies which attempt to survey the development of slavery in East Africa by comparing it to slavery in the southern United States. Such exercises are methodologically and historically unsound because the development of slavery on the East African coast in the nineteenth century was one of the consequences of the expansion of the capitalist mode of production in the United States and Europe.

With regard to slavery in Zanzibar, F. Cooper's study completely ignores the imperialist dimension. His work is essentially based on a legalistic and ideological analysis of the master/slave relationship.[9] An analysis of the relations of production between slaves and slaveholders cannot be carried out by reference to what is written in the Koran and other Islamic texts, just as relationships between British capitalists and their workers cannot be based on what is written in the Bible or labour codes. This formalistic empiricism is further aggravated by the use of cultural and ideological criteria in order to define social classes, as exemplified in this passage from Cooper's work:

> Most important, the upper stratum of Zanzibari society was not defined by success as planters or as traders. What defined them is best expressed by the term still used by Arabs and Swahili today, *heshima*, meaning, literally, respect.[10]

The problem of analysing production relations, class relations, and the ideology resulting from their combination, can only be examined by asking, first, which mode of production predominates? Such a question cannot be answered by describing how the Arab masters treated their slaves. That approach is rooted in subjectivism. It is not the treatment that a producer − be he unfree or free − receives from the owner of the means of production that determines his position, but rather the contrary: it is his position in relation to the owner of the means of production that determines the treatment he receives. This can only be identified by examining all the forces at work, and that means the local forces as well as those which can be traced back to the capitalist metropoles.

It was precisely because of this link between Zanzibar and the imperialist countries that the Arab slaveholders or landowners were no longer able to reproduce their once dominant position. Their 'commanding' role was now dependent on management of overseas capital by local agents, namely the British consuls and governors of the Protectorate.

Thus, from 1873 onwards, Zanzibari social formation was dominated by the capitalist mode of production, although it was based on slave labour with the surplus product being appropriated by Arab landowners who were intermediary agents. The surplus was actually shared between the landlords, the merchants, and the imperialist bourgeoisie. The relations of production between slaves and masters combined elements of both a slave mode of production and a feudal mode. The contrast between the two types of relations becomes clear when we explain the manner in which labour power was reproduced by the slave owners. It is typical of slave relations that the labourer is a product, or commodity, purchased by money.[11] The slave owner was entirely responsible for the reproduction of his slave through the provision of food, shelter and clothing. Under feudalism, on the other hand, the serf is forced by economic or extra-economic means to reproduce himself. The increasing use of extra-economic means, allowing the labourer to keep part of his product to reproduce himself, introduced elements of the feudal mode of production into the slave mode. It is because this latter form of reproduction was institutionalised in the relations of production that A. Mose has erroneously identified feudal relations as dominant.[12] However, the relations between slaves and slave owners were no longer those that determined the extraction of the surplus. By the end of the nineteenth century, the surplus was not extracted by the slave owners but by the ruling bourgeoisie of the capitalist metropoles in collaboration with the merchants and the Sultan, who received a portion of it in the form of a 25 per cent export tax levied on cloves.

Although the economic life of the island was ultimately determined by an absentee ruling class, the continuing extraction of the surplus depended on how effectively the relations between the former slaves and their masters continued to operate. This was a serious question since the actual labour processes involved in the production of cloves necessitated a large reservoir of labour to satisfy the requirements of the planters which peaked at harvest time. As long as slaves were available, there was no labour problem to speak of on the island.

But once it had been decided in the capitalist metropoles that slavery must come to an end, and serious pressure accompanied by sanctions was applied to carry out the policy, the transition from slave to free labour, and from pre-capitalist slave owner to capitalist landowner, became the primary concern of the bureaucratic representatives of the absentee ruling class. The empirical evidence of this preoccupation can be found in the numerous letters, reports and memoranda that were exchanged between the bureaucrats stationed in Pemba and Zanzibar and their colleagues in London.[13]

20

From slave labour to free labour

The process of transition from slave labour to free labour in Zanzibar pivoted on the question of labour supply. Merchant capital was increasingly penetrating the relations of production, through money lent to landowners who were losing their slaves because of the 1873 and 1897 decrees. The majority of these landowners were unable to repay their debts, because of their inability to obtain a yield from what they had borrowed. This illustrates most vividly why, for Marxists, capital must be seen as a relation and not simply as a sum of money. Obviously, money was available, but the element that transformed money into capital — labour — was not easy to obtain. For capital to be productive, a constant supply of free labour is required. If it is not available, the state will often resort to various means of making it available — including force if necessary, as was the case in Zanzibar. It might seem strange to say that labour supply was a problem in an area where slaves or former slaves would constitute a natural and inexhaustible labour source, yet all the evidence indicates this was the case. It is worth remembering that the same problem occurred in other areas which underwent this kind of transition. When slavery was abolished in the West Indies, the capitalists there were confronted with a labour crisis, which they did not anticipate. The remarks made by Marx on that problem could be applied to the Zanzibar situation:

> *The Times* of November 1857 contains an utterly delightful cry of outrage on the part of a West Indian owner. This advocate analyses with great moral indignation ... how the *Quashees* (the free blacks of Jamaica) content themselves with producing only what is strictly necessary for their own consumption ... how they do not care a damn for the sugar and the fixed capital invested in the plantations, but rather observe the planters' impending bankruptcy with an ironic grin of malicious pleasure.... They have ceased to be slaves, but not in order to become wage labourers, but, instead, self-sustaining peasants working for their own consumption.[14]

The arguments for and against abolition

The reasons for abolishing the legal status of slavery were not based on humanistic or moralistic grounds, notwithstanding the vast literature to the contrary. Whereas the expanded reproduction of capital required an ever expanding labour population, the reproduction of slave labour was becoming financially prohibitive.

21

Furthermore, the large slave population — estimated in 1895 at 140,000 out of a total of 200,000 — required a repressive apparatus with the means to suppress any attempt at revolt.[15] But the ultimate reason for the abolition of slavery was rooted in the knowledge that free labour would be more efficient than slave labour.[16] Although the principle of abolition was never seriously questioned by those involved in its implementation, the pace and manner of carrying out the decree were a matter of well-articulated disagreements. However, progressive enforcement became the established policy simply because a slave could not become a free person until he had completed lengthy procedures which involved a great deal of paper work. One of the results was to discourage a good number of slaves from even thinking about their freedom, let alone taking the initial step of applying for it:

> The effort to obtain freedom is now so great that very few are applying of their own accord.... A slave now to obtain his freedom must leave his master's *shamba* and run the risk (no light one) of being arrested as a vagrant, while he is endeavouring to find an employer....[17]

Some of the officials responsible for implementing the decree argued that the slaves were not interested in applying for freedom. They could not see that dampening the slave's enthusiasm had been one of the main objectives of this institutionalised form of obstructionism. Furthermore, those who spoke about the apparent lack of enthusiasm tended to ignore the fact that when the decree was publicised it did lead to assertions of freedom among the slaves, one of which was the refusal to work for plantation owners. This happened, notably, among slaves who continued to work on the *shambas* of their owners and who went on strike to demonstrate to their masters that the old days of being treated like objects were over.[18] Since abolition had become a legal fact, many of the arguments concentrated on how to make it workable without causing too much damage to the Zanzibar economy. Thus, candid observers squarely advocated a progressive implementation of the decree because they feared that immediate enforcement would 'completely disorganise our transport while considerably increasing the expense of procuring men for caravans'.[19] Some went further to argue that the transition from slave labour to free labour would result in revenue losses for the Protectorate as high as two-thirds.[20] Hence they suggested that:

> In the interest of the solvency of this Protectorate ... some measures may be simultaneously adopted for gradually intro-ducing Chinese or Indian coolie labour ... so that when the

period of transition is completed and negro labourers are no longer available, Asiatics may at once take their place.[21]

There were very few to argue that abolition would not create difficulties. Most observers exhibited a solid grasp of the problems that were bound to occur with the abolition of the legal status of slavery. Two kinds of problems were anticipated: legal-political and economic. The advocates of a slow transition insisted that sudden freedom for the slaves could incite them to violent retaliatory attacks against their former masters. As a preventive measure, they suggested that 'it be necessary to have an armed force sufficient to cope with and put down any disturbance which may arise'.[22] In other words, the problem became one of how to forge a legal and political apparatus which would replace smoothly a system which had ensured that the slave population behave in a predictable manner and submit itself to the unconditional rule of the masters.

It should be mentioned that the slave population on the islands was not a homogeneous one and that very often these arguments were coloured according to which section of the slave population was being discussed. Three categories of slaves can be distinguished: (1) those who worked for a wage outside the household; (2) domestic slaves; and (3) the *shamba* or agricultural slaves.

The first type consisted of slaves who had acquired a skill such as

> masons, carpenters, *chukuzi* (coolies at customs), *biashara* (vendors of food), *vibarua* (daily labourers at coal godowns, etc.), house boys, water girls, and generally all those who are occupied in town by Europeans, or merchants of various nationalities, in fact all in receipt of regular wages.[23]

Slaves in this category worked 'outside' for pay, and, in return for this relative freedom to move around, were required to give their master five days' worth of their earnings while keeping the rest for themselves. On the other hand, the master was no longer required to provide lodgings, food or clothing. When abolition of slavery was decreed, the relationship between slaves in this category and their masters had deteriorated to the point where 'many masters were glad if they could get only half of what their slaves earned.'[24] For them, the 1897 decree merely confirmed or legalised a status which was no longer that of a slave, and it is not surprising to see that the granting of freedom to this category is applauded because, it was said:

> These are intelligent, industrious, and useful members of the community; with very few exceptions they turn out well.... They appreciate the advantages of freedom.[25]

23

The second category of slave consisted of the *masuria* or concubines, and the general working slaves of the household. For this group, abolition might even have been seen with hostility:

> There is but little doubt that the *masuria* enjoy considerable advantages over the other slaves. Certainly they have no days they can call their own, but against this they have but little real work to do, they have their food and clothing and are in the way of obtaining very important advantages. Should one be fortunate enough to bear a child to her master, her future freedom and independence are secured, her child will inherit from its father, and she will enjoy the benefits of the inheritance.[26]

Finally, there was the most important category: the *shamba* labourers who were expected to work five days a week. Generally assigned daily tasks,

> which when finished, the worker was at liberty to do as he pleased. In return for this labour the slave was given a piece of land large enough to build a house upon, and sufficient to provide him with what produce he needed for supplying with food and clothing.

In contrast to the first category, this one was judged by the same writer as 'unintelligent ... devoid of resource ... [with] no ideas beyond doing as little as possible and getting as much as possible to eat and drink'. To grant them freedom, the writer concludes, 'would be a cruel action on the part of any government, and crime and starvation would be sure to result.'[27]

Abolition and the labour question

It should be clear now that the question of the abolition of slavery was not one which involved simply the class of slaves or former slaves. The decree of 1897 disrupted much more than their social and economic existence. It also unsettled class relations and affected other classes, especially the class of non-producers that had lived off the labour of the slaves. To touch on the legal status of slavery, therefore, was tantamount to tampering with the fundamental structure that held the Zanzibari social formation together. The official quoted below may have sought to dramatise when he anticipated what might happen on the island, but the impression he conveyed to his superiors in London is a fairly correct assessment of the situation as a whole:

> Until some substitute, therefore, has been found for domestic slave labour, the immediate emancipation of the agricultural population would entail disaster. Indeed, were it suddenly to be

24

introduced, instead of being gradually brought about by the force of circumstances, I do not see how these islands could be saved from misery, and perhaps famine, unless some system, not far different in effect, but more acceptable to all concerned, of State control over labour were framed to take its place.[28]

The starting premise of the above writer, need it be added, was that the 'slaves are very well treated by the Arab masters of Zanzibar' and, therefore, nobody should worry too much about changing the status quo.[29] Changes, if they had to be made, should be introduced as slowly as possible.

It is interesting to note the many ways in which the labour problem in Zanzibar was formulated. The interest resides in the fact that the way in which the problem was framed invariably determined the solution. In a slavery report for 1900, Farler represented the labour question for Pemba Island in the following terms: 'How to arrange that the free slaves shall be so distributed as to keep the plantations in good order and gather crops.'[30] For Zanzibar, Sir Lloyd Mathews attributed the economic deterioration of the island directly to a shortage of labour:

> The plantations of these islands [he wrote in 1901] were fully cultivated and profitable prior to the decree [of 1897]. Now, many of them are out of cultivation for want of labour, others are worked at a loss, and labour is getting scarcer every day.[31]

And he continued:

> I cannot blind my eyes to the fact that it [i.e., the decree abolishing the legal status of slavery] has not been of benefit to these islands up to the present. How to turn it into a benefit is a question we have to solve.[32]

All these arguments reveal how important slave labour was to the agricultural economy of Zanzibar. In spite of what may have been written to the contrary, the Arabs (whether slave owners, landowners or both) were not merely interested in being treated with *heshima* by their slaves, but expected above all to be provided with their daily subsistence by slave labour. The problem of transition was one of ensuring that freed slaves realised they were not being freed in order to revert to domestic production. Their new status meant that they were free to make their labour power available for purchase as a commodity. With the abolition of slave labour, it was feared that the slaves would simply produce their own food — as many of them were already doing under slavery — and no more. Should this happen, it was predicted that:

> The owners would, as a rule, be unable to make a living out of the compensation which might be granted to them, and being

unable to do any work themselves would be thrown on the state or starve.[33]

Some of the writers on the subject seemed to be concerned about the fate of the entire population when they raised the spectre of famine and starvation.[34] Yet it is clear that most of them were much more worried about what might befall the plantation owners specifically:

> Were it [i.e., abolition of the legal status of slavery] to be at the present moment enforced, it would involve the bankruptcy of all the landowners, the ruin of many Indian traders, and of the whole foreign mercantile community, as well as the inevitable bankruptcy of the government.... Were the strong tie which binds master and slave together to be broken, the emancipated slaves would no longer work upon the clove estates.[35]

Prior to 1897, the labour problem was dominated by debates (in writing) over how to enforce without much disruption the abolition of slave labour. After this date, the problem is characterised by a constant preoccupation with how to resolve labour shortages. To meet that objective, two different approaches were pursued: one was based on economic mechanisms and the other consisted of legal and political coercion. The former was based on the argument that good wages would cause labourers to flock to the plantations. But should this economic incentive fail, coercive measures were in order. The specific solutions advanced to solve the labour supply problems, therefore, varied from non-repressive to repressive.[36] Some advocated the establishment of so-called 'permissive freedom'.[37] Other administrators suggested labour bureaus.[38] Then there were the arguments for outright prohibition of entertainment that made labourers 'unfit to work the next day', such as 'dancing whole nights during all nights of the week except Thursday'.[39]

One of the most important reasons why the abolition of slavery was followed by serious labour shortages had to do with the kind of relationships that had developed over the years between the masters and slaves. In many cases, the slaves were allowed by their masters to cultivate for their own subsistence. Some were given two days during which they could work for themselves, others were given three. This meant that slaves could provide for themselves without depending on their masters, creating a serious labour shortage. At harvest time labour demands reached their peak. It was during one of these clove picking seasons that a British official reported thus: 'I frequently came across cases in which all the slaves of an estate refused to work for pay on their own three days of the week.'[40] An economic means used to resolve this shortage was the introduction of a piece-work system. This seems to have satisfied some of the *shamba* owners, especially the richer ones. Commenting on the advantages of the piece work system, one of these landowners declared that:

He has never before harvested such a quantity of cloves as he has this year, and, moreover, hitherto many cloves have remained on the trees unpicked until they were spoiled, while this year [1899] every tree has been clean picked.[41]

Contributing to the 'labour problem' was the fact that Zanzibar provided caravan porters for mainland expeditions to the interior of the continent. Thus the labour force was diminished through a pattern of labour recruitment which used Zanzibar as a labour reservoir for the mainland. When Stanley and other explorers planned their travels inland, they always recruited their porters from Zanzibar. Stanley himself was said to have estimated the number of required porters at 20,000 a month:

Even if this is exaggerated, Sir G. Portal, writing to the Marquis of Salisbury in September 1891, complains that the porters sent out from Zanzibar in the various expeditions amounted to many thousands per annum.[42]

This drain on the labour force in Zanzibar had a paradoxical result:

So great was the drain of labour that it gave a considerable stimulus to the slave trade, Sir G. Portal stating that 'the Arab land-owners are put to such straits for labour that they are willing not only to give high prices, but also to run considerable risks in order to obtain new slaves.'[43]

On the depletion of the labour population due to the termination of the slave trade, officials anticipated that economic incentives alone would attract people from the continent to go and settle in the Protectorate:

As soon as slavery in the islands is known to be a thing of the past, free natives may be expected to come to the islands from Usambara, Shimba, the Umba district, and Giriama in search of food and wages, and these immigrants will probably settle for good where they find security and what to them are luxuries.[44]

Things did not develop this way and the problem of reproduction of labour power remained serious. Its resolution meant that the transition from slave labour to free labour would have to include a period of forced labour because the economic incentives proved to be unenticing. One of the most popular forms of forced labour was the contract which aimed at tying the labourer to the land by giving him a plot on which he could both build a house and cultivate a *shamba*.[45] This was precisely the kind of paternalist relationship that the landowner and the slave had reached when abolition was introduced.

How 'free' labour became 'forced' labour

While it was easy to decree an end to the legal status of slavery, it was never a simple matter to insure a regular supply of non-slave labour. The shortage in Zanzibar provoked different kinds of responses. Some encouraged labour recruitment from the mainland.[46] Many landowners simply switched from clove to coconut plantations since the latter required much less labour to maintain and harvest.[47] Yet, in spite of these moves, the shortages persisted because the badly needed labour had to be suited to waged work. The difficulties of relying on undisciplined labour were noted by a German colonial official who pointed out in 1895 that it was difficult to get 'the natives to understand time contracts, the negro serving just as long as he feels inclined, and then running away.'[48] One of the main problems faced by potential employers in Zanzibar was that, once freed, some slaves were satisfied to stay at home and attend to their own affairs. Living conditions were not yet such that the agricultural worker (i.e., the former slave) was of necessity required to go and work for a wage.[49] There were, nevertheless, a good number whose freedom resulted in their labour power being exchanged for a wage.[50]

Nor did the free Wahadimu population provide a solution to the labour problem. Much more than any group on the islands, the Wahadimu were still close to what could be termed a domestic communal mode of production. It was for that reason that an agricultural officer lamented that:

> These people [i.e., Wahadimu] who correspond to the small peasant proprietors were of little use during clove picking.... The Wahadimu are ... not to be counted a factor in the solution of our labour difficulties unless some sort of pressure is brought to bear upon them.[51]

The continuation of the four-three system which operated under slavery — the agreement to work four days a week for the *shamba* owner and three days for themselves — was described as 'well-liked' by the former slaves because to have done otherwise would:

> have placed these people upon the wages sheet (and thus) would have brought them under the more rigorous discipline which we are bound to exercise with a large staff of paid labourers. It

would have involved their working 6 days a week, longer hours, and have rendered them liable to dismissal on misbehaviour or incompetence.[52]

In fact, this preservation of the four-three schedule was a way of keeping labourers constantly available. This also illustrates how the transition from slave labour to free labour will always assume forms which are determined by a combination of the existing modes of production. What appears as a very good system for the former slaves is in fact a very exploitative one. The reproduction of the labourer continues to be effected by the means which emerged under the previously dominant mode of production, at no cost to the employer.

The increasing encroachment of the British administration was paralleled by an increase in labour requirements, primarily because labour was no longer required simply in agriculture and by the traders in town, but also by the state apparatus which needed to improve the infrastructure of the Protectorate through new buildings and roads. Toward the end of the period under study, the labour shortages became so critical that:

> In 1907 every possible forcible method was used. The people were driven from their homes, the Assistant Collectors were ordered to go about the villages and drive them in, the *Masheha* were suspended or made to go and pick cloves themselves till they produced a certain number of labourers.[53]

Aside from purely economic reasons such as not needing the income from wages, workers were unenthusiastic about clove picking because of deplorable working conditions. Sometimes they were not even told how much they would be paid. The workers also complained that they were improperly treated by the Arab and Indian *shamba* owners. Accommodation was extremely poor, some saying that they were not even provided with a shelter to sleep under. Other workers complained that they had to walk from two to three miles in order to get to the nearest shop to buy their food; finally, there was the complaint that the government prevented them from returning home when they wished to go.[54]

The clearest overview of the labour situation in Zanzibar throughout this period is provided by a government report published in 1923:

> The history of labour in Zanzibar down to the year 1897 is the history of slavery and its gradual suppression by various treaties and legislative measures culminating in the Decree of Seyyid Hamoud in April 1897.... The history of labour subsequent to 1897 is a tale of shortage, disinclination on the part of the Arabs

to pay money wages, and administrative effort to organise the available supply. The introduction of Indian labour was at one time or another canvassed, but never materialised. In 1904 and 1906 and at other subsequent times recourse was had to recruitment of labour on the mainland. Mainlanders have also come voluntarily, settled in appreciable numbers and are now the chief source of supply for cultivation of plantations.[55]

From pre-capitalist slave ownership to capitalist land ownership

Whereas the transition from slave to free labour resulted in the semi-proletarianisation of the former slaves, the same process transformed the Arab landowner and slave holder into a semi-capitalist or, to be more precise, a manager for absentee European capitalists and/or Indian moneylenders. In view of their financially incapacitating dependence on Indian moneylenders, the survival of the Arabs as a class may seem surprising. The landowners managed to retain ownership of their land, in spite of it being heavily mortgaged to Indian financiers, for two reasons: the support of the colonial state apparatus, and the Indian traders' lack of interest in land ownership and agriculture.

The transition in forms of labour had drastic consequences for the labouring as well as for the propertied classes. Those who studied the problem of transition saw it as one of maintaining production. This required not only the establishment of free labour, but also a change in the economic practice and ideology of the former masters. Under the circumstances, the objective of the colonial state was to transform masters and slaves into capitalists and wage workers respectively:

> The Arabs have to learn to appreciate the advantages of paid labour, and the slaves have to be taught that not only is indolence a vice, but that they will never be able to estimate justly the true value of freedom or independence until they understand the value of their labour, and are willing to apply themselves to it. *This means a complete revolution in the ideas and habits of both masters and slaves* [my emphasis].[56]

The problem of the Zanzibar economy, then, was that while capitalist conditions of production increasingly prevailed, there were no capitalists as such in the productive sector. The problem became how to make the former appropriator of labour behave like a capitalist; or, failing that, how to replace him by others already able to operate a plantation system under capitalist conditions. Thus as early as 1894, three years before the total abolition of the legal status of slavery, the Earl of Kimberley advised his correspondent in Zanzibar, Hardinge, to encourage

> the acquisition of property by Europeans, which by promoting the organisation of a system of free labour, by immigration or other means, would lessen the danger of a failure of the supply of labour when labour is no longer available.[57]

Having no money of their own, the Arab planters had turned to the Indian moneylenders whose major interest as a class lay in making money through speculation on interest and mortgages, not in productive activities. Some plantation owners attempted to stay out of the clutches of these speculators by cutting their operating costs, but this usually resulted in the further deterioration of the *shambas.* Consequently, rather than seeing such a state of affairs develop, a government official declared he would

> like to see such properties either handed over on perpetual leases to sound capitalist associations, or cut into small holdings with provisions in the lease that they would not be further subdivided, and that the small-holder would be a resident on the land.[58]

And to make sure there was no misunderstanding about the form of production envisaged, it was added that

> we do not want a class of small-holder who will regard their holdings merely as their sole means of support for the family, or merely as the garden in which they can grow their family food-supply (and that is the chief difficulty we have to contend with in dealing with natives). We want him to become a plantation owner on a small scale, rising by his industry to larger ownership, and in addition, of equal importance, to provide a source of labour to neighbouring plantations.[59]

In other words, the government was interested in creating small capitalists.

Even though he was economically at the mercy of the Indian moneylenders, the Arab planter remained more important to the government and the British colonising power than the traders. Trading activity did not produce any surplus value. Creation of surplus value, the basis of profit for the capitalist, must come from generative activity which, in the case of Zanzibar, was clove production. The necessity to bail the planter class out of its heavy indebtedness to the Indian moneylender was the more urgent given the absolute lack of interest in agriculture shown by the traders in general.[60] The latter's only interest was to squeeze as much money from the planter as he was ready to cough up.

Obviously, the state's concern for the labourers and the planters derived from pure material interest. Those two classes, especially the former, were the basis of the Zanzibar economy and state finances. To equate the interest of the Arab planters with that of the state was not mere sentimental talk; it was linked to the large revenues that came from clove production, especially in the form of a 25 per cent tax *ad valorem* which had been levied since 1887.[61]

It must be explained at this point that the planter class was not a homogeneous one. The abolition of slavery accelerated a process of differentiation which had been going on for some time. When officials of the state expressed concern for the planter class, therefore, it was only directed at the 'salvageable' (i.e., more prosperous) section of this class. Hardinge expressed this very clearly when, anticipating what would be the probable effects of the abolition of slavery, he wrote to the Earl of Kimberley in 1895:

> Many owners would become a burden on the State. I am thinking not so much of the Arab planters, as of many members of the middle and lower classes.[62]

He quoted representatives of the latter as saying:

> We have nothing apart from our slaves; if you take them away, you take away both our capital and our income, and when they are gone, where are we to find the money to pay our servants?[63]

In other words, the penetration of capitalist relations in Zanzibar was resulting in a simultaneous process of pauperisation and enrichment.

Conclusion

Throughout the period under study, the outstanding feature of Zanzibar is the process of its subjugation to imperialist forces. This meant that the contradictions between various classes were not allowed to mature. The strategy of the British colonisers was to manage the contradictions so they would not develop to disrupt the economic and political system being imposed. In practical terms, such maturation would have led to the disappearance of the planter class along with the abolition of slavery. Instead, the state was used to preserve the class in question. However, it could only delay the historical process at work; it could not stop it. With the removal of the ruling British bureaucracy and the end of formal colonial rule, the contradictions that had been suppressed for almost a century came to the fore and were resolved in the bloody confrontation of January 1964.

Notes

1. See D. Wadada Nabudere, 'Imperialism, the national question and the politics of class formation in Uganda', a critical review of M. Mamdani's *Politics and Class Formation in Uganda*, mimeo, University of Dar es Salaam, January 31, 1977.
2. G.A. Akinola, 'The Sultanate of Zanzibar, 1870–1890,' unpublished Ph.D. dissertation, University of London, 1973, pp. 42–3.
3. *Ibid.*, p. 32.
4. *Ibid.*
5. The chronology of the various treaties is taken from *Documents relatifs à la répression de la traite des esclaves publiés en exécution des articles LXXXI et suivants de l'Acte général de Bruxelles, 1896*, Bruxelles, 1897, pp. 186 ff. (hereafter, *Documents-Acte general*); see also *File on Correspondence with British Representatives and Agents abroad, 1880*, Kirk to Salisbury, Zanzibar, February 23, 1880, Zanzibar Archives (hereafter ZA).
6. See the discussion in B. Hindess and P.Q. Hirst, *Pre-Capitalist Modes of Production*, London, Routledge & Kegan Paul, 1975, especially pp. 150–62.
7. Only a full reading of one of the treaties can show how closely the commercial and political interests were tied together.
8. For a discussion see G. Kay, *Development and Underdevelopment, a Marxist Analysis*, London, MacMillan, 1975. Also K. Marx, *Capital*, Vol. III, Moscow, Progress Publishers, 1974, Chapter 20.
9. On comparative history, note the following statement: 'If Malindi was the Alabama of the East African mainland, Mombasa was the Virginia.' On ideological analysis: 'Islam also helped shape coastal paternalism as a set of ethical principles and laws.' Both statements come from F. Cooper, 'Plantation Slavery on the East Coast of Africa in the 19th Century', Ph.D. dissertation, Yale University, 1974, pp. 269, 278.
10. *Ibid.*, p. 156.
11. B. Hindess and P.Q. Hirst, *op. cit.*, pp. 111–12.
12. A. Mose, *Die Herrshende Feudalklasse Sanzibars und die Kapitalistischen Kolonial Machte*, dissertation zur Promotion A, Karl Marx Universität, Leipzig, 1974.
13. Many of them were collected and published in *Documents-Acte général*, cited above.
14. K. Marx, *Grundrisse*, London, Penguin Books, 1975, pp. 325–26.
15. Letter from R.W. Pigot to A. Hardinge, Zanzibar, August 1, 1895, File E. 1, Vol. 1, Mainland Protectorate 1895, ZA.
16. Report by D. O'Sullivan on the island of Pemba, May 30, 1896, in *Documents-Acte général*, 1896, p. 229.
17. Letter from H. Armitage to Basil S. Cave, H.B.M. Consul, Zanzibar, Chaki-Chaki, Pemba, June 3, 1899, in File B 48, 1899, Vol. II, Miscell. 184 to 359, ZA.
18. Report on slavery, 1896–97, in File B 41, ZA.
19. A. Hardinge to the Marquess of Salisbury, Mombasa, January 29, 1896, in *Documents-Acte général*, 1896, p. 198. Also Salisbury to Hardinge, Foreign

Office, February 10, 1897: Instructions to Hardinge respecting the Abolition of the legal status of slavery in the islands of Zanzibar and Pemba, in *Documents-Acte général,* 1897, p. 180.

20. A. Hardinge to the Earl of Kimberley, Zanzibar, February 26, 1895, in *Documents-Acte général,* 1895, p. 168. Also Hardinge to Kimberley, Zanzibar, March 13, 1895: 'Last year we exported 108,321 bales of copra worth 1,034,755 rupees.... Abolition will entail a reduction of this amount by just about two-thirds,' in *Documents-Acte général,* 1895, p. 179.
21. A. Hardinge to Kimberley, February 26, 1895, *Documents-Acte général,* 1895, p. 150.
22. R.W. Pigot to A. Hardinge, Mombasa August 1, 1895, *Documents-Acte général,* 1895.
23. Alexander to Sir Lloyd Mathews, Zanzibar, March 16, 1899, *Documents-Acte général,* 1899, pp. 96–7.
24. *Ibid.,* and also Report by J.T. Last, Zanzibar, January 25, 1898, *Documents-Acte général,* 1898, p. 83.
25. Alexander to Mathews, *op. cit.*
26. Report by J.T. Last, Zanzibar, January 25, 1898, *op. cit.*
27. *Ibid.,* p. 83.
28. Rodd to Rosebery, Zanzibar, December 31, 1893, *Documents-Acte général,* 1895, p. 124.
29. *Ibid.,* p. 126.
30. Slavery report for 1900 by J.P. Farler, *Documents-Acte général,* 1901, p. 192.
31. Memorandum on labour by L. Mathews, Zanzibar, January 19, 1901, *Documents-Acte général,* 1901, p. 196.
32. *Ibid.,* p. 196.
33. R.W. Pigot to A. Hardinge, August 1, 1895, *op. cit.*
34. Report by J.P. Farler, Zanzibar, 1898, in which it is argued that the decree on abolition should work slowly 'to prevent the ruin of the owners' and 'for the good of the slaves themselves', *Documents-Acte général,* 1898, pp. 112–3; also J.P. Farler to L. Mathews, Zanzibar, June 16, 1899, *Documents-Acte général,* 1900, p. 85.
35. Rodd to Rosebery, *op. cit.*; also Kimberley to Hardinge, Foreign Office, November 27, 1894, where the Zanzibar situation is compared with the one that prevailed in India in 1843 when the Indian Act was passed abolishing the legal status of slavery, *Documents-Acte général,* 1895, p. 160.
36. Salisbury to Hardinge, Foreign Office, February 10, 1897, *op. cit.,* p. 181, which reads in part: 'to anticipate any danger to public order, it may be thought advisable to increase the native police force at the disposal of the government.'
37. Memorandum by Consul Smith on slavery in East Africa, in *Documents-Acte général,* 1895, ZA. The term 'permissive freedom' was coined by Lugard in his *Rise of Our East African Empire,* Edinburgh and London, Blackwood & Sons, 1893.
38. Slavery report for 1900 by J.R. Farler, *op. cit.*; also report on the island of Pemba by D. O'Sullivan, 1899, in *Documents-Acte général,* 1901, p. 165; also Memorandum on labour by L. Mathews, *op. cit.,* pp. 200–1.
39. Slavery report for 1900 by J.P. Farler, *op. cit.,* p. 193; also report by

O'Sullivan on the island of Pemba, May 30, 1896, *op. cit.*, p. 228.

40. J.T. Last to L. Mathews, February 6, 1899, *Documents-Acte général*, 1899, p. 72.
41. Report by J.P. Farler, Pemba, January 31, 1899, *Documents-Acte général*,1899, p. 64.
42. British and Foreign anti-slavery Society to Rosebery, September 1893, *Documents-Acte général*, 1895, p. 113; also Belgian consul to Euan Smith, Zanzibar, July 14, 1891, requesting permission to recruit free men to replace those who are returning home, File CC 1, 1891, ZA.
43. British and Foreign Anti-slavery Society to Rosebery, *ibid.*
44. Memorandum by Consul Smith on slavery in East Africa, 1895, *Documents-Acte général*, p. 139.
45. Memorandum on labour by L. Mathews, Zanzibar, January 19, 1901, *op. cit.*, pp. 197−8; also report by D. O'Sullivan on the island of Pemba, 1899, *op. cit.*
46. A.S. Rogers to Sir Charles Eliot, Zanzibar, May 13th, 1904, Outward Miscellaneous Correspondence, 1904, ZA.
47. R.N. Lyne to Rogers, Zanzibar October 31, 1904, Inwards Miscellaneous Dispatches, 1904, ZA.
48. Hardinge to Kimberley, Zanzibar, February 26, 1895, *op. cit.*, p. 166.
49. *Zanzibar Annual Report*, Agricultural Department, 1901, p. 27.
50. *Zanzibar Annual Report*, Agricultural Department, 1899, p. 20.
51. *Zanzibar Annual Report*, Agricultural Department, 1898, p. 32.
52. *Ibid.*, p. 31.
53. *Zanzibar Annual Report* by the Financial Member of the Council, 1911, p. 16.
54. *Ibid.*, p. 14.
55. Zanzibar Protectorate, *Report of the Commission on Agriculture, 1923*, pp. 37−8.
56. Report by J.T. Last, Zanzibar, January 25, 1898, *op. cit.*, p. 93.
57. Kimberley to Hardinge, November 27, 1894, *op. cit.*, p. 145.
58. *Zanzibar Annual Report*, 1909−10, p. 143.
59. *Ibid.*, p. 144.
60. *Ibid.*, p. 143.
61. Between 1872 and 1876 no tax was levied on cloves; from 1876 to 1886, $1−$2.5 per *frasila*, and in 1886, 30 per cent. See Hardinge to Salisbury, Zanzibar, May 4, 1896, in *Documents-Acte général*, 1896, p. 211, ZA.
62. Hardinge to Kimberley, Zanzibar, March 13, 1895, *op. cit.*, p. 185.
63. *Ibid.*

Two

The Formation of a Colonial Economy 1915–1945

ED FERGUSON

The distinctive features of a colonial capitalist mode of production appeared in Zanzibar between 1915 and 1945. This new system was based on the exploitation of free labour by capital through a money relationship. It took place as labourers and peasant proprietors sold their commodities – labour power, copra and cloves – to landlords, merchants and the state in return for cash. What made this capitalism was the appropriation of surplus value by capitalists from producers in the transaction. Because the majority of producers in colonial Zanzibar did not become a landless proletariat as in classical capitalism, the term 'colonial capitalism' has been used for this stage of development. The purpose of this chapter is to explain how colonial capitalism functioned to exploit labourers and enrich capitalists and the state in Zanzibar between the beginning of World War I and the end of World War II.

Production and appropriation

When slavery was abolished in 1897, shortly after the islands of Unguja and Pemba had been made the British Protectorate of Zanzibar, measures were taken to ensure that the transition to free labour would not upset property relations. Owners received monetary compensation for the property they lost in persons, while their control of clove plantations was not disturbed. Many ex-slaves, unable to find land outside the plantation sector, were bonded with former masters as squatters on the old estates. They were joined by peasants and migrants to form the labour force in the export sector of the colonial economy.

36

The Formation of a Colonial Economy

The production relations introduced under colonial rule were those of capitalism, but they would not be the classical relations between landless proletarians and capitalists that had appeared as the core of industrial capitalism in Western Europe. There, through the spontaneous process of class struggle, an acquisitive bourgeoisie came into being through the accumulation of property. Peasants were deprived of land and instruments of production, and this propertyless class was forced to seek work from the capitalists who had accumulated the means of production. In Zanzibar, capitalist relations of production did not originate from domestic class struggle. They were introduced from outside and guided in their evolution by the colonial power, Great Britain.

The state anticipated that the former slaveholding class, which was preserved as a puppet ruling body, would become a dynamic class of capitalist landowners. A standard currency was required to make possible the exploitation of labour power and accumulation of capital. During the pre-capitalist era the Indian rupee had been introduced in an irregular manner by the sultans to facilitate the circulation of commodities, but now it was needed in production as well.[1] In 1908, the colonial state made the silver rupee of India the acknowledged coin of the Protectorate because of the close commercial ties with that mighty British colony and the powerful role of its merchants in the Zanzibar economy.[2] The British sovereign was made legal tender at 15 rupees to the pound sterling to aid accumulation by monopoly capital in the United Kingdom.[3]

Slave relations had been abolished because capitalist relations were more productive of goods and profits, for reasons best explained by Karl Marx:

> In contrast to the slave, (free) labour becomes more productive because more intensive, since the slave works only under the spur of external fear but not for *his existence* which is *guaranteed* even though it does not belong to him. The free worker, however, is impelled by his wants.[4]

Greater productivity had become especially important to industrial capitalists in Great Britain. Since the bulk of raw materials and cheap food required in large quantities for consumption by machines and workers would come from abroad, it made economic sense to introduce the system of free labour to the colonies. Equally important, the introduction of a wage overseas would provide the purchasing power required to create a world market for the mass products of industry.

The transition from slave to wage labour in Zanzibar was accompanied by some dislocations in the labour supply, but this

37

made no adverse impact on the volume of clove and copra exports following abolition in 1897. Table 2.1 shows that the average quantity of clove exports remained steady for a decade and then began to rise, while the increase in copra exports was immediate. This upward trend for both commodities became a pattern for the period to 1945 as the table demonstrates.

Table 2.1 *Clove and copra exports: quantity averaged over 5 and 15 year periods[5] (in 1,000 tons)*

Period	Cloves		Copra	
	5 year period	15 year period	5 year period	15 year period
1896–1900	5.7	(Begin	5.0	(Begin
1901–1905	5.7	1901)	7.4	1901)
1906–1910	7.3	–	7.1	–
1911–1915	8.6	7.2	8.0	7.5
1916–1920	7.6	–	7.7	–
1921–1925	9.4	–	9.5	–
1926–1930	9.0	8.7	11.3	9.5
1931–1935	10.0	–	12.0	–
1936–1940	9.7	–	9.0	–
1941–1945	9.8	9.8	8.8	9.9

This steady rise in volume has been overlooked by historians in the past.[6] Copra data have been ignored because the commodity was produced outside the dominant plantation sector. The increase in clove exports, however, has remained hidden from investigators because of the way colonial statistics were reported. The administration presented annual data on yields that fluctuated sharply every few years.[7] Since official reports were of annual harvests, the statistics show an irregular rise and fall in volume over periods of less than five years; long-range tendencies have neither been observed nor calculated. To move beyond the limitations of colonial data and track broad trends in output it is necessary to recast the way official statistics are presented. If annual output is averaged over periods of five or fifteen years the short term variations disappear and trends become recognisable. The average annual volume calculated over five-year periods demonstrates a general increase up to the Depression of the early 1930s, after which there is a slight decline for clove exports and a sharp drop in

38

copra exports for the decade ending in 1945. The impact of the Depression is most evident and will be explained below. The conclusion from Table 2.1 to be emphasised at this point is the constant rise in quantity for these two basic exports demonstrated by the data for intervals of 15-year duration between 1901 and 1945.[8]

It remains to be explained how this increase in volume was achieved. Two reasons are apparent. The first is an increase in the number of productive trees. This is difficult to document for coconut palms since they were widespread throughout the islands. It is much easier to make an estimate for clove trees because data was compiled by the administration. Immediately after World War I, local administrators were concerned because many plantations were being neglected by absentee owners in Zanzibar Town. A Commission on Agriculture was appointed in 1923 to assess the situation and its conclusion was presented in the annual report for Zanzibar issued by the Colonial Office the following year:

> The average age of the clove trees in the Protectorate ... is much higher than it should be owing to the failure systematically to replant. There are not sufficient young trees to maintain indefinitely the present output of cloves. The really suitable land in both islands has long ago been put under cloves and regeneration of these areas is therefore the only means of maintaining the supply. So far, filling in the gaps caused by deaths, is the only method in operation.[9]

This argument for revitalising the existing clove sector because further expansion could not take place outside of it was supported by evidence from an administrative survey of trees in 1922. The census concluded that on the two islands there were some 3 million live trees planted on about 48,000 acres. Since clove trees were planted at intervals of 21 feet this sector could support approximately $4\frac{3}{4}$ million trees; clearly there was room for expansion. A bonus scheme to encourage replanting began the following year.[10] Payment had been made for roughly 200,000 new plants when the programme was discontinued five years later, suggesting a total of approximately $3\frac{1}{4}$ million clove trees in 1928.[11] Official figures for 1932 estimated the number at $3\frac{1}{2}$ million, and the figure for 1935 remained roughly the same.[12] There are no higher estimates for the period to the end of World War II, so it is apparent that some half a million new trees were planted from the early 1920s to the mid-1930s.

The second explanation for the growth of clove and copra exports is the increase in the number of labourers producing these commodities. Four categories of workers were involved. There were the squatters who worked on the plantation in return for a wage and a food plot. They were augmented by mainland workers who migrated annually to Zanzibar. These were primarily Wanyamwezi and Wasukuma people with a history of working for money as porters on the mainland trade routes. The demise of the caravan trade in the late nineteenth century was an incentive for them to migrate to Zanzibar to weed plantations as wage labourers. The third group was the large number of peasants from within the Protectorate. They grew their own food on land outside the plantation sector and went seasonally to pick the crops for landed capital — large and small — in return for a wage. Some of them became peasant proprietors who introduced the fourth type of worker, the unpaid family labourer. According to G.D. Kirsopp, the Chief of Customs in Zanzibar, these formed a sizeable portion of the labour force by the mid-1920s. Kirsopp estimated that by 1926 the majority of the 18,000 clove units in the Protectorate were held by more than 13,000 male smallholders who used the unpaid labour of more than 26,000 women and children.[13] He concluded his *Memorandum on Certain Aspects of the Zanzibar Clove Industry* with the observation that the number of unpaid family labourers engaged in clove production 'is probably not less important than the sum total of the outside [i.e., paid] labour employed.'[14]

Since the Zanzibar peasantry had not been made propertyless, it is appropriate to ask why they went to work for a wage. This question is particularly intriguing because direct taxation, which was the standard tool elsewhere in Africa throughout the colonial era, was used only intermittently in the Protectorate. A hut tax was introduced at the beginning of the century; waived for those who went to harvest, it was resisted by others. When it was abolished in 1911, there was an increase in the flow of labour from the mainland.[15]

State coercion and the attraction of imported goods were much more important factors contributing to the expansion of the labour market. The administration had made widespread use of force to get free peasants to harvest cloves prior to World War I, and new laws were passed during the war to ensure that pickers would be available for the harvest. The Native Labour Control Decree and the Regulation of Adult Male Persons Decree, for example, legalised compulsory labour. Individuals arriving from the mainland were registered and directed where they were needed for cultivation. A clove picking contract was introduced to recruit and retain domestic labour for the harvest. It stipulated the length of time, quantity to be picked, and the piece rate to be paid. While these were not mandatory, peasants requesting small advances of money prior to the harvest found that a contract was often a precondition for the loan. Violation of its terms was punishable under the Masters and Servants Decree (1925) which specified these offences and punishments:

> Failure to begin work after contract; absence; drunkenness; carelessness; use of any vehicle without permission; abusive language to employer or headman; refusal to obey a lawful order; giving a false name or address on engagement. These are punishable with a fine of half a month's wages, or in default, one month's imprisonment. The employer may be compensated from a servant's wages for loss caused by his fault. Desertion while an advance is owing is punishable with a fine of Rs. [rupees] 100 or six months' imprisonment.[16]

The desire for imports might have been stronger among Zanzibari peasants than others in East Africa at the beginning of the colonial era. The level of commodity consumption by merchants and slave owners in Zanzibar had been relatively high in the pre-colonial era, and the introduction of capitalist relations meant that peasants could perform wage labour to acquire new goods. It did not take long for imported cloth, sugar, and kerosene to become basic needs, and the purchase of these commodities was a powerful force pulling the peasantry into capitalist production relations.

Once engaged, most peasants remained wage labourers, but there were those who acquired property and became exploiters of labour and consumers of commodities on an enlarged scale. It was the acquisition of property by peasant entrepreneurs that revitalised the plantation sector in the 1920s. Their success was a result of the mobilisation of unpaid family labour. The exploitation of kin was different from capitalist exploitation: surplus value was extorted through the wage relationship, while it was surplus labour that was appropriated through family ties.

It is assumed that kin exploitation was intensified by the entrepreneur to gain further property, for that is the character of expansion in simple commodity production; but this is not easily documented. Certainly the proprietor was moving towards becoming a petty capitalist through the acquisition of more land, trees and the eventual employment of wage labour. This exploitation of unpaid family labour to produce cash crops was the fertile soil in which appeared capitalist exploitation and accumulation among the peasantry.

The export price for these crops did not follow the same growth pattern documented for output between 1915 and 1945, which is an indication of the dependent nature of the colonial economy. The total average export price for any one year was reported as the annual value of the crop. Cloves commanded a much higher price than copra because the Protectorate held a leading position among

41

producers who monopolised the world's supply from sites in the Indian Ocean. Standing in sharp contrast was Zanzibar's minor role in world copra production: when domestic output reached its peak in the 1930s, it was only 1 per cent of the world total.[17] Table 2.2 presents the movement of export prices for cloves and copra over a fifty-five-year period to 1945.

Table 2.2 *Domestic production of cloves and copra for export: yearly average quantity, value and export price* [18] *(in 1,000 tons and £1,000 sterling)*

	Cloves			Copra		
Period	Quantity	Value	Price per ton	Quantity	Value	Price per ton
1891–1895	7.0	146	21	—	—	—
1896–1900	5.7	139	24	5.0	59	12
1901–1905	5.7	221	39	7.4	93	13
1906–1910	7.3	320	44	7.1	111	16
1911–1915	8.6	400	45	8.0	154	19
1916–1920	7.6	562	74	7.7	216	28
1921–1925	9.4	857	91	9.5	232	24
1926–1930	9.0	729	81	11.3	252	22
1931–1935	10.0	534	53	12.0	118	10
1936–1940	9.7	627	65	9.0	92	10
1941–1945	9.8	678	69	8.8	134	15

The data reveals an upward movement in export value, or the price paid per ton for the crop at point of export, up to the end of World War I. The trend for copra was reversed in 1920, after which there was a steady decline in price until World War II, when the temporary loss of South-east Asian sources caused an upturn in price. The peak for clove export was in the early 1920s, followed by a sharp decline for the decade ending in 1935; the slow rise after that was also stimulated by the loss of South-east Asian suppliers during World War II.

The relationship between volume and value can be demonstrated clearly by calculating the average export price for the two crops over time spans of fifteen years. Table 2.3 presents these data for three intervals between 1901 and 1945.

These long-term trends show that the intermediate period, 1916–1930, was one of relative prosperity for property owners, merchants and brokers in the export sector because the value of

The Formation of a Colonial Economy

Table 2.3 *Clove and domestic copra exports: annual average quantity, value and export price for 15-year periods*[19] *(in 1,000 tons and £1,000 sterling)*

	Cloves			Copra		
Period	Quantity	Value	Price per ton	Quantity	Value	Price per ton
1901−1915	7.2	314	44	7.5	120	16
1916−1930	8.7	716	82	9.5	233	25
1931−1945	9.8	613	63	9.9	115	12

cloves and copra exports was advancing more rapidly than output. But this pattern was broken by the onset of the Depression: while the total quantity of exports continued to rise during the period 1931−1945, there was a sharp decline in the total value of the crops to the point that copra producers were receiving less than they were at the beginning of the century.

Two factors shaped these tendencies. The value or price paid for export crops was dictated from outside by the capitalist world market, while worker productivity, reflected in the quantity exported, was a domestic issue closely monitored and controlled by the wage policy and practice of the Protectorate administration. The Depression which began in the metropolitan economies in the late 1920s was transferred to the colonies through drastically cut prices to overseas producers of food and raw materials. Copra had entered into the diet of industrial workers as an edible oil and the slash in proletarian wages in Western Europe and the United States created a demand within these economies for even cheaper consumption goods from abroad. The early climb in clove prices was reversed in the mid-1920s by monopoly capital for a different reason: new uses for clove oil in cosmetics and flavouring had been discovered.[20] This change from the narrow, high-priced spice market to the broader industrial market had a twofold impact on clove exports to industrial countries. On the one hand it stimulated the flow in that direction: the United Kingdom and the United States increased their portion of the total to roughly 45 per cent by the beginning of the Depression. On the other hand, it led to a decline in prices to these buyers, who threatened to substitute inexpensive synthetics if lower clove prices were not forthcoming. The administration met their needs by introducing a grading system with a category of inexpensive 'industrial clove'.[21]

43

The impact of these price fluctuations on the Zanzibari population varied according to class: the rise in export prices illustrated in Tables 2.2 and 2.3, for example, was not accompanied by a uniform increase in wages for labourers, profits for capitalists, and revenue for the colonial state. It is possible to calculate the benefits from price increases that accrued to each of these groups. The task must begin with an explanation of how value is produced through capitalist relations of production.

Capitalist society is the highest form of commodity production. Everything is made for exchange or sale on the market rather than for personal consumption. Even the capacity to labour is sold as a commodity on the market. Commodities acquire their value through the human labour expended upon them, provided, of course, that there is a market for them in which the money price can be realised.

In classical capitalism the working class, having been stripped of land and tools, is forced to seek work from the capitalist for a wage as a means of staying alive. The fact that they are propertyless in the world of production ensures that they will come forth to sell their capacity to work in order to purchase their means of consumption. Thus economic coercion replaces physical coercion as the principal means of drawing labour to the point of exploitation.

The capitalist purchases this unique commodity — labour power — to work the means of production which he owns and controls. A wage is paid to workers in return for the use of their labour power for a specified period of time. The wage in capitalism should be clearly understood as payment for the workers' ability to labour, not as the value of what their labour produces, which is quite a different thing. The value of labour power is determined like any other commodity: by the average amount of labour it takes to produce it for the market. Translated into concrete terms, the 'average amount of labour' means the average amount of goods such as food, clothing, housing, etc. workers require to exist so they can return to work for the capitalist the following day, and raise a new generation of labourers at home as well.

Workers are employed by capital to make commodities. During the period of employment they create greater value than they are paid as a wage, or to put it differently, the portion of the work day during which they create the equivalent of their wage is necessary labour time, while the rest of the work day is surplus labour time. It is this surplus or uncompensated labour that is called surplus value. From this comes the capitalist's profit when the commodity is sold; it is the basis of his existence.

Since capitalism is a system based on accumulation, it is

necessary for capital to continually look for ways to increase the extraction of surplus value from labour to raise profits. Capital has devised three techniques for this purpose.[22] One is to reduce the necessary labour time. The other two involve an increase in the worker's output of commodities during surplus labour time. Let us look at how these three techniques are used in the standard capitalist mode and in its variant in Zanzibar.

As stated earlier, necessary labour time is that portion of the work day during which the worker produces the equivalent in value of the wage. For the wage to be lowered, the value of labour power must be reduced. In concrete terms this means that the cost of consumer goods must fall so it will cost less to produce and reproduce the labour force, which explains the drive by industrial capital for cheap sources of food from overseas to keep down the cost of consumption goods for workers at home. In theoretical terms, there is a reduction of necessary labour time and a lengthening of surplus labour time.

Capitalism approached this problem differently in Zanzibar. The aim was to avoid creating a landless working class, for if access to land could be maintained, the cost of producing and reproducing labour power would not have to be borne entirely by capital through the wage. Labourer and family would meet their own consumption needs through subsistence production. This was especially attractive where labour was required seasonally, for the wage would be paid to maintain the labourer on a temporary basis. By this means the colonial state reduced necessary labour to an extreme minimum from the beginning, thereby making the working day almost equivalent to surplus labour time. The proportion of surplus value in the total value of commodities produced would be substantial. This has been called the 'cheap labour policy': cheap, because labour retained an excessively small proportion of the total values it created.

The two techniques for increasing the productivity of the worker differ in that one was used in early capitalism prior to the Industrial Revolution, when the level of productive forces was low, while the other was characteristic of mature capitalism with highly developed productive forces in machinery. Both had the consequence of increasing worker productivity, but each achieved that objective by manipulating different factors in the labour process.

In early capitalism (1450–1700) it was the labourers themselves who were made to work more intensely to increase their output of surplus value. This was achieved by lengthening the working day and by payment of the wage in the form of a piece rate, or piece wage. These were the initial means for increasing the production of surplus value, and the state played a central role in coercing the labour force and implementing policy. This was because the workers were inclined to labour only as long as necessary to meet their meagre needs. Of course little surplus value could be created under these conditions, so the state intervened to extend the work day by law.[23] Labourers resisted and the length of the work day came to be determined by class struggle. Karl Marx remarked on how the peasants resisted becoming proletarians:

> It takes centuries ere the 'free' labourer, thanks to the development of capitalistic production, agrees, i.e. is compelled by social conditions, to sell the whole of his active life, his very capacity for work, for the price of the necessaries of life, his birthright, for a mess of pottage.[24]

In mature capitalism it is primarily the constant innovation of more productive technology, in addition to the speed-up of work that heightens labour's output of goods in the same amount of time. In Zanzibar, this second method was not used because the level of productive forces was never developed through the introduction of machinery and new skills.

The principal technique introduced by the colonial administration to create more surplus value was payment by piece wage. Because agricultural production required seasonal rather than annual labour, and because of the low level of productive forces based on semi-proletarian labour, this became the most successful means to intensify labour's output of commodities and surplus value. There were additional reasons for the use of the piece wage under colonial conditions. Marx identified the specific advantages of this form of payment:[25]

1. It is an exact measure for *intensity* of labour. Only the working time embodied in an amount of commodities determined beforehand and experimentally fixed is paid as such.
2. The *quality* of labour is controlled by the work itself. It must be of average perfection if piece-work is paid in full.
3. *Supervision* is superfluous since intensity and quality are controlled by the wage itself.
4. It creates *competition.* Given piece-wage, it is naturally the personal interest of the labourer to strain his labour-power as intensely as possible; this enables the capitalist to raise more easily the normal degree of intensity of labour.
5. The wide scope that piece-wage gives to individuality, tends to develop on the one hand that individuality, and with it the sense of liberty, independence, and self-control of the labourers; on the other, their competition with one another. Piece-work has, therefore, a tendency, while raising individual wages above the average, to lower this average itself.

The Formation of a Colonial Economy

Before demonstrating how this form of payment was used to cheapen the price of labour, it is necessary to explain how the magnitude of the original piece wage was determined. This is revealed in a letter dated September 7, 1898, from Sir Lloyd Mathews, Treasurer and First Minister of the Zanzibar Government, to R.N. Lyne, the Director of Agriculture.[26] Although the letter was written after abolition, many slaves had not gained their freedom; they are referred to as '*shamba* labour' by Mathews, who also uses the term for ex-slaves who had become squatters:

> Special enquiries have been made regarding clove picking and payment of labourers. Last year the people picked on the Zanzibar [Government] estate from 4 to 8 *pishi* per day from 8 a.m. to 4 p.m. This is a small quantity, an average of 6 *pishi* daily, but it must be remembered that last year's crop of cloves was very scanty and does not give a fair average of what can be done when there is a full crop. 10 *pishi* can easily be picked during 8 hours when there is a full crop. A free man who works solely for himself gathers 12 *pishi* per day and a *shamba* labourer 9 *pishi* — but the master or *msimamezi* has to be with the slave to keep the work going. A free man working solely for himself could — from 6 a.m. to 6 p.m. allowing one hour's rest at midday — gather 15 *pishi* if there is a good crop and probably an average of such a man's working through the season would be about 12 *pishi*. *Shamba* labourers are naturally indolent and as yet are unaccustomed to work well and do not appreciate it when it is even for their own benefit solely. My conclusions are that a few free men energetic and strong would average 12 *pishi* per day but that the ordinary labourers would not make a greater average than 9 *pishi* daily, probably less.[27]

After pondering the question of an average quantity, Mathews deliberated at length on what might be the initial size of the piece wage:

> The price for picking cloves has varied considerably, ranging from 3 to 6 *pice* per *pishi*. The price varying according to quantity of crop and also probably to amount of labour to be obtained. A fair price for picking cloves can only be based on what may be regarded as a fair living wage for the picker. There is no doubt that 12 *pice* per day is sufficient to purchase the food usually taken by *shamba* labourers and the lower classes of free working peoples. So that 16 *pice* daily would do this and also pay for their sleeping quarters but this is scarcely sufficient. All ought to be in a position to earn at least 20 *pice* per day and more if they like to exert themselves. The high prices of 5 or 6 *pice* per *pishi* are quite unnecessary during a season such as the present is likely to be and 2 *pice* per *pishi* is too low — as it would scarcely produce to the

pickers the 20 *pice* daily. The price for picking must be 3 or 4 *pice* per *pishi*. This even by picking 7 *pishi* per day would produce to the pickers a fair living wage of 21 *pice* per day at 3 *pice* per *pishi*. The following might be tried as payment for picking cloves and might be an incentive to the pickers to work harder and for more hours — and all after that be paid for at the rate of 4 *pice* per *pishi*. The spur would be to get the first 6 *pishi* done as soon as possible, in order to get working at the higher price picking.[28]

Table 2.4   *Clove production: piece work task and wage for weeding*[29] *(in cents of rupee)*

Year	Task per day (in sq. yards)				Cents per day		Quantity of labour expended
	343	490	588	735	Given wage	Adjusted wage	
1915	X				49	49	100
1916	X				63	63	71
1917	X				63	63	71
1918	X				75	75	53
1919	X				75	75	53
1920		X			81	57	84
1921		X			81	57	84
1922		X			69	48	98
1923		X			59	41	116
1924		X			59	41	116
1925				X	69	32	135
1926				X	69	32	135
1927				X	63	29	141
1928				X	63	29	141
1929				X	63	29	141
1930				X	63	29	141
1931				X	56	26	147
1932				X	56	26	147
1933				X	56	26	147
1934				X	44	21	157
1935				X	44	21	157
1936				X	44	21	157
1937				X	44	21	157
1938				X	44	21	157
1939				X	44	21	157
1940				X	44	21	157
1941				X	44	21	157
1942				X	44	21	157
1943			X		62	36	127
1944			X		67	39	120
1945			X		73	43	112

To demonstrate how the piece wage was used to intensify labour exploitation, the task and price paid per unit must be examined throughout the period under discussion. The standards for payment in both clove and copra production were set on the government plantations. While the volume of products from these estates was estimated to have been only 2 per cent of the total annual output, they became the testing ground for wage policies that employers of labour throughout the Protectorate were encouraged to follow.[30] Table 2.4 presents the appropriate data for the activity of weeding clove plantations.

The basic unit of measurement for this task work was a *pengele*, the space enclosed by four trees planted approximately 21 feet or 7 yards apart, making an area of 49 square yards. In 1915, the task was 7 *pengele* or an area of 343 square yards a day. The wage for this task was approximately 49 cents of a rupee. In 1918 it rose to 75 cents, while the task remained unchanged. Since mainland workers tended to do this work, the wage increase can be explained by labour shortages caused by the war. Although the wage went up again in 1920, it actually signalled intensified exploitation because of the enlarged task. This technique, whereby the state used piecework payment to intensify the exploitation of labour power, can only be understood if the size of the task is compared with the wage. This can be illustrated by examining the period from 1920 to 1925, during which clove export prices, and profits, reached their highest level.

The state initiated and guided the stages of the process. The first step was to introduce an enlarged task accompanied by a higher wage. In 1920 the new task became 10 *pengele*, or 490 square yards, and the wage went up to 81 cents of a rupee. However, when this task and wage is measured against that for 1915 the new wage is the equivalent of only 57 cents. The new task for 1920 was proportionally greater than the wage increase; compared to the figures for 1919, the change actually amounted to a wage reduction.

There was no change in task size through 1924, but the wage was cut in 1922 and again in 1923. Then, in 1925, the task was increased by 50 per cent to 15 *pengele* with an accompanying wage increase of only 17 per cent to 69 cents of a rupee. Measured against data for 1915, the adjusted or real wage for 1925 was 35 per cent below that of a decade earlier. The overall decline in weeding wages from 1915 to 1945 can be followed in the 'adjusted wage' column of Table 2.4.

The final column of the table, titled 'quantity of labour expended', is a more graphic way of illustrating how the exploitation of labour was intensified. If we take the data for 1915 as a baseline of 100 units of labour power put out for that wage, the change becomes apparent. A worker exerted less labour power over the following seven years: that meant the work load was lighter. From 1923, however, the intensity of labour increased to the point where the weeder had to do roughly 50 per cent more work during the Depression years for what was the equivalent of a 1915 wage.

Intensified exploitation of labour is also visible in the piece rates for the different steps in copra production, as revealed in Table 2.5.

Table 2.5 *Copra production: piecework tasks and wage[31] (in cents of rupee)*

Year	Climbing & picking per tree	Collecting & transport to camps per 1,000	Husking per 1,000	Breaking & drying per 1,000
1925	3-4	300	—	—
1926	—	—	—	—
1927	3-4	300	—	—
1928	3-4	250	225-250	225-250
1929	3-4	250	150	200-250
1930	2.3	225	125	200
1931	2.0	200	100	175
1932	2.0	200	100	175
1933	1.6	200	82	150
1934	—	—	—	—
1935	1.3	150	63	125
1936	—	—	—	—
1937	2.3	200	73	147
1938	2.3	200	73	147
1939-44	—	—	—	—
1945	4.0	400	117	217

While the rates for 1915–24 were not published, and annual data are incomplete, the trends are clear. Payments for climbing and picking were cut sharply during the Depression years; by the end of our period they returned to approximately the 1925 rate. A similar trend is observed for collecting and transporting coconuts, with the 1945 rate 25 per cent above that of 1925. There was a downward trend for husking, breaking and drying throughout the 20-year period.

Picking cloves was the most important task in the export sector. Harvested cloves usually constituted about three-quarters of the total exports, with copra making up the balance. What made labour for clove harvests so exceptional was the need to rapidly mobilise a sizeable labour force to pick the clove buds as they ripened from July to September, and December to February. The basic unit of measurement is the *pishi* of approximately 4 pounds of green cloves. The piece wage per *pishi* tended to rise as the season progressed. Table 2.6 gives the starting rate, the range from beginning to highest, as well as the median piece rate over 5 and 15 years beginning in 1901.

Table 2.6 *Clove production: piece work wage for picking averaged over 5 and 15 year periods* [32] *(in cents of rupee for 1* pishi *of 4 lbs.)*

period	Starting		Range		Median	
	5 year period	15 yr. period	5 year period	15 yr. period	5 year period	15 yr. period
1901−05	5	—	1	—	6	—
1906−10	5	—	11	—	11	—
1911−15	5	5	14	9	12	9
1916−20	5	—	14	—	12	—
1921−25	7	—	16	—	15	—
1926−30	7	6	7	12	11	13
1931−35	6	—	7	—	10	—
1936−40	6	—	8	—	10	—
1941−45	8	7	8	8	12	11

Certain conclusions can be drawn from the data in this table. The average piece work wage paid at the start of the harvest rose so little over the period as a whole that the increase of 2 to 3 cents of a rupee was too small to be significant. Since wage rates are ultimately determined by class struggle, the relatively static starting wage for half a century suggests a higher level of class consciousness and action among landowners than among the peasant labourers. This conclusion should be tempered by the consideration that it was the state which set the starting rate in the interest of the landholding class.

The range between the low and high, or opening and closing wage for a season, with the median being the midpoint, requires some explanation before a tentative interpretation of the data can be advanced. There is no way to establish with certainty the volume of cloves harvested at the starting wage when the crop is full, or the closing wage when there are fewer cloves to be picked at higher reaches, or the amount picked at any wage between the two. Since the wage range for the year is known, it is necessary to calculate a 'middle' or median wage. The range and median are significant indicators of the extent to which capital had to heighten the starting wage in order to retain or recruit picking labour. These data can also be interpreted to suggest the level of peasant resistance to wage labour, as well as the potential for an independent source of income.

The interpretation given to these two parts of Table 2.6 is that the range was narrow and the median low when labour was scarce. From 1901 to 1915 the supply of labour was forthcoming primarily because of state coercion and the availability of imports for purchase. Harvest labour became more difficult to recruit between 1916 and 1930 as alternative sources of income opened up to the peasantry through the acquisition of small units of clove trees by proprietors who retained picking labour as unpaid family members on their own clove *shamba* for at least a portion of the initial harvest which had to be picked rapidly before the buds blossomed. Copra prices were also at their peak in this period, offering a source of income from coconuts grown outside the clove sector. It is suggested that these alternatives were a manifestation of peasant resistance to wage labour, or peasant individualism, rather than an indication of a higher collective identity as wage labourers. The drastic fall in copra prices during the Depression and the general increase in the cost of consumer goods pulled peasants back into the paid labour force of the clove sector in the final period.

The broader consequences of the trends in task and piece rates for export crops remain to be demonstrated. What was the relationship between the export price paid to capital and the wage paid to labour and how can it be analysed? The objective must be to create an overall wage bill that takes into account the piece rate variations and reflects the total labour costs for annual production in each of the export industries. This involves certain methodological issues. How can a total wage bill be calculated when the size of the labour force is never stated? Even if that is given, how can the wage proportions be known for different tasks, such as weeding and picking, in the total wage bill? Furthermore, can a wage bill be created when an unknown portion of the total harvest was produced for market by peasants using unpaid family labour?

It seems possible to provide fairly accurate estimates and tentative conclusions by indirect means. To do so requires clarification of three issues. First, what is the size of the wage labour force? Second, how can task percentages of the total be calculated when there are rate differences between them, such as those for weeding and picking cloves, or collecting and husking coconuts? Third, how can a procedure be devised to calculate the total wage bill for each industry once the first two issues have been resolved?

The fact that the wage was paid by piece rate simplifies the problems immensely. The total quantity of commodities produced in each sector is known. From those figures the number of piece payments for tasks can be calculated. It took approximately 6,000 coconuts to make one ton of copra.[33] Since all tasks were based on the number of coconuts, it is possible to estimate the total number of tasks completed and payments made. The tasks involved in clove production are weeding and picking. Since clove trees are planted at intervals of 7 yards it is possible to estimate the total number of tasks of 49 square yards, a *pengele*, done twice a year when the total number of clove trees is known. Based on the government tree survey of 1922 it is estimated that there were roughly 3 million clove trees from 1916 to 1930, and 3½ million from 1931 to 1945. Cloves were picked in units of 4 pounds, a *pishi*, so the total number of *pishi* picked in any one year can be calculated from the total quantity produced.

It is assumed the merchant paid the property owner the government picking rate plus a small additional amount. Theoretically, the payment would be composed of the equivalent in value of the piece wage per *pishi* and a portion of the surplus value embodied in the cloves. The same two parts are embodied in the payment received for coconuts. The surplus value portion of the payment made by the merchant to the property owner was to cover any other production expenses, repayment of loans to merchants, and the remainder was profit.

The merchant paid the same price to landowners for cloves or coconuts, whether paid or unpaid labour was used. Since the piece wage embodied in the price is equivalent to the necessary items of consumption to maintain and reproduce the labourers, it is consumed for that purpose whether paid in money wages directly to the labourer or to the land owning peasant who has to maintain his unpaid family labour. The point of interest here is that by owning his own small unit of productive land and using his family as unpaid labour, the small peasant holder can realise surplus value by selling the collective product to the merchant for a profit. This makes it possible to acquire more land which he will work by exploiting wage labour. To this extent he is sowing the seeds of direct capitalist exploitation. But since the entire family may also be benefiting from the surplus value received which is used to

53

acquire more property (wealth) it is debatable if unpaid family labour can be classified as 'exploited' in the same way as hired wage workers who have no hope of acquiring any wealth from their labour.[34]

The objection might be raised that government wage rates were not followed uniformly by individuals who purchased labour power, and rates varied through the season. To anticipate this problem the assumption is made that median government rates were the norm throughout the Protectorate. This should result in an overestimation rather than underestimation, based on the assumption that private employers would tend to pay less, rather than more, than the piece rates laid down by the administration.

The result of this procedure for estimating the total wage bill for clove production is provided in Table 2.7.

Table 2.7   *Average clove wage bill per ton produced* [35]

Period	Total quantity (in 1,000 tons)	Total wage (in £1,000 stg.)	Wage per ton (in £ stg.)
1916–1920	7.6	140	18.4
1921–1925	9.4	183	19.5
1926–1930	9.0	135	15.0
1931–1935	10.0	138	13.8
1936–1940	9.7	137	14.1
1941–1945	9.8	172	17.6

Table 2.8   *Average copra wage bill per ton produced* [36]

Year	Total quantity (in 1,000 tons)	Total wage (in £1,000 stg.)	Wage per ton (in £ stg.)
1928	9.4	35.5	3.8
1929	11.6	38.7	3.3
1930	12.8	36.1	2.8
1931	11.8	28.7	2.4
1932	11.8	28.7	2.4
1933	12.2	26.6	2.2
1934	–	–	–
1935	11.7	20.1	1.7
1936–37	–	–	–
1938	9.0	20.2	2.2
1939–44	–	–	–
1945	8.8	28.8	3.3

The figures in Table 2.7 show a small increase in the total clove wage bill for the early 1920s after which it declines for a decade during the Depression. It begins to pick up slightly in the late 1930s and more substantially during World War II.

Because the piece rates for copra production are incomplete, the trend in that industry cannot be shown for the same period. Table 2.8 shows the results for the period from 1928 to 1945. Here there is a decline of almost 50 per cent in the total wage bill over the seven-year period, 1928–35, after which there is a small increase to 1938 which had become more substantial by 1945, although the pace of this latter trend cannot be determined.

While it is clear that wage cuts were made to maintain or increase the level of surplus value, it should be emphasised that wages were raised for the same reason. The wage rate might be increased because labour cannot be attracted at prevailing rates, and surplus value cannot be produced if there is no labour power to exploit. This was the case in the early 1920s. Or, the wage might be increased because labour could not be reproduced in the necessary condition of well-being (an unhealthy labour force is less productive). This is a partial explanation for the increase in the late 1930s and 1940s, by which time the cost of living for wage earners had risen sharply. A further explanation for the increase during World War II was the collective fear of capital that labour unrest which had begun in the late 1930s throughout the British Empire would threaten its hold over labour, so small concessions were made to prevent possible disturbances in the Protectorate. Wage increases had very little to do, therefore, with a better price received by domestic capitalists for the export crop on the world market; no such 'sharing' of profits takes place between capital and labour. Rather, the wage rate is simply a matter of maintaining and increasing the rate of surplus value, and for that reason an explanation must be given of that crucial concept.

The difference between the total wage bill and the value of exports in any particular year is the surplus value produced by the labour force. Since all value is created by labour, the portion beyond that returned to the producing class as wages is identified as surplus value. It goes to the expropriating classes of landowners, merchants and the colonial state. While it is their sole source of profit, all of it does not become profit, for a portion is used up as operating expenses. The manner in which this surplus value is consumed by these strata will be explored in the next section. First, an attempt must be made to estimate the actual amount of surplus value produced on an annual basis in Zanzibar.

The method for arriving at that figure is to calculate the difference

Table 2.9 Clove production: estimated annual total wages as percentage export value[37] (in £1,000 sterling)

Period	Total picking wage	% export value	Total weeding wage	% export value	Total wages	Total export value	Export value less total wages	Total wages as % export value
1916–20	102	18%	38	7%	140	562	422	25%
1921–25	158	18%	25	3%	183	857	674	21%
1926–30	116	16%	19	3%	135	729	594	19%
1931–35	120	22%	18	3%	138	534	396	26%
1936–40	122	19%	15	2%	137	627	490	22%
1941–45	148	22%	24	4%	172	678	506	25%

between the total wages, or wage bill, and the total value of exports in each industry. Table 2.9 presents these calculations for the clove industry by showing the total wages as a percentage of the total export bill. The difference between that figure and 100 per cent is the percentage of surplus value.

The data indicates that total wages in clove production were in the approximate range of 20 per cent to 25 per cent of the total value of the crop exported in the period as a whole. The balance of 75 per cent to 80 per cent was surplus value.

Most striking in Table 2.9 is the disparity between the total wages for picking and weeding. This is of considerable interest for a number of reasons. First, because the quantity of work done in cultivation was greater than that in picking, yet the weeding wage is so much lower. Second, while it might be argued that the higher picking rate for less work was a result of skills required for the activity, this was not the case, as no training was required for either task. In other words, the labour used in both sectors was the same: simple average labour.

Since the wage differential cannot be explained by skills or 'labour of a higher or more complicated character than average labour ... [hence] a more costly kind' required for the harvest, a deeper probe must be made into the source of this wage differential.[38] To do so the two dissimilar tasks must be converted into a common unit for comparison. Conversion into time required to complete a task will achieve this objective. The average number of tasks performed in a given period of time was known to administrators, so it is possible to calculate the amount of time it took to do a picking task and a weeding task. From this, it is possible to calculate the difference in wage per hour between weeding and picking. Table 2.10 shows what percentage the weeding wage was of the picking wage when both tasks were performed for one hour.

Table 2.10 *Clove production: weeding wage compared to picking wage for one hour of labour*[39]

1916–20	1921–25	1926–30	1931–35	1936–40	1941–45
52%	22%	18%	18%	15%	22%

The reason for this wage differential was capital's pursuit of surplus value. In that quest the profit is greater when the cost of labour power is reduced. This was achieved through the division of labour that prevailed in this sector. The starting picking rate

Table 2.11 Copra production: estimated annual total wages as percentage export value [40] (in £1,000 sterling)

Year	Total picking wage	Total collecting wage	Total husking wage	Total breaking & drying wage	Total wages	Total export value	Total wages as % export value
1928	4.9	10.6	10.0	10.0	35.5	235	15%
1929	6.1	13.1	7.8	11.7	38.7	261	15%
1930	4.4	13.0	7.2	11.5	36.1	241	15%
1931	3.5	10.6	5.3	9.3	28.7	150	19%
1932	3.5	10.6	5.3	9.3	28.7	143	20%
1933	2.9	11.0	4.5	8.2	26.6	105	25%
1934	–	–	–	–	–	–	–
1935	2.3	7.9	3.3	6.6	20.1	120	17%
1936–37	–	–	–	–	–	–	–
1938	3.1	8.1	3.0	6.0	20.2	92	22%
1939–44	–	–	–	–	–	–	–
1945	4.4	13.3	3.9	7.2	28.8	133	22%

remained relatively stable and did not decline only because the large amount of domestic peasant labour required for the harvest would not come forth at a lower wage. But a much reduced wage for weeding could be paid to domestic labourers stigmatised as ex-slaves and migrant labour recruited from the more depressed regions of the mainland where the demand for caravan labour was in decline. There was nothing natural about this particular arrangement, for ex-slaves and migrant labourers were quite capable of picking cloves, and did so when the opportunity presented itself. Nevertheless, a complex interplay of ideological, social, and class forces was at work which created and perpetuated a separation of tasks that kept down the wage bill for clove production.

Table 2.11 shows the estimated total wage for copra production, although for a more restricted period because of limited data. Here the evidence for the copra industry shows that over this more limited period, wages ranged from 15 to 25 per cent of the total export value of copra, leaving 75 to 85 per cent of the total as surplus value.

If complete data were available for the copra industry it would be possible to combine the wage totals for cloves and copra to determine the total wage bill for domestic production of exports and present it as a percentage of total export value. This would provide the total amount of surplus value created in domestic production for export. While this copra data is incomplete, the combined evidence does suggest that the quantity of surplus value produced by the Protectorate labour force in the export sector in any one year was around 75 per cent of the total value of export commodities. To express it in another way, the labour force received approximately one-quarter of the value it produced, while the remaining three-quarters went to landowners, merchants and the state. How was the surplus product divided up between these sectors of the exploiting classes? What were the proportions received by each? How was it used? An attempt will be made to answer these questions in the following section.

Distribution, consumption and accumulation

The total value created by the labour force in any particular year was distributed in varying amounts between landed capital, merchant capital and the state. What united these sectors was the fact that their income, profits and revenue were derived from the surplus value produced by the labour force. Peasants, squatters and workers were the source of labour that gave exchange value to cloves and copra. If only 25 per cent of the total value was returned to them as wages, as has been estimated, the other 75 per cent was distributed between the appropriating strata. Just how that took place and the use to which each put its portion is a task for investigation.

The colonial state's existence depended on surplus value which was the ultimate source of almost every category of state revenue. This explains its interest in the development of capitalist relations of production which generated not only the commodities but the surplus value embodied in them. When the Protectorate was created in 1891 the principal source of revenue was the 25 per cent duty on clove exports. This was a means of redistributing surplus value from merchant and landed capital to the state. Since only a small portion of imports was consumed domestically, there was only a minor loss of revenue when the 5 per cent import tax was abolished in 1892 to make Zanzibar a free port in an attempt to maintain its past position as the market centre for East Africa.

Re-exports, which constituted the bulk of trade goods passing through the Zanzibar port in the late nineteenth century, were an important means of accumulation for merchants and bankers who operated outside the Protectorate, but they did not yield revenue for the state since re-exports were exempt from taxation. Under these circumstances it became the state's objective to secure its finances by stimulating export production which would create the income for the consumption of more imports. The greater volume of export-import trade would yield more revenue. This priority of increasing domestic production for export was consistent with the need of industrial capital to promote production and consumption of commodities on a world scale.

After World War I, when colonialism had taken root on the African continent, the fate of Zanzibar's re-export trade was of no great fiscal concern to the administration. A decline in the volume of re-export trade through the Zanzibar harbour would have no significant impact on commodity circulation in East Africa as a whole, for what was lost to traders in Zanzibar would be gained by merchant firms in Britain's mainland possessions.

The rise in commodity production and consumption by means of the export-import trade had become a conspicuous feature of the colonial economy by the 1920s, accompanied as it was by a decline in re-exports. Table 2.12 shows the rising percentage of imports consumed domestically, rather than being re-exported, as a result of the increase in export production between 1896 and 1945.

Table 2.12 *Domestic consumption and production: annual average as percentage total imports and exports* [41] *(in £1,000 sterling)*

5 year period	Imports			Exports		
	Total value	Value consumed domestically	% consumed domestically	% domestic origin	Value domestic origin	Total value exports & re-exports
1896—00	1134	282	25%	20%	215	1067
1901—05	1029	345	34%	33%	336	1020
1906—10	929	419	45%	47%	453	963
1911—15	876	532	61%	63%	578	923
1916—20	1921	716	37%	41%	826	2031
1921—25	1827	952	52%	57%	1177	2052
1926—30	1593	989	62%	63%	1045	1650
1931—35	890	687	77%	77%	699	902
1936—40	961	706	73%	75%	761	1016
1941--45	1157	691	60%	65%	854	1320

The figures for 1896—1900 reflect the domination of re-export trade which was characteristic of the nineteenth century pre-colonial economy: only a quarter of imports were consumed domestically. By 1941—1945, when the colonial economy was well established, the value of imports was approximately the same, but the portion consumed domestically had grown to three-fifths of the total. It was only the rising volume of commodities produced for export that made this increased consumption of imported commodities possible. The state built up its revenue from this heightened trade. While its primary role was to serve external capital by creating a greater volume of cheaper exports through capitalist production relations, this generated the desired increase of surplus value at the same time. Since state revenue was derived almost entirely from surplus value, it became a question of some consequence how that additional amount would be distributed among the appropriating strata of the Protectorate.

The state obtained its portion of surplus value through taxes, fees, licences, rents and all the other categories of revenue. The most important source was customs revenue from trade. This tax on exports and imports came to yield at least a half of government income during this period as shown in Table 2.13.

Political Economy of Zanzibar

Table 2.13 *Average yearly customs revenue as per cent total revenue* [42] *(in £1,000 sterling)*

Period	Customs revenue				Total revenue	Customs revenue as % total revenue
	Export duty		Import duty			
	Value	Total	Value	Total		
1916–20	119	35%	65	19%	341	54%
1921–25	197	39%	106	21%	508	60%
1926–30	132	27%	132	27%	494	53%
1931–35	116	24%	131	28%	475	52%
1936–40	111	23%	155	32%	480	55%
1941–45	125	21%	169	29%	583	50%

The table also shows a declining ratio of export duty to import tax as a result of the policy decision made primarily in the 1920s to shift the greater portion of tax revenue to consumers of imports. The import tax which had been abolished in 1892 was reintroduced at 5 per cent in 1899 and was raised to 7½ per cent in 1907. In 1921 it was increased to 10 per cent, then to 15 per cent in 1927. The following year the 25 per cent export duty on cloves was reduced to 20 per cent with payment in cash substituted for payment in kind.[43]

The most likely cause of this moderate shift in taxes from exports to imports in the decade following World War I was the transition in property ownership and the large amount of surplus value being appropriated by merchants and moneylenders. Control of the means of production in clove trees was moving from plantation owners to peasant smallholders. Because an increasing percentage of clove exports was coming from small property owners, the tax burden on them was lightened as an incentive to increase output. The loss of a portion of export revenue was regained through the greater tax on imports of which merchant capital was a key consumer. By this means surplus value would be redirected to the state from merchants and moneylenders.

How much surplus value was taken from private capital by the state? There are two aspects of this question that need to be answered. First, the amount of surplus value in annual revenue must be identified. Second, the percentage this made up of the total surplus appropriated by landed and merchant capital must be estimated.

Almost all state revenue was derived from surplus value. The small portion that was not came from two sources. It is assumed

Plate 6   The Bububu railway crossing the bridge at Saateni. The seven-mile line linked the plantation area with Zanzibar Town. It was uprooted in the late 1920s when it was superseded by the ubiquitous lorry.

that interest and port fees were paid from outside Zanzibar and cannot be considered surplus value. This amounted to less than 10 per cent of annual revenue. The other source to be excluded covers court fees, licences for *ngomas*, canoes, and boats, and taxes such as those on domestic food sold in the market. The amount of the wage bill paid out for these purposes is unknown. If they were one quarter of the wage bill, for example, that would be 12½ per cent of the revenue, meaning 77½ per cent, or just over three-quarters of the annual revenue was surplus value. The firm conclusion that can be drawn is that at least 90 per cent of state revenue came from the labour force directly through its wage and indirectly from the surplus value pulled from the hands of private capital. While the exact size of each is not known, the major portion was surplus value.

The unknown amount of wages paid to the state for fees, etc., makes it difficult to arrive at a conclusive estimate of the amount of surplus value reaped by the state from private capital. If, for example, a quarter of labour's wage went to the state for those expenses, then we would arrive at the following approximations as the state's portion of surplus value: 40 per cent from 1916 to 1930;

60 per cent from 1931 to 1945. If the seemingly high amount of half of labour's wage went on fees, etc., then the state's portion of total surplus value is reduced to 33 per cent for the earlier period and 55 per cent for the later period. It can be said with confidence that the state's portion of surplus value grew from less than half that created before 1930 to more than half the total created during the Depression and World War II.[44]

State expenditures of revenue went to maintain the material infrastructure and reproduce class relations. All categories of expenditure served these two requirements. The greatest allocation in the annual budgets was for salaries and pensions to those who staffed the state apparatus from the Sultan through European officials to lesser functionaries at the provincial and local levels. The Sultan's annual salary of almost ten thousand pounds was twice that of the British Resident.[45] Salaried state employees below the royal family and European officials constituted an emerging petty bourgeoisie which staffed all levels of the state apparatus — administrative, judicial, medical, educational, and public works. Often more skilled than their superiors, they were less well paid.

Pensions for retired European and non-European officials remained the largest expenditure in the annual budgets after salaries and public works. In 1938, a typical year, the amount set aside for this purpose was 12 per cent of the total budget, a figure that declined only slightly to 11 per cent by 1945.[46] That exceeded the sum set aside in 1945 for either medicine or public health and was almost double the allocation for education in the Protectorate.[47] The total sum identified for health and education had not changed substantially since 1931.

Employees who performed wage labour for the state were in quite a different category from those receiving salaries. The largest number worked for the Public Works Department (PWD). Between one thousand and three thousand persons were paid a wage to maintain the roads and facilities required to get commodities to and from the ports. The trend for PWD wages can be observed in Table 2.14 (page 66).

Payment for PWD labour power was made in the form of a time wage rather than the piece wage. It is likely that the type of work dictated this form of payment: closer supervision of the work process itself in a situation where objectives were achieved in stages over time, rather than in uniform units. The time wage was kept roughly on a par with the estimated daily income for piece wage labour in clove picking to avoid the withdrawal of labour from the value producing sector. Wage reductions were made accordingly.

Plate 7   A lorry in the Zanzibar market, having brought coir rope, firewood and other produce from the countryside.

Plate 8   The building of the new harbour, 1923. It shifted port authorities from Shangani to Malindi.

Plate 9   The Protectorate Council under the chairmanship of the Sultan. It was merely advisory with token Arab and Indian representatives, seen on the right.

Table 2.14   *PWD: Daily Minimum Wage* [48] *(in cents of rupee)*

Year	Average no. employed	Unskilled		Skilled	
		Female	Male	Native	Indian
1898	—	—	31	—	—
1899–1910	—	—	—	—	—
1911	—	—	69	—	—
1912–24	—	—	—	—	—
1925–26	1,400	63	75	100	100
1927	2,205	63	63	100	100
1928	2,316	63	63	100	100
1929	1,510	63	63	100	100
1930	—	—	—	—	—
1931–32	842	50	63	100	225
1933	1,126	50	50	100	225
1934	—	—	—	—	—
1935	1,148	50	50	100	100
1936	—	—	—	—	—
1937	—	50	50	100	100
1938	3,000	50	50	100	100
1939–41	—	50	50	—	—
1942	—	56	56	—	—
1943–44	—	—	—	—	—
1945	1,400	70	70	140	140

While PWD labour was not engaged in the production of surplus value, it was required for its realisation through transport to the point of sale. It serviced the most essential aspect of the material infrastructure for export production.

Very little of the surplus value which was drawn to the state as revenue was for accumulation through investments and loans. A balance of assets which approximated the annual expenditure was kept on hand. While loans were not made internally, the state made free use of its revenue as gifts and loans without interest to Britain during wartime. The sum of £70,000 sterling was given to Britain between 1915 and 1918, 'as a contribution to HMG towards the expense of the war', while an additional £221,000 was loaned interest free.[49] This practice had become general colonial policy by World War II, when colonial administrators were encouraged to build up surpluses for Britain's use. The loss to the colonies, and gain to Britain, were reported to Parliament by the Secretary of State for the Colonies:

> At the end of 1945, a total of 48,846,000 Pounds has been raised in the Colonies and re-lent to His Majesty's Government to assist the war effort. Of this total 16,113,000 was lent to His Majesty's Government free of interest.[50]

While Zanzibar's contribution was surpassed by those of many other colonies, the practice supports the argument that the colonial state represented class interests rather than those of an undifferentiated public. State revenue was created by the labour force, appropriated by the landed and merchant classes, and redistributed in varying amounts to the state primarily through taxes. It was put to use to perpetuate the exploitative relations of capital and wage labour. It is a strong case for the colonial state to be seen as an instrument of class oppression.

What portion of the surplus value remained with landowners, merchants and moneylenders and was not redirected to the state? It was estimated that the amount taken by the state grew from less than half to more than half between 1916 and 1945. Therefore, the direct appropriators retained the larger share up through the 1920s until the Depression when the state reduced the portion kept by private capital to less than half the total surplus value.

These are merely estimates meant to be suggestive and cannot be considered conclusive by any means. Statistical data can convey illusions of certainty and finality. There are problems in making such estimates, but a greater likelihood of underestimating rather than exaggerating totals. The wage bill, for example, was lower than estimated to the degree that private employers or merchants paid wages below those on government plantations. Certainly that happened, so it is probable that the wage bill is an overestimate and that the total amount of surplus value going to merchants and landed capital was larger than the above estimate.

It seems likely that the greater part, by far, of this total went to merchant capital. That is because merchants, by definition, used their profits for accumulation by reinvestment rather than for consumption as was characteristic of pre-capitalist landed classes. Whether they be feudal lords or slave masters, the landed classes used the surplus generated by serfs and slaves to support a pattern of luxurious and ostentatious living.

The lives and fate of merchants and slave owners were closely bound together in the pre-colonial era. They were dependent on one another for the production and sale of cloves and copra. However, each sought a greater portion of the surplus product, forcing them into opposition, and the slave owners were no match for the merchants. The latter controlled the price for crops and imported commodities and had money to loan as well. The ultimate consequence was that slave owners became debtors and merchants became creditors. Of course loans were made not only to satisfy slaveholders' consumption needs; they were an additional way for merchants to use their money as capital. Loans were advanced to be repaid in a greater amount as principal plus interest. A variation on this form of capital accumulation was the practice of receiving a portion of harvested cloves as partial repayment on a loan. Slave owners were seldom able to liquidate their debts to moneylenders and the latter gained an increasing share of the surplus product in the pre-capitalist era.

Capitalism expanded this debtor-creditor relationship in the colonial era as the groundwork was laid for a new strata of landowners to appear in the clove and copra sectors of the economy. The creation of wage labour and the stimulus of commodity consumption led to social differentiation within the peasantry and the rise of a property-accumulating segment within it. Merchants were now in a position to liquidate the heavy debts owed by plantation owners by dividing the estates and selling them in small units. There were those in the administration who wanted to halt this process and conserve the plantations. The Commission on Agriculture argued this line in its 1923 report: it wanted cheap credit facilities extended to plantation owners to pay off creditors.[51] But this argument was rejected by the government which favoured smallhold ownership. Kirsopp, the Chief of Customs in 1926, presented the case for peasant production:

The Formation of a Colonial Economy

The agricultural economy of this island is in fact in a fairly rapid transition. The counterpart of Arab decline has been native advancement.... If the clove industry of Zanzibar is to be retained in the hands of the present producers it can, I suggest, only survive as a peasant culture. Our agricultural problem is not, therefore, the regeneration of the original plantation system so unsuited to modern conditions, but the building up of a system of small holdings on lines best adapted to economic production.[52]

The real problem, in the eyes of the administration, was that this new stratum of peasant smallholders had become heavily indebted to merchant creditors in a comparatively short period of time. The administration made its move to reverse this situation a few years later, when the impact of the Depression produced a conflict of class forces that threatened accumulation on a world scale as well as within the Protectorate.

The crisis of accumulation that hit industrial capitalism in the late 1920s, causing the Depression that followed for more than a decade, was extended to the colonies through a demand for cheaper commodities. The Protectorate administration worked out a plan to reduce wages and force up productivity, but these objectives could not be achieved while merchants and money-lenders dominated the smallhold producers. So, state power was used in the 1930s to break the hold of commercial and lending capital on the peasantry by restricting its ability to accumulate.

A series of legislative measures were passed from 1934 to 1939 to achieve this objective. The Produce Export Decree (1934) cheapened clove exports to Europe and the United States by introducing grading. The Clove Exporters Decree (1934) limited the number of exporters through costly licensing. The Alienation of Land Decree (1934) prohibited further transfer of land into the hands of merchants and provided for a moratorium, or suspension of payments, on debts. The Clove Growers' Association Decree (1934) created a government body to control the clove and copra industry. The Clove Purchasing Decree (1937) granted that body a monopoly on buying and selling export crops, although it was relaxed the following year because of clove boycotts in India in support of the Protectorate merchant class with its close ties to that country. As a result of the Land Protection (Debt Settlement) Decree (1938), the government took over all peasant debts by buying out creditors. The Land Alienation Decree (1939) put further restrictions on property transfer: it specified that a seller of land 'must always keep sufficient property for the proper maintenance of himself and his dependents'.[53] This prevented the rise of a true proletariat.

The power of merchants to accumulate was blocked by these measures as well. Their acquisitive role in Zanzibari history accounted for both their success and ultimate failure. They had proved to be more dynamic than landed capital prior to the Depression: they accumulated the lion's share of surplus value as a result. But they did not have state power. When the grip of merchants and moneylenders on peasant production clashed with the interests of metropolitan capital in the Depression, the colonial state proved loyal to the latter and moved to drastically limit the access of the former to surplus value. The decline of merchant capital gave new life to a peasant economy deeply enmeshed in capitalist relations.

What were the general consequences of colonial rule for those who worked for a wage in Zanzibar? It has been argued that the exploitation of wage labour was the source of life for the capitalist classes of landowners, merchants and the state. Only a small portion − perhaps 25 per cent − of the value labourers created in export production was left in their hands. What assessment can be made of how this met their consumption needs, which, after all, constituted a principal reason for them to become involved in commodity production?

Many imports to Zanzibar had become general necessities in the years between World War I and World War II. Because the annual income derived from export production was relatively small, peasant producers and wage labourers could buy comparatively few imported goods with cash from this source alone. To supplement their meagre income from the export market, they increasingly went to the domestic market with a novel objective. No longer were useful consumption goods of equal value exchanged directly. The purpose of the new transaction was to sell in order to receive goods and cash as well. To do this, consumer items of greater value had to be sold in order to receive money along with goods; the incoming cash was to make up the difference in exchange value between the commodities bought and sold. It will be argued that the combination of low cash income from the export market and these new transactions in the domestic market were important factors contributing to the impoverishment of labour in Zanzibar from 1915 to 1945.

The observations of administrators during the Depression support this argument. A 1937 government survey entitled *Nutritional Review of the Natives of Zanzibar*, reported on local market exchanges that reflect the dietary decline of the peasantry:

All the valuable foodstuffs go to the town. It is a strange situation

70

arising from economic forces. The African must clothe himself as well as feed himself, and he can only do this by trading his valuable foodstuffs to the well-to-do and buying for himself a cheaper food, using the balance on the transaction for clothes, repairs to houses, fishing nets and lines and other essential outgoings. Eggs are not eaten, because they can be sold, and often are not sold because they are potential chickens commanding a higher price. Milk is not drunk but bartered. The only fish eaten is that which cannot be absorbed into the available market. Everything is sold to buy rice.[54]

Ninety per cent of the rice consumed in the Protectorate by this time was being imported rather than grown locally, and it was costly to consume.[55] Peasant consumption of domestic brown rice − more nutritional than imported polished rice − was costly as well: peasant consumption had fallen off because it required fertile soil which they no longer possessed nor could afford to rent. Furthermore, the substantial labour time required to raise it could conflict with the labour requirements in the export sector.

As a result, cassava replaced rice as the staple for rural and urban wage labourers in the colonial era. The change of diet was observed by administrators in the 1930s:

Rice is an arduous crop.... It is not surprising that cassava, which yields up to six tons an acre, and which needs little more than planting and gathering, is preferred as a crop by the native, and that he relies upon what he can earn in the clove season to purchase what rice he can afford, falling back on his home grown cassava under almost famine conditions when his money is spent.[56]

The appearance of cassava as a dietary staple contributed greatly to the rise of nutritional deficiency in this phase of the Protectorate's history. In contrast to rice, cassava has practically no nutritional value. This was known to the British administration from its experience in the colony of India where the shift from rice to cassava had already taken place. The Indian experience contributed to the formation in 1936 of an advisory body in Britain to study nutrition in the colonial empire. The unhealthy consequences of cassava consumption are clearly stated in its report:

In Travancore, in South India, the staple crop used to be rice. Rice is still grown on the low-lying lands and considerable quantities are imported, but with the increase in population in recent years, this state has had to find food crops which will grow on higher lands, and cassava now forms an important part of the food supply. The energy yield per head of population is probably no less than it used to be but there has been a marked deterioration in health, which it seems must be due to the fact that a large proportion of the population now lives on cassava and not rice as their staple foodstuff. Cassava contains a much lower quantity of the protective factors than rice and therefore nutrition was bound to suffer if means were not found of replacing in the diet the various elements in the composition of rice which are not found in cassava.[57]

In the Protectorate, a correlation between low wages and poor nutrition had been documented for Zanzibar Town by 1935. A study of the income and diet of 'poorer natives' concluded that 498 of 652 interviewees 'spent no more than a shilling per head per week on food', a sum that was only one quarter of the government's estimate of the cost of living for a labourer.[58] According to the same survey, the common diet among 'poorer people' consisted of 2 ounces of bread for breakfast, nothing for lunch, and cassava for dinner in 'any amount that can be afforded up to two pounds or more.'[59]

The growing impoverishment of Zanzibar's labour force was part of a general pattern that had appeared in Britain's colonial empire with the introduction of capitalist production. What brought it to the attention of officials in the 1930s was the potentially adverse impact that wage cuts might have on the productivity of the labour force. The possible connection between low wages, malnutrition and declining productivity in the Depression was argued and the Secretary of State for the Colonies initiated a three-year study of the nutrition of colonial labourers in 1936. The following conclusions and recommendations were published in 1939:

> It is an unfortunate fact that the world prices of primary commodities are subject to more violent fluctuations than those of manufactured articles.... The colonial producer must, it appears, continue to expect to see a wide variation in his income from many crops.... Wherever possible the labourer should be able to supplement his wages by produce from his own garden.[60]

In Zanzibar the slight wage increase for Protectorate labour during the war (see Tables 2.4−2.6), was dwarfed by an 81 per cent rise in prices between 1939 and 1946.[61] Measures were taken to intensify the 'cheap wage' policy under wartime conditions. The 'Grow More Crops' campaign and the provision of food plots to those on the islands without visible means of livelihood were a mere tactic to cheapen the reproduction of labour power. It was the logic of colonial capitalism in Zanzibar: to make production relations highly profitable while inhibiting the appearance of capital's nemesis, the landless proletariat.

Notes

1. Richard F. Burton, *Zanzibar; City, Island, and Coast*, Volume I, London, Tinsley Brothers, 1872 (Johnson Reprint Corporation, 1967), p. 405.
2. C.A. Bartlett, *Statistics of the Zanzibar Protectorate, 1895–1935*, Zanzibar, Government Printer, 1936, p. 4. The units of one rupee were 64 pice or 16 annas. Later, the rupee was subdivided into 100 cents.
3. One rupee exchanged for one shilling four pence at the exchange rate of fifteen rupees for one pound sterling up to 1926. That rate changed with government devaluation of the rupee beginning in 1927, from which year one rupee exchanged for one shilling six pence. The East African shilling replaced the rupee as currency from 1936 at approximately the prevailing exchange rate. Accordingly, all calculations in this chapter are made on the basis of one rupee = one shilling four pence from 1891 to 1926, and one rupee = one shilling six pence after 1926.
4. Karl Marx, *Capital*, Volume One, New York, Vintage Books, 1977, p. 1031.
5. Data for cloves to 1935 from C.A. Bartlett, *op. cit.*, and 1936 to 1945 from Zanzibar Government, *Annual Trade Report for 1963*, Zanzibar, Government Printer, 1964. Data for copra to 1935 from Bartlett, *op. cit.*, and estimates for 1936–45 based on method in note 18.
6. For example, Frederick Cooper, *From Slaves to Squatters: Plantation Labour and Agriculture in Zanzibar and Coastal Kenya, 1890–1925*, New Haven, Yale University Press, 1980.
7. R.S. Troup, *Report on Clove Cultivation in the Zanzibar Protectorate*, Zanzibar, Government Printer, 1932, p. 20.
8. While tendencies may continue beyond 1945, all calculations in this present study end with that year.
9. Colonial Office, *Annual Report for Zanzibar, 1924*, pp. 8–9, and Zanzibar Protectorate, *Report of the Commission on Agriculture, 1923*, Zanzibar, Government Printer, 1924, p. 3.
10. Colonial Office, *Annual Report for Zanzibar, 1923*, p. 8.
11. Colonial Office, *Annual Report for Zanzibar*, for years 1924 to 1928.
12. Colonial Office, *Annual Report for Zanzibar*, 1931 *and* 1932, *and B.H. Binder, Report on the Zanzibar Clove Industry*, Zanzibar, Government Printer, 1936, p. 2.
13. G.D. Kirsopp, *Memorandum on Certain Aspects of the Zanzibar Clove Industry*, London, Waterlow and Sons Ltd., 1926, p. 10.
14. *Ibid.*
15. This direct tax was not reimposed again, except briefly from 1934 to 1938. Mahmoud Hemeid Jabir, 'The plantation economy during the protectorate period in Zanzibar', a dissertation submitted in partial fulfilment of the requirements of the degree of Master of Arts in the University of Dar es Salaam, 1977, pp. 74–5. A debt of gratitude is owed to Mr. Jabir for making available a copy of this highly informative work.
16. From G.St.J. Orde Browne, *The African Labourer*, New York, Barnes & Noble, Inc., 1967 (reprint of 1933 edition), p. 181.

17. C.A. Bartlett, *op. cit.*, Table VIII, footnote.
18. Data to 1935 from Bartlett, *op. cit.*, Table VI, and 1936–45 from Zanzibar Government, *Trade Report for the Year 1963*. All clove exports are of domestic origin. All copra originating elsewhere and re-exported from Zanzibar is excluded. Figures for quantity and value are calculated by adding the annual totals for 5-year period and dividing sum by five to get yearly average. Yearly average price for 1,000 tons is calculated by dividing yearly quantity by value; it is assumed to be the amount paid for 1,000 tons by exporting firms at the Customs House in Zanzibar Town.

    1891 and 1892 data on clove export value are unavailable. Estimates for those years are arrived at in the following manner. Total quantity for 1891 was 5,900 tons; for 1892, 6,000; for 1893, 5,900. Value of the latter was £139,000 sterling. That figure is used as a conservative estimate for total annual value for previous two years.

    Data for domestic copra were not available for 1891–95. Domestic copra exports averaged 75 per cent of total copra exports from 1896 to 1935. Copra figures for 1936–40 and 1941–45 are estimates based on the assumption that they are 75 per cent of the total copra export (domestic and re-exports) reported in Zanzibar Protectorate, *Trade Report for the year 1940*, and Zanzibar Protectorate, *Trade Report for the year 1945*.
19. *Ibid.*
20. Troup, *op. cit.*, pp. 5–6, and W. Grazebrook, *The Clove of Commerce*, London, Commercial Calculating Company, 1925, p. 27.
21. B.H. Binder, *op. cit.*, p. 10.
22. The techniques are analysed in detail in Part III, 'The production of absolute surplus-value,' Part IV, 'Production of relative surplus-value,' and Part V, 'The production of absolute and relative surplus-value,' in Karl Marx, *Capital*, Volume I, Moscow, Progress Publishers, 1954.
23. See Chapter X, 'The working-day', in *ibid.*
24. *Ibid.*, p. 258.
25. *Ibid.*, Chapter XXI, 'Piece-wages'.
26. Zanzibar Archives, Secretariat File, No. 10543.
27. *Ibid.*
28. *Ibid.*
29. Data from Zanzibar Protectorate, *Blue Books*, annually, and Mahmoud Hemeid Jabir, *op. cit.*, Table 2.3B. Wages reported in shillings are converted at R1 ‒ Sh1/4d to 1926, and R1 ‒ Sh1/6d after that year. Jabir gives range of 7¼ to 8½ annas per day as 1915 wage. At R1 ‒ Sh1/4d the range is 45–53 cents per day. The median of 49 cents per day is used in this table. Basic task unit is *pengele*, area enclosed by 4 trees, approximately 7 yards by 7 yards, or 49 square yards. 'Adjusted wage' is given wage adjusted to 1915 task of 343 square yards. Method: given wage is divided by task to get cents of rupee per square yard. Multiply that figure by original task of 343 square yards to arrive at a wage adjusted to original unit of labour expenditure. 'Quantity of labour expended' by worker to receive equivalent of 1915 wage is used as

index of 100 units of labour power. Calculated annually by determining percentage difference between adjusted wage and that of original year, 1915, and then adding or subtracting that percentage to/from index of 100 as required. It is assumed to indicate the intensity of labour for equivalent of 1915 wage: less labour is put out if it falls below index; more labour is put out if it rises above 100.

30. Troup, *op. cit.*, p. 21.
31. Data from Zanzibar Protectorate, *Blue Books*, annually, except 1930 figures from *Report on the Agricultural Department for the year 1931*. The *Report on the Agricultural Department for the year 1933* gives 1.6 as the climbing and picking wage for 1931−32, and 150 as the collecting wage for 1933. 'During the year 1940 ... the price of coconuts fell from Shs17/- a thousand to Shs6/- at which price it was hardly worth collecting them, and the yield to the owners did not permit the employment of labour in extensive cultivation.' 'Labour Report for 1940', drafted by Provincial Commissioner, Zanzibar, October 9, 1941 in Secretariat File: No. 10543: 'Clove Labour', Zanzibar Archives.
32. Data from Jabir, *op. cit.*, and Colonial Office, *Annual Report on Zanzibar*, London, HMSO, annually. First 15-year period is 1901−15 for starting wage, wage range and median wage. Colonial Office, *Annual Report on Zanzibar* for 1931−35 gives a starting wage of 5 rather than 6 cents, and a range of only 5 cents rather than 7.
33. *Annual Report on the Agriculture Department for the Year 1932*, Zanzibar, Government Printer, p. 11.
34. The methodological steps to estimate the total wage bill for clove and copra industries are given in notes 37 and 40.
35. Quantity from Bartlett, *op. cit.* and Table 2.3. Wages from Table 2.9.
36. Quantity from Bartlett, *op. cit.* and Table 2.3. Wages from Table 2.11.
37. Total wage includes all payments for picked cloves made to independent producers as well as wage labour. Wage rates from Table 2.4 and Table 2.6. Total export value, 1916−35, from Bartlett, *op. cit.*, and 1936−45 from Zanzibar Government, *Trade Report for Year 1963*. Method for calculating total picking wage follows these steps: (1) calculate total quantity exported in tons for period and divide by 5 to establish annual average; (2) multiply by 560, the number of *pishi* of 4 pounds in one ton, to convert total to *pishi*; (3) double that total since wage is paid for green cloves which weigh approximately twice as much as the dried cloves which are exported; (4) eliminate annual wage variation between starting wage and maximum wage by using median wage, half-way between starting and maximum wage, for five-year period as an 'average' wage for each year within period; (5) multiply total from step 3 by step 4 to get total wage bill in cents of rupee; (6) divide by 100 to convert total from cents of rupee to rupees; (7) establish number of rupees in one pound sterling for each year by using conversion rate above, and divide by that number to convert total wage bill into pounds sterling. Method for calculating total weeding bill: (1) establish number of tasks per acre; (2) multiply by wage in cents of rupee; (3) convert to cents of shilling by using conversion rate above; (4) convert to shillings

per acre (5) multiply by 48,000 acres, the number of acres under clove cultivation according to government *Blue Books*; (6) multiply by 2 since weeding done twice per year; (7) divide by 20 (20 shillings = £1) to convert answer into pounds sterling.

38. See Marx, *op. cit.* (Moscow), pp. 51 and 191 for analysis of unskilled labour, or simple average labour, and skilled labour.

39. Method: (1) estimate the total number of tasks for weeding and picking each year and establish five-year averages. Total number of weeding tasks, *pengele*, is estimated at 3 million for 1916 to 1930 and 3.5 million for 1931 to 1945. Multiply by 2 since weeding is done twice a year. Total number of picking tasks, *pishi*, is approximately 5 million for 1916 to 1930 and 5.5 million for 1931 to 1945. (2) Estimate average time for one weeding task and one picking task. It is estimated that an average of 10 *pishi* can be picked in 8 hours, based on letter from Sir Lloyd Mathews, Treasurer and First Minister of the Zanzibar Government, to R.N. Lyne, Director of Agriculture, Zanzibar, September 7, 1898, in Zanzibar Archives, Secretariat File, No. 10543; *Blue Book for 1925*; and Colonial Office, *Annual Report for 1936*. It is estimated that 10 *pengele* can be weeded in approximately 4 hours based on *Blue Book for 1945*; Colonial Office, *Annual Report for 1951*, and *Annual Report for 1959–60*; and Frederick Cooper, *op. cit.*, p. 109; only *Blue Book for 1925* differs. Therefore, the amount of time it takes to complete one weeding task is approximately one half that taken to complete a picking task. (3) Determine the percentage of total weeding time to total picking time for each five-year period. (4) Adjust total weeding wage in Table 2.9 upward by percentage difference found in step 3 for each period. This gives total wage for each of the tasks adjusted to contain equal amounts of labour time. (5) Find what percentage this total weeding wage is of the total picking wage.

40. Total wage includes payment to independent producers as well as wage labour. Statistics unavailable for all years. Data from Bartlett, *op. cit.* for quantity and value domestic copra exports to 1935. 1937 and 1938 quantity and value is estimated yearly figure for period 1936–40 as explained in note 18. 1945 quantity and value domestic export estimated at 75 per cent total copra export for that year. Method for calculating total picking wage: (1) 1 tree produces average of 30 nuts; so 200 trees produce 6,000 nuts which is the number estimated to produce 1 ton of copra. (2) Multiply picking wage per tree by 200 to get cents of rupee paid out for picking coconuts for 1 ton copra. Use median wage where range is given, such as 3.5 cents for 1928. (3) Multiply cents of rupee per ton copra by total tonnage for year, then divide by 100 to convert to number rupees paid for total picking wage for that year's tonnage. (4) Divide total rupees by 13.33, being number of rupees in one pound sterling at exchange rate of R1 = Sh 1/6d, to convert answer to pounds sterling. Method for calculating total collecting, husking, breaking, and drying wage: (1) multiply wage rate per 1,000 by 6 to get cents of rupee paid out for the 6,000 nuts required to produce 1 ton copra; (2) divide by 100 to convert from cents of

rupee to rupee per ton; (3) multiply rupee per ton by total quantity for year to get total rupees paid out for that tonnage; (4) convert to pounds sterling as in last step for picking.

41. Data from C.A. Bartlett, *op. cit.* and Zanzibar Protectorate, *Annual Trade Reports for 1945 and 1948.* Bullion and specie import and re-export figures excluded from table. 'The movement of silver between this Protectorate and India is for the adjustment of a fluctuating trade balance', according to Zanzibar Protectorate, *Annual Trade Report for the Year 1925.* Data for value of domestic copra exports, 1935−40 and 1941−45, are unavailable. Estimate for total value made according to explanation for Table 2.2, to which is added 42, the average amount total domestic exports exceeded total clove and copra exports for five-year periods, 1896−35.

42. Data from Bartlett, *op. cit.*, and Colonial Office, *Annual Reports on Zanzibar* for the years 1936, 1937, 1938, and 1946. Total revenue for 1932 from Bartlett, while import and export figures are estimates arrived at by using average percentage for 4-year period, 1931, 1933−1935. Total for 1936 is from Colonial Office *Annual Report,* while import and export figures are estimates derived from 1937−40 average percentage.

43. Raymond Leslie Buell, *The Native Problem in Africa,* New York, The Macmillan Company, 1928, pp. 276−277.

44. In the hypothetical case where none of the labourer's wage went to the state, the proportions of surplus value going to the state would be approximately 45 per cent in the earlier period and 67½ per cent in the later period.

45. Zanzibar Protectorate, *Blue Book for the year ending 31st December 1938,* Zanzibar, Government Printer, 1939.

46. *Ibid.*

47. Zanzibar Protectorate, *Blue Book for the year ending 31st December 1946,* Zanzibar, Government Printer, 1948.

48. 1898 daily wage is rural rate (town rate is 38 cents), derived from monthly wage of Rs8 in country and Rs10 in town as reported in Frederick Cooper, *op. cit.,* p. 81. Cooper does not give the number of days worked per week. This calculation is based on assumption of 6 working days per week, thus dividing monthly wage by 26. If only 5-day work week, then monthly wage is divided by 21.75 to get daily country wage of 37 cents and town wage of 46 cents. Monthly wage of Rs18 for 1911 in Cooper, *ibid.* Daily wage calculated on assumption of 6 working days per week. If a 5 day-work week, then daily wage is 83 cents. Data for 1925 onwards from Zanzibar Protectorate, *Blue Books* unless noted otherwise. Female unskilled wage for 1925 and 1926 is actually listed as 62 cents, which was 10 anna. In 1927 it is listed as 10 anna. My conversion table has 62.5 cents being 10 anna rounded upward. 63 cents has been entered for 1925 and 1926 to show that wage remained unchanged in 1927, although reported in different unit. Wage reduction for 1927 made in November 1926, Correspondence in File 11456, 'Cost of Labour: PWD and Agriculture Departments', Zanzibar Archives. Reduction same date in Pemba from 100 to 75, and 75 to 63 on June 1,

1928. Wage differential between country and township labour introduced in 1933: 50 cents in country, 56 in Zanzibar Town; Executive Council March 16, 1933 in File 11456, Zanzibar Archives. Wages for 1939 to 1941 from letter to Secretary of State for Colonies from British Resident, Zanzibar, September 10, 1942, in Secretariat File No. 11479, Zanzibar Archives, as is 1942 data for increase to 56 cents in country and 63 cents in Zanzibar Town. Cost of living allowance is added to minimum wage in 1945, and applies to both sexes; differential between country and township remains. Therefore, figure is minimum wage 'plus cost of living allowance, 40 per cent and 50 per cent approximately without and within township respectively,' making unskilled labour 70 cents in country and 84 cents in Zanzibar Town. 1945 data on skilled wage is minimum for either 'Native' or Indian, 'plus cost of living allowance, 40 per cent and 50 per cent approximately without and within township respectively...' making skilled labour 140 cents in country and 150 cents in Zanzibar Town.

49. Great Britain, *Colonial Reports — Annual Zanzibar Reports for 1915, 1916, 1917, and 1918*, London, HMSO.
50. Great Britain, Colonial Office, *The Colonial Empire (1939—1947), presented by the Secretary of State for the Colonies to Parliament, July 1947*, London, HMSO, 1947, p. 105.
51. *Report of the Commission on Agriculture, 1923*, pp. 3—5.
52. G.D. Kirsopp, *op. cit.*, p. 1.
53. Reported in Zanzibar Protectorate, *Report of the Action which is being taken on the first report — Part 1 — of the Committee on Nutrition in the Colonial Empire*, (CMD 6050), Zanzibar, Government Printer, 1940, p. 6.
54. Zanzibar Protectorate, *Nutritional Review of the Natives of Zanzibar*, Zanzibar, Government Printer, 1937, p. 9.
55. Zanzibar Protectorate, *Report of the Action...*, p. 10.
56. Zanzibar Protectorate, *Nutritional Review...*, p. 19.
57. Economic Advisory Council, Committee on Nutrition in the Colonial Empire, *First Report — Part 1 — Nutrition in the Colonial Empire*, (presented to Parliament by command, July 1939, CMD 6050), London, HMSO, 1939, p. 18.
58. Zanzibar Protectorate, *Nutritional Review...*, p. 7, and Great Britain, Colonial Office, *Annual Report of Zanzibar Protectorate 1935*, London, HMSO, p. 21.
59. Zanzibar Protectorate, *Nutritional Review...*, p. 9.
60. Economic Advisory Council, Committee on Nutrition in the Colonial Empire, *First Report...*, p. 46.
61. Great Britain, Colonial Office, *Annual Report on Zanzibar for the Year 1947*, London, HMSO, 1948, p. 8.

Three

The Struggle for Independence
1946—1963

B.D. BOWLES

1

The structure of Zanzibar's political economy during the colonial period had arisen not by accident, but out of the needs of colonial production. Zanzibar became an underdeveloped area as a result of this process. The process itself was unusual in that cloves and copra, the major exports, were not primarily raw materials for industries in the metropolis, Britain, but were exported mainly to the similarly underdeveloped areas of India and Indonesia. By the middle of the twentieth century such a trans-Indian Ocean trade had become an important supplementary part of the capitalist world trading system. Indeed, one can see India acting in some ways as a sub-metropole.

But all this does not detract from the fact that what happened in the world of trade was to a very large extent determined by the interests of British capital, that is, those in whose interests the colonial economy operated. But British capital operated in a situation created by history and not in a vacuum. Clove production was introduced by Zanzibar's first colonisers, the Arabs, and some of the earliest profits were made by merchants carrying on an entrepôt trade, in particular the slave trade. Production is always likely to be more important than trade, and the last remnants of the entrepôt trade were disappearing during the late colonial period. Clove and copra production became dominant. In spite of unsuccessful efforts by some colonial administrators to diversify Zanzibar's economy (only, as one would expect, into other export crops such as cocoa), even copra declined in importance and cloves became virtually a monoculture. This meant that the

79

pressure on producers from both the owners of the means of production, that is, the clove plantation owners, and the merchants deprived of other sources of profit, became increasingly great. The tendency was for the merchants to reduce buying prices of cloves and for purchasers of labour to reduce wages.

Cloves cannot be harvested without a large but temporary labour supply. Their cultivation requires a small amount of constant labour on weeding, and enormous amounts of labour for a relatively short period of six to eight weeks at picking time. Hence clove production is peculiarly appropriate to a migrant labour system. This system, where a peasant migrates for a part of the year to an industry or plantation run on capitalist lines, was typical of colonial economies. Late in the nineteenth century it was realised that while slaves were useful for constant weeding purposes they were less economical and less useful than temporary paid pickers. The constant labour was provided by mainlanders, temporary labour by Zanzibaris. The conversion of indigenous people into a reserve labour supply (the process by which they were forced to offer themselves on the labour market) took place over a long period. It was achieved less by increasing cash or forced labour demands on peasants (these were tried and failed) than by the impoverishment of the areas in which they were forced to live. Fertile land was appropriated by landowners; peasants had eventually to move to the less fertile areas. While in Pemba a peasant could usually support himself and his family off land in any part of the island, in Unguja a patch of the barren coral rag could not support a family. A peasant had to supplement his income by fishing or, increasingly, by becoming a labourer. It is therefore not surprising, that in Pemba the chances of survival of the peasant class were high and in Unguja its survival unaided was unlikely. Indeed, in Pemba there was increasing differentiation among peasants: some peasants became individual landowners and employers of clove-picking labour. Social relations in the island of Unguja were different from those in the island of Pemba. This is not because there were African landowners in Pemba. That only changed the racial composition of the landowning class, not relations between that class and other classes. The difference was in the existence of a rich peasant class in Pemba, and the relative insignificance of a semi-proletarianised peasant-labourer class in Pemba. Thousands of peasant labourers were in fact transported every year from Unguja to Pemba during the clove-picking season.[1]

The landowning class controlled this labour and exploited it. Large landowners, who did not themselves work on the plantations but owned more than 1,000 clove trees each, numbered 810 by

1949. Small landowners who owned between 60 and 1,000 clove trees, and who usually worked alongside wage labourers, numbered 11,800. Many of the former were resident in Zanzibar Stone Town, while the large majority of the latter lived and worked on plantations in Pemba. Arabs made up 485 of the 810 large landowners and 3,875 of the 11,800 small landowners. Both these sets of figures make nonsense of the frequently asserted claim that race and class coincided in Zanzibar. The majority (by number) of those owning more than 60 clove trees was African (8,140 out of 12,610, or 65 per cent).[2]

The size of the labour force used may be calculated roughly. The average annual yield of a clove tree was six pounds of dried cloves. There were nearly 4 million clove trees. An average picker picked some 400 pounds of dried cloves in a forty-day working period. This means that 60,000 workers were required. We must first subtract from this number those 11,800 who worked alongside their wage labourers. This leaves some 48,000 wage-earning clove pickers, of whom some 8,000 worked in Unguja and 40,000 in Pemba. This compares with estimates by the colonial administration made for 1957 (a record year) of a total of 50,000 wage-earning clove pickers.[3] The majority of the clove pickers came from Unguja. While about 7,000 were probably residents of Pemba and a similar number came from mainland Tanganyika temporarily for the clove picking season, about 34,000 residents of Unguja would have been engaged in clove-picking in an average season. This is some 62 per cent of the number of adult males in Unguja, an extremely high proportion. Though some of these were squatters, the vast majority were temporary, 'migrant' workers, transported by government steamers to Pemba for the clove picking season. A large number of peasants in Unguja could not sustain themselves on their land, and had been forced to depend upon earnings from clove picking. A further large number of clove pickers were casual workers resident in Ngambo, the working-class area of Zanzibar Town. They were unemployed for much of the rest of the year and were ex-peasants who had permanently given up the struggle to make a living off the land.[4]

Conditions of work and living for temporary clove pickers in Pemba were extremely poor. Picking clove buds might take all day and removing the stems might take half the night, a colonial labour report admitted. Picking had to be done in any weather, and it almost always involved climbing the tall clove trees. Employers provided no ladders. Ulcers on pickers' legs occurred frequently, and if a man fell from a tree there was no possibility of compensation for injury or death. Workmen's compensation legislation did not exist until 1948, and then did not apply to temporary workers. Representatives of the plantation owners, especially the rich peasants who claimed they would not be able to afford to pay compensation, made their objections known in the Legislative Council and the huge loophole was left. Living conditions were equally bad. Employers 'usually' provided temporary accommodation in the form of rough shelters erected on bare ground, and any form of sanitation or water provision was rare. The colonial labour department began to prescribe regulations for the accommodation of workers in the belief that a healthy worker would be more efficient, but department reports admitted that these regulations were not being carried out.[5]

Wage rates varied enormously. For example, the table below gives the estimated annual wage of a clove picker, as well as the estimated yearly profit of the owner of a six-acre *shamba*, between 1947 and 1959.[6]

Year	Wage in shillings	Profit in shillings
1947	54	475
1952	1,080	5,760
1953	864	1,296
1957	318	2,765
1959	104	890

All rates were piece rates, according to the *pishi*, or container, of picked clove buds with stems removed. This in itself illustrates the weak position of the worker since it forced him to work enormously long hours. He did, however have some room for manoeuvre over the rate. He could desert a 'mean' employer for a 'generous' one. The administration tried to prevent this by means of contracts, but workers successfully avoided these and the attempt failed. Employers in a hurry to have their cloves picked before the buds blossomed were to some extent vulnerable to worker pressure and wages did tend to go up in years of good crops and high prices. But, as the table shows, wages were forced down very sharply in years of low prices. It is noteworthy that, while in 1953 the employers, caught out by an unexpected drop in the price of cloves, had low profits while wages were high, by 1957 wage rates had been forced down so as to keep up the level of profit. While piece rates had risen to Sh1/- a pound in 1952 they had been pushed down to 7 cents a pound by 1960.[7] And quite apart from the changes in wages, the difference between the two sets of figures illustrates the way in which an owner, in years of low prices, received some nine times what a labourer received. Some owners hired overseers and never even visited their plantations.

Usurers battened off both groups. A report published in 1950 discussed what it called the universal practice of credit amongst agricultural 'producers'. It was referring to the plantation owners who borrowed money from moneylenders as an advance on the future clove crop. The interest charged on this loan was 25 per cent, but in fact, the report said, the actual interest was much higher since the borrower bound himself to sell to the moneylender at a fixed low price. There were fourteen registered moneylenders in 1950 but the report claimed that a thousand probably existed. Legislation aimed at reducing interest rates had clearly done very little to improve the situation. The colonial administration regarded usury in much the same light as they had earlier regarded slavery, and for the same reason: it was inefficient and destroyed the incentive to increase production. By 1960 the situation had changed very little for many landowners, but the clove price boom of the early 1950s had freed most small borrowers from permanent indebtedness, that is, debts running on from year to year. This had the important result that the conflict between small landowners (of whom there were many in Pemba) and small money lenders had been moderated. I have been unable to find similar information about pawnbrokers who used the same methods on the labourers. There were 37 licensed pawnbrokers in 1949 whose profits were said to be considerable. It is likely that the number of their 'customers' declined when pickers' wages rose in the early 1950s, and increased again when they fell in the late 1950s. Pawnbrokers' shops were one of the objects of attack in 1964.[8]

More typical of capitalism than moneylending was the operation of merchant capital. Most cloves were exported by private traders resident in Zanzibar, who usually made a profit of about 10 per cent if they had no choice over when to sell. But increased profits were often made by holding back cloves until the world price rose, in other words by speculating on future trends in the world price. The colonial administration claimed that these fluctuations were damaging to the producer. They meant that there was a reduced incentive to produce more if price rises could not be foreseen. In many colonies they introduced price assistance schemes which were said to have as their main purpose the ironing out of these fluctuations, and fostered cooperatives which were said to be for the benefit of producers. In Zanzibar the real intent of administrative interference is a little clearer. The Clove Growers' Association (CGA) was formed in the 1930s, clearly by administration initiative. It was never in anything but name a cooperative association run by 'growers' themselves (these growers were seldom the producers, anyway). Soon it was proposed that the CGA, really a department of the administration, should have a monopoly of clove exporting. It was intended therefore to push the private traders out of the market altogether, with the object of taking the profits. The administration already received a high revenue from the export of cloves in the form of the export duty 'inherited' from the Sultan. Now it intended to be, like Seyyid Said, a trading prince itself. Opposition from the private traders, who were able to use their contacts to impose a boycott of Zanzibar cloves in India, succeeded in defeating this proposal. The traders had been able to hit where it hurt most, that is at the ability to export cloves at all, by taking advantage of the fact that cloves were not exported primarily to the colonial metropole. Henceforth the Clove Growers' Association could not monopolise, but only share in, the private traders' profits to be made out of cloves. This sharing was ensured by legislation directing exporters to buy a proportion of their cloves from the CGA (and that proportion was to be fixed by the administration). For example, in 1959 the CGA was buying cloves at 70 cents a pound and selling them to exporters at Shs2/55. This enormous profit was partly the result of a crisis in the affairs of the CGA which will be examined later, but there is no doubt that the CGA was attempting to secure for itself a major part of the surplus value accruing from clove production. Estimated figures for 1960 are given for an acre of cloves yielding 250 pounds: Zanzibar merchants' profit, Shs25/-; clove pickers' wages, Shs52/50; owner's profit, Shs137/50; administration tax, Shs162/50, and CGA profit, Shs410/-.[9]

The CGA had ceased to be in any sense representative of plantation owners or clove producers. It had become an extractive trading organisation operated by the colonial state. While it did not exercise the monopoly of clove trading which theoretically it possessed (since it had the legal powers to force clove exporters to purchase all their cloves from itself), it did possess and use a statutory monopoly of clove stem (as opposed to clove bud) purchases and of clove distillation (a process by which clove stems were converted into oil). It also monopolised trading in new export crops which the colonial Department of Agriculture wished to introduce, such as cacao, derris, kapok and tobacco, though none of these became established. From 1946 to 1949 the CGA held a monopoly of the export of coconut products to the British Ministry of Food on a purchasing contract. Finally it acted as a commercial bank on the island of Pemba and controlled the transfer of funds from one island to the other.[10]

The colonial state may next be considered as an extractive agency, though it also had the function of moderating conflicts between classes in Zanzibar society. We have already observed the huge proportion of the income derived from clove production in Zanzibar itself absorbed by the administration in tax and by the state-operated CGA in profit in 1960. Both these should be seen in the context of the overall aims of colonial rule in Zanzibar. First, taxation supported colonial officials at a level of income far higher than that of all but a tiny minority of the people of Zanzibar. In times of adversity the maintenance of that official level of income was the primary aim in the minds of the colonial officials. For example, in 1947 the Chief Secretary announced the need for austerity and the docile acceptance of inevitable shortages, and in the same speech accepted a report recommending higher salaries for colonial officials.[11]

Ultimately, however, there was a more important call upon the resources of Zanzibar under colonial rule. The colonial officials were not ends in themselves, a dominant class absorbing and consuming a surplus. They were the representatives of a state headquartered in London. One of the interests of that state in the immediate post-war period was financial, that is, support for the exchange value of sterling as against the dollar. The holding of reserves of sterling in London helped to maintain that exchange value, and the reserves of every British colony were held in London. It was therefore a prescribed policy for British colonies to build up as large a reserve as possible, by a taxation rate which brought in a revenue higher than expenditure, and by a surplus in the overseas balance of trade caused by an excess of exports over imports. The reason for this was stated as 'self-interest' by the British Resident in 1952: 'We are entirely dependent upon sterling. It is, therefore, no more than self-interest to do everything we can to improve the position of sterling.' On another occasion a British official had spoken of 'our duty and privilege' to assist in 'restoring the world to health' after it had been 'ravaged by war'. It was a common colonial assertion that the interests of all the people in a colony, the metropole and indeed the whole world were the same. The administration's surplus balances reached 2.5 million pounds by 1955, almost all of which was invested in Britain. During the years 1950 to 1955 there was a net favourable balance of trade of 6.2 million pounds, the credits being held by the Crown Agents in London. The benefits to Britain rather than Zanzibar are clear. Quite apart from losses through the depreciation of the invested capital and devaluation of sterling, the capital was being utilised in Britain for the benefit of the British ruling class.[12]

While the colonial state represented the interests of that absentee class in the economic sphere, it also performed the function of maintaining its own power in Zanzibar. One of the ways the colonial officials achieved this, as in other colonies, was by the use of a Legislative Council. Racial representation of privileged groups within the colony encouraged those groups to think in terms of racial interests, and hence divided them. Before 1946 those represented were Europeans, Arabs and Indians. In 1946 the first African member was appointed. Representation of Africans was kept small until 1958 and consisted of privileged Africans, educated teachers or officials and small clove plantation owners from Pemba. A further division was encouraged between the residents of Pemba and those of Unguja. The former expressed the sense of deprivation of the relatively rich inhabitants of Pemba as compared with the rich inhabitants of Unguja. They complained of the lack of electricity, hospitals and tarmac roads in Pemba.[13]

On the other hand the Legislative Council usually enabled such conflicts of interest to be resolved peacefully. Potentially the most serious conflict of interest among the privileged groups was that between the clove plantation owners or landowning class and the clove exporters or merchant class. Arab representatives of the former frequently clashed with Indian representatives of the latter. It was often, in the specific case of Zanzibar, a contradiction between an indebted class and a creditor class. The colonial state frequently intervened to assist the former through subsidies and legal protection against bankruptcies, but it had to balance its favours to some extent since it had the same interest as the merchants in efficient production. The common interests of all members of the Legislative Council, the factors which enabled most disputes to be resolved peacefully, were first, low levels of taxation, and second, as high a level of security and stability as was consistent with the first aim.[14]

But by 1950 the Legislative Council was already ceasing to be of use to the colonial state in resolving internal disputes. A good example is the discussion of the Copra Bill in 1950. Relations between landowners and merchants were of much the same character in coconut production as in clove production: competition for a share of the surplus, complicated by indebtedness of landowners to merchants. Coconuts were usually processed into copra and the process until 1950 was monopolised by Zanzibar merchants. In that year the colonial administration proposed to intervene in copra processing and build a coconut products

86

factory. Representatives of the existing mill owners in the Legislative Council protested vigorously; like good capitalists they wanted to be left alone to share the benefits of their 'enterprise'. Representatives of the sellers of coconuts, the landowners, welcomed the administration proposal. They accused the merchants of keeping prices artificially low; at the same time they were somewhat suspicious of the administration and would have preferred a factory under their own control. It was the sort of situation in which, on the mainland, the administration encouraged cooperatives like the Kilimanjaro Native Coffee Union. Here, however, the merchants were evidently in a stronger position to protect their interests. The administration went ahead with its factory but limited its production to a maximum of a fifteenth of coconuts then grown. Landowners' suspicion mounted: it was a time when they foresaw a decline in state assistance, and a watering down of their privileges such as Legislative Council membership. In 1952 the Arab Association resolved on a boycott of the Copra Board because it included 'non-growers' and in 1953 the Association boycotted the Legislative Council itself.[15] This was significant in that it forced colonial officials to make a decision about whose support they needed most: they could no longer play a balancing role.

We have seen in previous chapters the decisive part played by the colonial state in changing the mode of production in Zanzibar and incorporating the islands into a capitalist trading system. By 1945 that change had been largely achieved and the role of the state began to alter. The state tried merely to reproduce the existing system of production and its consequent social relations by a legal system based on the rights of property owners and the physical protection of property owners by police. Extremely few legal obligations were laid upon property owners, and few attempts were made to provide legally for cooperatives and other modified forms of property.

An education system which virtually confined state-assisted education to the sons of the privileged classes in Zanzibar also helped to entrench the status quo. Batson observed that in 1948 out of 265,000 persons on Zanzibar, 190,000 had had no schooling. In the rural areas of Unguja only 7,900 out of 36,900 children under fifteen years of age had attended or were attending school, and in the rural areas of Pemba only 4,700 out of 43,600. The number of those ever having reached the fifth year of schooling was 5,000 in Zanzibar as a whole.[16] This position changed remarkably little in the period before independence.

If the colonial state wished to prevent change, the same was not

Plate 10   A coffee seller in Zanzibar Town, a cosmopolitan centre in which Africans, Arabs, Indians and even Persians mingled.

true of other classes in Zanzibar society. Landowners, it has already been suggested, were suspicious of British intentions and demanded more positive support from the colonial administration. They decided finally to cut loose from their protectors and go it alone. Their efforts to pursue this policy will be examined later. For the moment we must examine a class who, unlike the landowners who wanted only more decisive measures in defence of the system, began seriously to question the rewards they gained from the system and threatened to undermine it. Wage workers were relatively few but they were concentrated in an area where consciousness of their position was being constantly thrust upon them. They lived mainly in Ngambo, the 'other side' of Zanzibar Town. It was the area of mud and wattle, battered tin roofs, segregated from the appropriately named Stone Town. At one end of the creek which served as the boundary stood the main police station, sentinel of the 'no-man's land' between. In 1945, the vast majority of the inhabitants of Ngambo were casual labourers. If employed they were paid daily rates and had no guarantee of employment beyond the day itself. Many of them were fairly permanently unemployed, but were always hoping for an improvement on their previous lives in the equally poverty-stricken villages.

The ethnic composition of the Ngambo people was varied, but there were two main divisions, mainlanders and indigenous Africans. The former were primarily Tanganyikans forced out of their home areas on the mainland by the need to earn cash to pay taxes. The majority of the 'mainlanders' in Ngambo had been present there for two or more generations. They were in fact the longest established section of the Zanzibar proletariat, though many 'mainlander' squatters in the rural areas of Unguja shared this distinction with them. The other group was indigenous ex-peasants, mostly later arrivals. They were there as a result of the alienation of land to rich landowners at the time of the Arab invasion, but their presence in Ngambo was much delayed by the fact that their grand-fathers had first tried to eke out a living from the much less fertile areas of Unguja which had not been alienated. In years of good clove harvests and relatively high pickers' wages this group could often maintain itself on the wages of six to eight weeks' work. They lived like peasants, on the yearly harvest income. But as the table on p.82 shows, wages after 1952 were falling and it became impossible to survive on clove picking as a sole occupation. Hence progressively the indigenous workers became the competitors of the 'mainlanders' for the available jobs in the town itself. This competition proved to be to the advantage of those who wished to make a nationalist appeal. 'The mainlanders are foreigners,' became their cry. In this way there was constant pressure to divide the proletariat on ethnic lines.

What made the situation worse, and had been the constant cause of peasants abandoning their land, was food shortage. It is surprising that in an area of such high rainfall as the islands of Unguja and Pemba there should ever have been famines. There was and always had been sufficient land to support the population of the islands in food. But the cultivation of cloves had three consequences, commonly these days associated with the process of underdevelop-ment. The first was the alienation of land for the clove plantations. This occurred on a large scale, as we have seen. Especially in Unguja this reduced the amount of fertile land left for food cultivation. True, food cultivation by squatters took place under the clove trees. But this food was partly consumed by the owners and the squatters, partly sold to the towns. The fairly fertile land on the edges of the plantations was used by peasants but even some of this was used for small clove or coconut plantations. Gradually more and more peasants were forced out on to the coral rag, where it is possible to cultivate pockets of land on a shifting basis. As time went by it became more and more difficult to allow a long enough recuperation period for fallow land; harvests became smaller and the risk of pre-harvest hunger greater. In the end some peasants were forced off the land altogether. In other areas, taxes were used to force peasants to take up paid employment. But in Zanzibar they were not necessary for this purpose.

The second consequence of clove cultivation was the tendency to rely on imported food. The colonial state made no effort to ensure that Zanzibar was self-sufficient in food. (It is only fair to point out that the state had made little effort for a hundred years in Britain itself to ensure this.) Merchants could obtain cheap supplies of rice from Burma and South-east Asia in the period before 1939 and officials encouraged them to do so. Prices of food (and hence production costs) could be kept low more easily in this way than by higher prices, subsidies or other financial incentives to producers of food. The combination of a lower than usual rainfall and the disruption of overseas supplies of food, as happened in Pemba in 1946, could produce famine. People were forced to gather wild edible fruits. This was only a difference in degree from the endemic food shortage which was gradually forcing peasants off the land. The problem in 1946 was that there was no work for them elsewhere. The clove harvest had also been affected by the lower rainfall and clove pickers were not required. As a result there was a frantic gathering of mangrove bark for sale which ruined the trees for a generation. It is clear that this situation is positively in the interest of employers with a constant need for labourers. What had gone wrong in 1946 was that they did not need labourers. In spite of this, according to a government official, plantation owners opposed measures being taken to increase the production of food, such as the compulsory planting of rice and cassava. By the time of the 1964 Revolution, the Afro-Shirazi Party claimed, only 11 per cent of the cultivable land was being used for grain production and 90 per cent of the grain needed for home consumption was being imported.[17]

The third consequence of clove cultivation, adding to the effect of the other two on food production, was the 'alienation of time'. Clove picking was virtually a necessity for any peasant who wished to gain a cash income. His own farm would be under crops or needing planting with crops at the same time as the clove harvest. The longer he stayed on the clove plantation, the less time (and inclination) he would have for preparing the ground for rice and planting seeds. It was said that a rice grower could earn more in a month of clove picking than in a year of rice growing. The effect of low rice prices (for the grower) was thus to impel him to neglect rice cultivation for whatever period he could earn money from clove-picking. His time was hence 'alienated' from food production. A food crop which had come to be widely grown instead of rice was cassava. It needed less attention and could be harvested at any time. It fitted in better, therefore, with colonial export crop production. This is why it was favoured by colonial administrators, in Zanzibar and elsewhere, in spite of its nutritional deficiencies.[18] The colonial administration further encouraged this 'alienation of time' by the device of contracts. These bound clove pickers to one employer for a stated period of between 40 and 60 days. Desertion from work being done under a contract was a crime and the police were deployed to catch deserters, whether or not they were returning to their fields to cultivate. These contracts were un-popular with clove pickers, as can be imagined, and it was only in years of scarcity that large numbers presented themselves for contracts.[19]

The employers had the stronger bargaining position in Zanzibar, for there were usually more workers than jobs. The pressures of food shortages in the villages were greater than the pressures to increase employment. This was markedly so in the period 1947—48 after the famine of 1946. The administration itself was the largest employer; it took on very few 'permanent' employees and treated the rest as casual labourers subject to dismissal at a day's notice even if they had worked five years continuously. Wages were Shs1/30 a day (with no increments) at a time when this amount would buy only two pounds of rice. Soap and coconut oil factory owners were able to force their workers to work long night shifts. The main port employer, the African Wharfage Company, in July 1948 offered marginally better terms to its permanent employees, a minority of its work force. They amounted to Shs1/70 a day, but they included six-month contracts. This offer, which was at first accepted, united the unskilled and skilled workers against the company. The unskilled workers resented not having been offered permanent terms, and the skilled workers resented the absence of a cost of living allowance offered to dockers in Dar es Salaam.[20]

A strike began in August 1948 among the workers of the African Wharfage Company. When the administration began to recruit other men to take the work of the strikers (taking a clear pro-employer stance, which in its position as a main employer it could scarcely avoid) the dockers' strike turned to a general strike among all African workers in Stone Town. The administration now acted remarkably quickly, promising an increase in its minimum daily wage to Shs2/-. It further promised to reduce the cost of living through price control, and appointed an inspector of prices immediately. It was now clearly in a position of physical weakness, for when the police attempted to arrest two strikers armed with sticks, a crowd of other strikers succeeded in releasing them, and the crowd went on to demonstrate outside the police station. Reinforcements were subsequently summoned from Dar es Salaam, but the vulnerability of the administration had been shown.

91

In a further interesting development, strikers were reported to be interfering with food supplies from the rural areas to the town. This demonstrated the vulnerability of Stone Town and elicited what the British Resident called a 'splendid spirit of cooperation between different communities in the capital'. In other words, employers of different races had realised their common class interests. The attempt showed the possibility of alliance in opposition to employers between the workers of Ngambo and the food producers of the rural areas. These latter were the squatters and peasants on the fringes of the fertile areas. The danger appeared clear to the administration at the time, but they subsequently found themselves in what appeared to be a stronger position. In the absence of effective unions it was difficult for the men to stay out for long and the strike ended before all employers had agreed to improve labourers' terms of service. During 1949 there were several cases of workers being dismissed on the pretext of the employer's inability to pay the higher wages agreed to; subsequent threats of strike action came to nothing. Administration price control proved to be ineffective, and the position of inspector of prices was vacant by July 1949. Workers had made some gains on the wages front but had achieved nothing tangible in their basic relationship with employers. They were still at the latter's mercy. Yet it was clear that better organised workers would be able to exercise some power.[21]

2

Much of the succeeding period, from 1950 to 1963, was concerned with the working out of a struggle which had come to the surface in 1948. It was between workers and employers, though it was complicated by the fact that the administration was one of the main employers. It was possible to believe that the strike had been primarily a conflict between mainlanders and indigenous people because the former were among the leaders in the strike. This was what Arab employers wanted to believe; and some Arabs subsequently began a political campaign to emphasise common interests among indigenous people. They claimed to be indigenous themselves, and that indigenous workers were as threatened as indigenous employers by mainlanders. Use of indigenous workers to fill jobs left by striking mainland workers was a practical way of pointing to common interests. This was the basis of much of the nationalism subsequently expressed by Arabs; it appealed to a common 'nationality' as subjects of the Sultan. On the other hand workers could believe that what had happened was a struggle between Africans and non-Africans. African workers wished to emphasise the common interest of Africans as against Arabs and Europeans. They worked through the African Association; but they came into competition with the Shirazi Association, whose members claimed a special identity for themselves, connected with Shiraz in Iran. These were the images people had of themselves. They have been widely adopted by writers about the period, as indeed about Zanzibar history as a whole. Yet the understanding and analysis of Zanzibar history depends on thinking of workers as they actually were, that is, workers, rather than mainlanders or Africans, and to think of employers as employers and not as Zanzibaris or Arabs and Asians. To do otherwise is to write the history of images. To prevent a victory for the workers, that is a revolution, it was necessary for employers to isolate the Ngambo workers (as mainlanders) from clove pickers and peasants. To win a victory, the workers had to win the support of clove pickers and peasants. For the workers the struggle was to win the support of this group, which was not a proletariat but a semi-proletariat. In so far as conditions explained earlier were further proletarianising this group, there was a certain inevitability about the way the struggle would go if the process was allowed to continue; this accounts for the sense of urgency felt by some of the employers.

The first sign of the way peasants would move came in 1951. At this time there were riots among a section of middle peasants in Unguja. Middle peasants were those who did not and could not employ labour, but had not been forced on to the labour market for clove picking every year. It was not possible for such people to escape from the effects of the colonial economy. They were not self-sufficient because they needed to buy clothes, pay for education for a few of their children, and so on. They were drawn into the colonial economy either by becoming small clove or coconut producers or by keeping cattle and chickens. In the former case, they could sell cloves or coconuts to the local shopkeepers; in the latter case, they could sell ghee and eggs, sometimes milk and meat, in the local markets, and some could provide transportation services with bullock carts. In the former case land and in the latter case animals were what helped these middle peasants to preserve a measure of independence. But this independence was being gradually and irretrievably eroded during colonial rule. Pressure on land was increased both by the desire to grow more crops for more cash and by the search for grazing areas for the cattle. Choices were imposed between crops and grazing, cash crops and food crops, and between selling and consuming food. The amount of land suitable for grazing was limited by the

Plate 11   The 'Siku Kuu' (Eid) fair at Mnazi Mmoja grounds. A common religion brought the people together but failed to unite them.

prevalence of tsetse fly on large sections of the coral rag. In the relatively small area of suitable land, along the fringes of the large plantation areas in Zanzibar island, peasants competed with each other and with their animals for space. Diseases spread very rapidly among cattle if they once established themselves.[22]

A group of middle peasants in an area of western Unguja not very far south of Zanzibar Town came into conflict with the colonial administration in 1951. They closed ranks among themselves using their common religion, Islam, as their rallying cry. The general threat to these middle peasants was proletarianisation, that is, the loss of their livelihood in their villages and their being forced upon the labour market. There were two specific threats: one was the loss of land, the second the death of cattle. Over a period between 1945 and 1950 the administration had compulsorily acquired several pieces of land for the purpose of extending the runway of the Zanzibar airport. The airport was being built in the same plantation-fringe area as the middle peasants occupied. At one point there was a proposal to acquire the land occupied by a mosque and destroy the building. The appetite of the administration for land seemed insatiable.[23]

The second threat was to their cattle. Kiembe Samaki and Mazizini are within four miles of Zanzibar Town, and peasants were able to sell milk and ghee in the town market. Yet their cattle were being attacked by various diseases: rinderpest, east coast fever and anthrax. Tsetse flies were also nearby. Measures taken by the Veterinary Department to deal with these diseases only increased the fears of the peasants. In 1944, 33 cattle were slaughtered by the department because they had contracted rinderpest. Then in 1949, the officials began compulsory dipping of cattle against east coast fever and other tick-borne diseases. Not only were peasants expected to bring their cattle for dipping weekly but also they were expected to pay a fee. In addition to this the effect was not altogether beneficial. As officials themselves later recognised, dipping prevents the building up of immunity, and a calf which is dipped regularly will be more and not less liable to death from the disease if at any time dipping ceases. Peasants who observed deaths after dipping accused the administration of wishing to diminish their herds, and were prepared, as Muslims, to see this as a deliberate attack by infidels.[24]

In this situation a flashpoint was reached when, because of the danger of anthrax, the Veterinary Department in 1951 introduced compulsory inoculation against the disease. The first incident was the refusal of two bullock-cart owners to allow their bullocks to be inoculated. They were arrested and fined, as a consequence of which the villagers decided on a boycott of administration activities. They also appealed to the workers of Zanzibar Town to support them, in return for peasant support at the time of the general strike in 1948. Next, nineteen villagers were arrested for refusing inoculation and taken to the High Court in town. A large crowd of villagers from Kiembe Samaki and other villages carrying sticks, surrounded the court building and, after the conviction of the nineteen, attempted to release them. They succeeded in ambushing the van taking eleven of the convicts to prison; having released these, they tried to break into the prison in order to release the others. Police fired on the crowd and five were killed.[25]

The significance of this incident was great. Peasants who claimed to have supported the general strike of 1948 by not taking their produce to the town market now took the initiative themselves and appealed (unsuccessfully) for worker backing. They subsequently formed an anti-colonial association named the National Party of the Subjects of the Sultan of Zanzibar (NPSS) in 1955, presumably somewhat disillusioned by the lack of support from non-indigenous workers. But the possibility of alliance between them had been grasped, and circumstances were to favour its realisation. The administration had been forced to use bullets and hence aroused further antagonism. Its weakness was shown by the fact that the rioters very nearly succeeded in breaking into the prison, that Special Constabulary and Tanganyika police reinforcements could only be called in afterwards, and that the police themselves were not altogether to be relied upon: one of those subsequently convicted for rioting was a police constable on leave.[26]

Middle peasants were those who feared being forced on to the labour market; their protest was against the process by which they were being proletarianised. Their feelings were aroused by particular actions of the colonial administration, which others might justify, like building an airport and inoculating cattle. But it is to the general effect of colonial rule that we should look in analysis.

The same point may be made about the actions of the people of Zanzibar in the period from 1957 to the Revolution in 1964. Colonial rule, and more specifically the colonial economy with its monocultural dependence upon clove production, lay behind the discontent of the period. The specific grounds of complaint, such as the conduct of the CGA and the struggle between mainland and indigenous workers, were symptoms rather than causes of it. We will examine the conduct of the CGA first.

In name and in theory the CGA was a cooperative, a union of clove growers aiming to act together in their own interest. In practice it was an administration trading organisation aiming to make a profit like any other trading organisation, but aiming also to influence the production of export crops in the same way as the Department of Agriculture. Its manager and its other European employees had high salaries; at one point the Director of Agriculture resigned to become its manager. It kept large balances, which were partly invested overseas. Some of the balances were also used for financing the purchase of the clove crop, that is, in advancing to planters money to pay their costs before the crop came in. It was acting as a moneylender. A little of its surplus was used to provide clove tree seedlings and roads along which cloves could be transported.[27]

Its main business, however, was not to distribute surpluses but to make them. This was done by large margins between its buying prices and its selling prices, because it could compel exporters to buy cloves from it at its own stated price. It was generally slow to change either buying or selling prices. This was in accord with British government policy, for the colonialists believed that growers' troubles were caused by fluctuating prices and 'speculation' among buyers. But a more basic problem was the market. Increases of production did not usually lead to higher prices since the market did not expand. In the case of cloves the market was actually contracting in the late 1950s. Both India and Indonesia, the main markets for cloves, were trying to reduce purchases in 1957 when there was a bumper crop in Zanzibar. The

CGA bought very large amounts of cloves which it could not sell. It bought them at the relatively high price of Shs2/- a pound, a low price in relation to the boom period earlier, but which it had been slow to change when that boom collapsed. In paying for cloves in 1957 it exhausted its available reserve balances and took an overdraft from a British bank of £3.5 million. In 1958 it reduced its buying price to Sh1/- a pound, but tried to maintain its high selling price in order not to make losses on its previous year's purchases. However, importing countries still wished to reduce purchases and moreover were aware of the large stocks held by the CGA. They refused to buy at the CGA's price and exports remained at a low level.[28]

In the case of a private company this would eventually have led to bankruptcy. In Zanzibar this was not allowed to happen. A report recommended a more flexible buying price in future but no other changes, and simply promised several years of austerity ahead because of the debt to a British bank incurred by the CGA. In other words the troubles of the CGA were to be laid at the door of the people of Zanzibar. The CGA had got itself into debt with a bank, and Zanzibar clove growers were to be made martyrs to the power of the bank. But behind the specific mistakes of the CGA was the excessive dependence of the Zanzibar economy as a whole on clove exports. Clove producers were on the whole landowners, and the troubles of the landowners could similarly be transferred largely to their workers. The table in this chapter demonstrated that workers' wages fell at a greater rate than landowners' profits.[29]

The struggle between mainland and indigenous workers was another symptom of the colonial crisis. It was connected with the growth of trade unions among workers in Zanzibar after 1948. These were small at first and had an erratic membership. But gradually their advantages became obvious. Building workers, for example, one of the most depressed groups, achieved a minimum wage of Shs3/60 a day by 1959, after a series of strikes and long negotiations directed by their union. But the achievements of workers through struggle should not be exaggerated. Prices rose almost in step with wages, though more erratically. Food continued to be mainly imported and periodic food shortages still occurred. The aims of union activity imperceptibly became different. Offensive was being forced into defensive, job security was becoming more important than better conditions.[30]

The causes of this were, once again, dependence on cloves. Falling clove prices after 1955, with the sudden drop in 1957, were forcing clove pickers into Zanzibar Town. Peasants who supplemented their meagre incomes with clove picking had been able to do this fairly satisfactorily in the early 1950s. But earnings were dropping drastically in the late 1950s and more and more peasants began to look for work in town. This happened most to Tumbatu peasants in the north of Unguja. They found themselves in competition with existing mainland workers. The process, as usual, benefited employers, since they were relieved of the pressure for higher wages. It also suited the Zanzibar Nationalist Party (ZNP) which wished to win the political support of the indigenous workers. The more they were in competition with mainland workers, the more others rather than themselves would gain. Productive activity hardly increased at all after 1957 since so much depended on cloves, and hence there were no new jobs waiting to be filled. This was a threat to the security of the existing labour force in Zanzibar Town. Employers and 'nationalists' joined hands in encouraging the new indigenous labourers to take the old jobs. The existing workers struck increasingly over dismissals, and unions tended to become divided into old unions of mainland workers and new unions of indigenous workers, the latter often organised by the ZNP. The level of skills in the Zanzibar work force had been so low that substitution was relatively easy.[31]

Employers in the crucial dock area were the first to try to change. Men calling themselves *wachukuzi wa kienyeji*, or indigenous porters, were introduced by the employers into the docks as cart pullers. There was a violent dispute with the existing porters, and the administration appointed an enquiry, which said that both groups of porters were pawns in a political game. But the political game continued. Two rival federations of unions soon existed: The Zanzibar and Pemba Federation of Labour (ZPFL) consisted almost entirely of mainlander workers; the Federation of Progressive Trade Unions (FPTU) included the indigenous workers. This ethnic conflict was, as it turns out, of considerable advantage to the existing regime as well as the existing employers, since revolution proved to be impossible while it continued. But the interest of the ZNP in workers' problems was in reality limited; eventually the FPTU led by Abdulrehman Babu seceded from the ZNP and united action by the working class of Zanzibar island became possible.[32]

Many elements of this situation recur in the relationships between squatters and landowners in Unguja. Political motives once again combined with economic circumstances. Owners of large clove plantations (there was quite a large number of these in the north-west of the island) had allowed squatters on their lands to cultivate small *shambas* as long as these did not include trees. The more energetic squatters could and did produce food crops on the *shambas* allotted them, since the land was the most fertile on the island. Most of the squatters were of mainland origin, many of them descendants of slaves. The more profitable the activities of the squatters became, the more anxious owners were to take the profits for themselves by evicting squatters and replacing them with paid labour. While clove prices were high, food production seemed to owners a waste of effort; now, in 1957 and 1958, when clove prices plunged down, it seemed a way of retrieving the income they were losing. This, yet another result of the depression of clove prices, coincided with a political motive. Most squatters were supporters of the Afro-Shirazi Party (ASP) and after the victory of that party in the 1957 elections, owners began to evict known supporters of the ASP. In accordance with the policy of the ZNP to encourage the replacement of mainland with indigenous labour, they tried to replace them with indigenous agricultural labourers. The ZNP employed labour organisers to form agricultural trade unions of workers willing to take over from squatters. The ZNP's appearance of concern for the rights of indigenous workers won them a fair amount of support, as witnessed in the 1961 elections. But the squatters were extremely bitter.[33]

The anti-colonial movement has been mentioned only briefly so far. This is partly because the movement was overshadowed by the struggles of and between workers, just as independence itself was later to be eclipsed by revolution. And it is partly because the nationalist movement can be analysed as the activity of people other than workers, to whose history we can now turn. The nationalist movement was divided, just as the workers were, on ethnic lines. The ZNP was founded in 1955 by a group of Arabs from the dominant landowning class. It has been alleged that they foresaw a revolution and acted to forestall it. It is more probable that they foresaw independence and acted in order to be sure of inheriting power. By 1955 it was clear that self-government of some description was coming to most African colonies, and that those who organised themselves in parties would be in a better position to secure power. In most African colonies it was the educated petty-bourgeois Africans who thus organised themselves, simply because that was the only differentiated African class which had been allowed to arise out of the colonial political economies. But in Zanzibar there was an indigenous or at least a non-European dominant class of landowners and only a weak African petty-bourgeois class. The dominant indigenous class, the landowners, was naturally the first to organise itself. All nationalist leaders sought allies from classes other than their own, since both the British and their own nationalist ideology forced this on them, the British by elections, and their own ideology by its use of the concepts of 'nation' and 'foreigner'. The ZNP recognised early on the advantages of a nationalist ideology in gaining the support of indigenous rich peasants, middle peasants and workers. It was the middle peasants of the airport area, who had been involved in the 1951 disturbance, who became its first supporters, and one of them became its chairman. Their anti-colonial grievances were sufficiently strong to create a common interest with the landowners, who had recently been involved in a confrontation with the colonial administration over constitutional arrangements, voting procedures and the like. This so called 'Arab' boycott had lasted seventeen months from June 1954 to November 1955. It was a natural development from this early alliance (in which the peasants played an increasingly subordinate role) to take the side of indigenous workers or indigenous poor peasants against the mainland 'foreigners'; hence the party's role in the struggles already recounted. The rich peasants, from whom they might have expected more, were difficult to win over, as will be seen.

The rival side of the nationalist movement was the ASP. Not founded until 1957, this party reflects the weakness of the African petty-bourgeois class in Zanzibar and its difficulty in achieving a unity between the educated Africans of Unguja and the rich African peasants of Pemba. The latter wanted to call themselves Shirazi, to emphasise the similarity of their origins with those of the Arabs; they persistently saw their interests in different terms from other Africans in Zanzibar. The African Association and the Shirazi Association had long been in conflict, and it was only at the last minute that an electoral pact was formed between them for the 1957 election. The ASP might be seen as an African or mainland worker party. It certainly used an African nationalist ideology, arguing, with Africans on the mainland, that oppressed Africans should unite against the oppressing Europeans. It supported the mainlander union organisations and squatters in their disputes. Its leader, Abeid Karume, had little formal education and had been a merchant seaman. But it is suggested here that the ASP, at least until the period of the 1964 Revolution, should be regarded as a petty-bourgeois party. Karume was by 1957 no longer a merchant seaman, but a motorboat owner. The party was organised for the purpose of inheriting power at independence (if necessary delaying it until there was a larger number of educated Africans to do so more effectively), and emphatically not for revolution. Its support in 1957 was clearly among the relatively well-off section of the Zanzibar population (excluding the landowners), as witness the results of the 1957 elections. The Afro-Shirazi electoral pact won five out of six seats on a very limited franchise where the vote was confined to those with certain educational and property qualifications.

There was a competition between the two branches of the nationalist movement for the support of the rich peasants of Pemba. As clove growers, their interests seemed bound up with those of the plantation owners, yet they recognised that their exclusion from power gave them common cause with mainland Africans. The electoral pact of 1957, and the founding of the ASP shortly afterwards, seemed to indicate the cementing of an alliance between the two petty-bourgeois groups. In 1959, however, Pemba members seceded and formed the Zanzibar and Pemba People's Party (ZPPP). This had virtually no support in Unguja. In the two elections of 1961 it won seats in Pemba only and held the balance between the other two parties. Its decision, reflecting the belief of the rich Pemba peasants that their interests lay in a maintenance of the status quo rather than any transfer of power to an African party, was to support the ZNP. The failure of the ASP to win a majority in the 1961 elections greatly frustrated its supporters since it ensured that the ASP would not inherit power at independence. There was street fighting between ASP and ZNP supporters in 1961. There were attacks on the 'Manga' shopkeepers who had been keen campaigners for the ZNP as well as agents of the landlords over squatter evictions. This meant that the revolutionary element, or at least those not willing to accept the British way of deciding the power struggle, was increased in the ASP, and it became a suitable candidate for receiving power if the independence settlement was overthrown.[34]

The British part in the independence settlement has now to be considered briefly. They are said to have rigged the 1961 elections: the ASP would have much preferred to come to power by electoral means. It appears that there is some truth in the accusation in a general sense, though the electoral results were due to the alliances already described. The colonial government in London appears to have been resolved in 1953 on the suppression of all militant nationalism, believing that this was necessary to preserve the existing relations of production. They arrested all but one of the members of the committee of the Arab Association in June 1953 because of an article in a newspaper. The Arab Association decided a year later on a non-cooperation campaign. They boycotted all administration activities and withdrew from the Legislative Council. This was virtually the only example of specifically nationalist struggle in Zanzibar and its effectiveness appears to have convinced the British that an independence solution must be found, yet could not be found without the cooperation of the existing dominant class of landowners. The

Plate 12   An experiment with democracy: women, many with babies on their backs, voting in a village in the 1961 election.

Plate 13   An experiment with democracy: men and women voting in Zanzibar Town in the 1961 election. Some brought their thermoses, and the coffee seller in the middle had a captive market.

Plate 14   The National Assembly after the 1963 election. Members of the government and the opposition posing beside the Speaker in the grounds of the Victoria Garden.

Resident announced in October 1955 that Zanzibar would proceed by appropriate steps to self-government. The boycotters then returned to the Legislative Council, but were encouraged to form a political party. However, by the time of the 1957 elections two party organisations existed and somewhat surprisingly the ZNP was heavily defeated. The British subsequently favoured a coalition between the ZNP and the ZPPP, both of which represented producers of cloves. The ZNP was assisted by the decision to give Zanzibar Stone Town two seats, while the size of its population indicated it should have one. This turned out to be decisive since the results were so close. In the first election the ZNP won both seats in Stone Town and the result was an 11–11 draw. In the second election the British created a further seat in Pemba with the consequence that a ZNP/ZPPP coalition took office as a result of a narrow 12–11 victory.[35]

Power was transferred to this coalition, but it was a limited power. It was limited by the lack of physical means for controlling the population. The British did not have any army resident in Zanzibar during this period. They armed the police, they created a Special Branch to deal with security problems and a Reserve Unit to quell riots. But the fact that the 1961 riots continued out of control for several days showed that these measures were not successful. British power had temporarily broken down and was only restored after the importation of British troops. The regime which took over power at independence in 1963 did not have even these inadequate means of keeping itself in power. There appears to have been no arrangement to call on British troops. Even the existing police force was weakened by the dismissal of many mainland policemen whose loyalty to the regime was doubted. In addition, the location of the institutions of government in Unguja, where the sharpest social contradictions were, and in a vulnerable position in Zanzibar Stone Town, tilted the strategic situation towards the possible success of a bid to overthrow the government.[36]

The riots of 1961 appear to have been very influential in demonstrating that the government in Zanzibar Stone Town could be overthrown. It was only necessary to wait for independence when it was assumed (rightly, as it turned out) that the British troops would no longer be available. The bitterness of African workers and squatters was also demonstrated by the riots. Workers whose conditions were deteriorating and whose very employment was under threat, and squatters in a parallel situation in the rural areas nearby, believed with full justification that the election results meant that power was being handed over to employers and land-lords. To overthrow the regime thus seemed possible and necessary. The mechanics of the overthrow are still unclear. Even its own publications do not directly claim that the ASP accomplished the overthrow. The argument that Abdulreman Babu's Umma Party or John Okello did the deed is unconvincing. In any case it should be unnecessary to detail the role of individuals. The Zanzibar government was overthrown by large groups of people, classes in alliance with each other in pursuit of their common interests. Mainland workers and squatters had long had their reasons. Mainland ex-policemen were merely specially knowledgeable and disaffected workers. Alliance with the middle and poorer peasants of Unguja appears to have been decisive, since these could have isolated the town workers and squatters. Both groups were affected more by the political economy of colonial Zanzibar, which was impoverishing and proletarianising them, than they were by the physical presence of the British. The indigenous workers were merely recently proletarianised peasants. Those who benefited from the colonial political economy lived primarily in Zanzibar Stone Town and in Pemba. The rich peasants of Pemba, decisive in elections, could play no role in a physical attack on Zanzibar Stone Town. That would be left to the residents of Ngambo and the nearby villages. Once overwhelming physical force was no longer in the hands of the minority, the majority overthrew them in January 1964.

Notes

1. See earlier chapters and Michael F. Lofchie, *Zanzibar: Background to Revolution*, Princeton, Princeton University Press, 1965, pp. 4, 47, 106.
2. E. Batson, *The Social Survey of Zanzibar*, unpublished, 1957—61, Volume 15. The similar group in Unguja is sometimes heterogeneous but much smaller in number: 1,550 indigenous Africans, 930 mainland Africans, and 770 Arabs. Of 230 owners of large and very large *shambas* in Unguja, 220 were resident in town. Compare Lofchie, *op. cit.*, p.14. See also Sheriff's chapter in this volume.
3. Batson, *op. cit.*; *Annual Report of the Provincial Administration 1957* (hereafter *ARPA*), p. 15; *ARPA 1958*, p. 11; *ARPA 1959*, p.18; R.A. Crofts, *The Zanzibar Clove Industry*, Zanzibar, Government Printer, 1959; Zanzibar Protectorate, *Debates of the Legislative Council* (hereafter *DLC*), November 26, 1957, p. 74.
4. Batson, *op. cit.*; Volume 16; *Annual Report of the Labour Department 1945* (hereafter *ARLD*), p. 1; *ARLD 1946*, pp. 2—4; *ARLD 1950*, pp. 10—15; *DLC*, November 12, 1957, p. 8.
5. *ARLD 1947*, pp. 1—10; *ARLD 1949*, pp. 5—10; *ARLD 1954*, p. 6; *ARLD 1957*, p. 10; *ARLD 1958*, p. 8; *ARLD 1960/61*, p. 7; *DLC*, December 24, 1949, pp. 56—61; *DLC*, December 13, 1957, pp. 189—94.
6. Sources: *ARPA 1947*, pp. 1—2; *Annual Report of the Department of Agriculture 1952* (hereafter *ARDA*), p. 1; *ARDA 1953*, p. 1; *ARDA 1957*, pp. 1—3; *ARDA 1959*, pp. 1—3; *ARDA 1960*, p.2. The estimates have been made by calculating the likely yield of cloves and multiplying by the price for that year; and by calculating the likely amount picked by a worker and multiplying by the picking piece rate.
7. *ARLD 1953*, p. 16; *ARLD 1957*, p. 14; *ARLD 1959*, p. 22.
8. Lofchie, *op. cit.*, pp. 104—113; *DLC*, February 8, 1949, p. 76; *ARPA 1952*, p. 1; *ARPA 1959*, p. 21; A.J. Kerr, *Report of an Investigation into the Possibilities of Cooperative Development in the Zanzibar Protectorate*, Zanzibar, Government Printer, 1950, p. 14.
9. *Standard Bank Review*, August 1958; *ARDA 1957*, p. 3; *ARDA 1958*, p.3; *ARDA 1959*, pp. 1—3; *ARDA 1960*, pp. 1—4; *Annual Report of the Clove Growers' Association*, 1956—1957, and 1957—1958.
10. Kerr, *op. cit.*, pp. 6—9; *DLC*, March 1, 1947, p. 84; *DLC*, June 16, 1947, pp. 110—117; *DLC*, February 12, 1955, p. 132; *ARDA 1946*, pp. 1—3; *ARDA 1947*, p. 7; *ARDA 1950*, p. 1; *Annual Reports of the Clove Growers' Association*.
11. *DLC*, October 29, 1947, pp. 14—16.
12. *Ibid.*, and *DLC*, November 20, 1952, pp. 5—13; *DLC*, November 30, 1955, p. 26; *DLC*, November 21, 1956, pp. 22 and 242; *DLC*, June 10, 1958, p. 233.
13. *DLC*, May 11, 1946, p. 115; *DLC*, September 6, 1948, p. 137.
14. See *DLC*, 1945—1953, *passim*.
15. *DLC*, September 16, 1950, pp. 141—55; *DLC*, December 17, 1954, p. 71.
16. Batson, *op. cit.*, Volumes 9 and 10; ASP, *Afro-Shirazi Party: A Liberation Movement*, Zanzibar, Printing Press Corporation, 1973, p. 9.
17. *ARDA 1946*, pp. 3—4; *ARLD 1946*, pp. 1—3; *ARPA 1946*, pp. 1—5; Zanzibar Government, *Fruits of the Zanzibar Revolution*, Zanzibar, 1965.

18. *ARPA 1950*, pp. 1–2; Zanzibar Protectorate, *Report on action which is being taken on nutrition*, Zanzibar, 1949, p. 22.
19. *DLC*, December 7, 1945, p. 81; *ARLD 1945*, pp. 1–4; *ARLD 1946*, pp. 3–6; *ARLD 1950*, pp. 2–6.
20. *DLC*, September 6, 1948, p. 132; *DLC*, December 17, 1948, p. 6; Zanzibar Protectorate, *Report of Labour Conciliation Committee appointed on September 2, 1948*, Zanzibar, Government Printer, 1948; *ARLD 1948*; Anthony Clayton, *The 1948 Zanzibar General Strike*, Research Report No. 32, Scandinavian Institute of African Studies, Uppsala, 1976, p. 28.
21. *DLC*, September 6, 1948, pp. 132–37; *ARLD 1948*, pp. 1–7; *Annual Report of the Zanzibar Police*, Zanzibar, Government Printer, 1948, p. 14; *ARPA 1948*, p. 27; *ARPA 1949*, pp. 22–6.
22. F.B. Wilson, 'Notes on Peasant Agriculture and Industries in Zanzibar Island', unpublished, 1939, pp. 27, 30; *ARDA 1949*.
23. Zanzibar Protectorate, *Report on the Civil Disturbances in Zanzibar on July 30, 1951*, Zanzibar, Government Printer, 1952, pp. 1–4.
24. *Ibid.*, pp. 1–7, 15; *DLC*, August 12, 1948, p. 106; *ARDA 1949*, pp. 3–5; *ARDA 1951*, pp. 4–8; *ARDA 1952*, pp. 4, 15, 20; *ARPA 1950*, p. 10; *ARPA 1951*, p. 24.
25. Zanzibar Protectorate, *Report... 1951*, pp. 7–19.
26. *Ibid.*, p. 19; Lofchie, *op. cit.*, pp. 147–51; *DLC*, August 8, 1951, p. 99.
27. *ARDA 1948*; *Annual Reports of the Clove Growers' Association, passim*.
28. *Ibid.*; Crofts, *op. cit.*; *ARDA 1957*, p. 1; *ARDA 1958*, p. 3; *ARDA 1959*, p. 3.
29. Crofts, *op. cit.*; *ARDA 1960*, p. 1; *ARPA 1960*, p. 3.
30. *ARLD, 1948–57, passim.*; *ARLD 1959*, p. 3; *ARDA 1960*, pp. 2, 7.
31. *ARLD, 1958–61, passim.*; Lofchie, *op. cit.*, pp. 186–8; *ARPA 1959*, pp. 3, 21.
32. J. M. Gray, *Report of the Arbitrator to Enquire into a Trade Dispute at the Wharf Area of Zanzibar, 1958*, Zanzibar, Government Printer, 1958; Lofchie, *op. cit.*, pp. 259–61; *ARLD 1960* and *ARLD 1961*, pp. 1–5, 9, 25–8.
33. John Middleton, *Land Tenure in Zanzibar*, London, HMSO, 1961, pp. 46–7; Lofchie, *op. cit.*, pp. 184–6; *ARPA 1958*, pp. 1–2, 11; *ARPA 1959*, p. 20; Afro-Shirazi Party, *The Afro-Shirazi Party Revolution*, Zanzibar, Afro-Shirazi Party, 19754 p. 44.
34. See Lofchie, *op. cit.*, pp. 131–255, for his interpretation of these events.
35. *DLC*, November 10, 1955, pp. 171–6, p. 188; *DLC*, November 18, 1958, pp. 10–13; Zanzibar Protectorate, *A Statement by the British Resident on Constitutional Development in Zanzibar, October 3, 1955*; Zanzibar Protectorate, *Report of the Supervisor of Elections in Zanzibar*, 1957, pp. 2–6; Zanzibar Protectorate, *Report of the Supervisors of elections on ... elections held in January 1961*.
36. *Annual Report of the Zanzibar Police*, 1958; Lofchie, *op. cit.*, pp. 203, 212, 265, 274.

Part Two

Class Formation

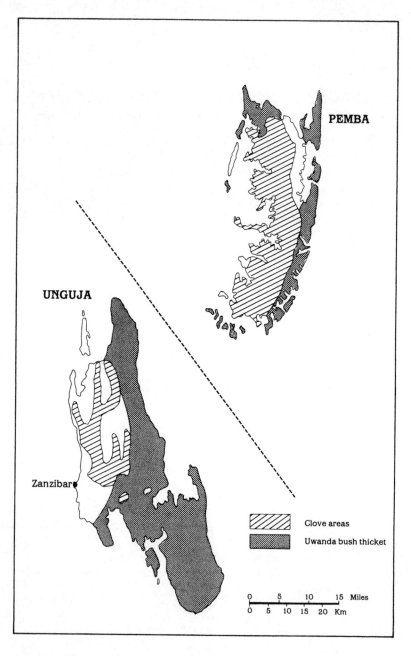

PEMBA

UNGUJA

Zanzibar

| | Clove areas |
| | Uwanda bush thicket |

0   5   10   15   Miles
0 5 10 15 20 Km

Zanzibar: Agricultural Areas

108

Four

The Peasantry Under Imperialism 1873–1963

ABDUL SHERIFF

The peasantry is a class in transition, owing its origin to the pre-capitalist epoch and disintegrating under the impact of capitalism. In analysing the characteristics and role of a peasantry, therefore, it is necessary to be concrete and historically specific.

The peasants are petty commodity producers who still own or possess definite rights in the means of production, especially land. They use family labour and, on the whole, produce their own subsistence, giving their economy a markedly individualised production and consumption.

> The smallholding peasants … live in similar conditions but without entering into manifold relations with one another. Their mode of production isolates them from one another. Each individual peasant family is almost self-sufficient.[1]

However, 'the development of the capitalist form of production has cut the life-strings of small production in agriculture,' destroying the peasant's self-sufficiency and impoverishing him.[2] While the development of large-scale industry destroyed the domestic industries of the peasants, the latter's increasing dependence on exchange of their own produce for manufactured commodities created an expanding sphere for merchant capital to occupy a monopoly position over producers and appropriate their surplus through unequal exchange. Moreover, occupying a precarious position in an expanding money economy, the peasant was driven by taxes, crop failures, divisions of inheritance and every natural and human calamity into the arms of 'capitalism's secondary modes of exploitation, that of the peasant against usury and mortgages'.[3]

109

Class Formation

Under the impact of capitalism the peasantry no longer remains a homogeneous group. It does not merely dissolve; rather, it disintegrates into different strata which permits the penetration of capitalism directly into peasant production.[4] As each calamity pushes peasants into 'Shylock's embrace' to become 'serfs of capital', some are expropriated wholly or partially.[5] The poor peasants are increasingly forced to sell their labour power to supplement their earnings. At the same time, the small segment that is emerging as rich peasants is in a position to buy not only the poor peasants' land, so gaining control over the means of production, but also their labour power, so appropriating surplus value which forms the basis for accumulation.

According to Lenin, differentiation of the peasantry under capitalism was a historically progressive force which facilitated the development of the economy to a higher level. The accumulation of land and capital by the rich peasants permitted them to extend their ownership of means of production (farm implements, manure), to invest a larger proportion of their income in agricultural production, to obtain loans at a lower rate of interest on the security of their larger properties, and to employ others, so enhancing the division of labour. In short, it facilitated the development of productive forces and production relations by socialising production. Secondly, whereas a self-sufficient peasantry constricts the development of the home market, differentiation of the peasantry creates an internal market not only in the means of consumption, especially food and clothing for the semi-proletarianised peasants and landless agricultural workers, but also in the means of production for the rich peasants. Furthermore, differentiation begins the process of proletarianisation, resulting in the appearance of the poor peasantry — seen by Lenin as a potentially revolutionary force which, in alliance with the urban proletariat, could lead to the overthrow of capitalism and raise society to a more advanced stage of socialist development.[6]

In the era of monopoly, however, capitalism ceases to be progressive; and the disintegration of the peasantry is slowed down and the partially decomposed class is frozen; preserved and reproduced, its social position facilitates the super-exploitation of its labour power.

> The existence of a small peasantry in every capitalist society is due not to the technical superiority of small production in agriculture, but to the fact that the small peasants reduce the level of their requirements below that of the wage-workers and tax their energies far more than the latter do.[7]

By this means, moribund capitalism is able to shift the cost of

110

reproduction of labour power to the peasant economy. In the case of the semi-proletarianised migrant labourer, capitalism pays only a 'bachelor wage' for the regeneration of the labourer's own physical capacities while at work, whereas his family, and even he himself when not at work, have to sustain and reproduce themselves at their own expense. Thus, not only is surplus value appropriated, but there is a transfer of value in the form of the cost of reproduction of labour power for which the capitalist does not pay. In the case of peasant cash crop production, the whole cost of production and reproduction of labour power is borne by the peasant household so that the commodities produced by the peasant can be sold far below their value. This was the basis of the alleged 'superiority' of peasant production under colonialism. In the case of the rich peasants the two forms of exploitation are combined, leaving them with the responsibility of organising production, enabling capital to exploit both their labour and that of the poor peasants they employed.[8] With agriculture so heavily exploited, the rich peasant is likely to divert his surplus capital into the more remunerative sphere of trade rather than reinvest it in agriculture. He therefore tends to be preserved as a rich peasant rather than become a capitalist farmer.

This is the theoretical background to our study of the peasantry in Zanzibar, which is organised into five sections. Prior to 1873, the peasant economy functioned more or less autonomously, despite the imposition of tribute by the ruling dynasties at Zanzibar (Section 1). With the abolition of the slave trade and of slavery, and the consequent shortage of labour for the clove plantations, capital had to bring the peasantry into the clove economy, either as a producer of labour to work on the plantations (Section 2), or as a smallhold producer (Section 4). At the same time, in the person of the merchant, capital penetrated deeply into the peasantry to create a perpetual flow of labour power that was no longer self-sufficient (Section 3). The final section (5), looks at peasant politics. This class, so often identified with a whole ethnic group – the so-called Shirazi – was no longer a homogeneous entity, nor was it composed solely of that ethnic group. It is not surprising that the politics of the peasantry should have appeared bewildering to the ethnically inclined analyst. Lenin had noted 'the inherently contradictory class structure of this mass, its petty-bourgeois character, the antagonism between the proprietor and the pro-letarian trends within it'.[9] The decomposition of this class actualised this contradiction through the political role of the different strata of the peasantry. The key to understanding the recent history of Zanzibar, like many other Third World countries, lies with the peasantry.

1. Marginalisation of the peasantry

When cloves were introduced to Zanzibar in about 1810, each island was composed of three geographical zones. On the larger island of Unguja, the first zone consisted of a series of parallel ridges in the north-western quarter of the island which, due to heavier rainfall and greater soil fertility, were apparently still forested. The neighbouring peasants had definite rights in these forests for hunting and collecting firewood. On the smaller island of Pemba which receives heavier rainfall, the hillsides in the western two-thirds of the island were heavily forested until the 1830s. The second zone consisted of a belt of low lands encircling these ridges and covering the western part of both islands. Much of this belt had already been cleared by the indigenous people for the cultivation of their food crops. Parts of this region, especially in Unguja, had passed into the hands of Arab landowners who established coconut plantations. The third zone consisted of the coral country (*uwanda*) of the eastern part of both islands, covering nearly two-thirds of Unguja and about a fifth of Pemba.[10]

After the introduction of cloves, especially in the feverish period of the 1830s when the price was still very high, it was in the lowlands that coconut trees were initially cut down to plant the more lucrative clove trees. That zone, however, was not the most suitable for cloves, and they became the poor clove areas. During the 1840s the forest zone began to be cleared, especially in Pemba, to establish the primary clove belt. Overproduction led to a collapse of the price for cloves from the late 1840s until the early 1870s, thus restricting clove production in Pemba to only a few pockets; it was not until after the hurricane of 1872 that the rest of the forest was cleared. With the establishment of the clove economy, it seems that the peasants lost their hunting and wood collecting rights in the forest belt, and may have been expropriated of their agricultural land in the lowland belt. This apparently forced some of the peasants to migrate to the stony coral region of the eastern part of the islands.[11]

The less fertile eastern zones of both islands emerged as the main peasant country during the nineteenth century. The economy there was self-sufficient to a considerable extent. Group co-operation played an important role in overcoming individual weakness in the struggle against nature. The land was communal property, with a distinction made between the family building site, *kiambo*, which was held by the kin group, and *uwanda* bushland which was common village property in which individuals had only use rights. The deeper soil of the *kiambo* permitted the planting of

Plate 15   A typical village on the east coast of Unguja. Note the makuti *huts and stone houses under a canopy of coconut palms.*

tree crops, such as coconuts where the soil was sandy. It was also under permanent cultivation with a rotation of food crops and a short fallow period. The *uwanda* was used to grow all the principal food crops through shifting cultivation. The bush was cleared through communal labour and the vegetation burnt to provide additional fertility. The land was cultivated for up to 5 years after which it was allowed to rest for 2 to 25 years depending on its quality and distance from the village. The plots were enclosed within stone walls, *bigili*, built with communal help, for protection from wild pigs. These structures became the property of the cultivator without conferring ownership rights to the land enclosed.[12]

Before the expansion of cloves, production of rice was extensive, especially in Pemba. The peasants cultivated the valleys *gratis*, while 'strangers' had to pay *ubani* (incense), a nominal portion of the harvest in recognition of land ownership by the local peasant community. Relatives normally helped in harvesting and took a share of the crop which was 'out of all proportion to the value of services rendered'; probably this was a form of redistribution to maintain equality among peasants and strengthen the social ties between them. With the acquisition of land for clove plantation in

113

the hilly areas, a large proportion of the rice plains, especially in
Unguja, were also appropriated, and peasants from adjacent *uwanda*
or seasonal migrants were obliged to pay rent in kind at harvest time
amounting to twice the amount of seed sown, i.e., about 5 to 10 per
cent of the harvest.[13]

Fishing was also an important sector of the peasant economy and
most of the settlements were located near the sea. The collection
and trapping of sea produce down to the low tide level and on the
sandbanks were governed by the same rules of tenure: the *kiwanja*
(plot) was owned by a kin group as in the case of the *kiambo*. Deeper
waters, however, were considered 'God's *waqf*' (endowment) where
anyone could fish with lines or drift nets, using *ngalawas* (outriggers)
or *daus* (dhows). An interesting conservation system, similar to the
fallow system on land, was used to ensure a continued supply of fish:
heavily fished localities were closed against fishing seasonally or for
a longer period by mutual agreement between elders of the various
villages concerned.[14]

The food production sectors of the peasant economy were com-
plemented by a sector producing means of production and manufactured goods such as implements and handcrafted items. There
was some division of labour and full-time specialists. Peasants used
the tree of the mangrove swamp for rafters (*boritis*) in house
construction, the coral stone for lime in masonry, and coconut
husks to provide coir rope for construction and domestic needs.
There were some carpenters and builders who were specialist
craftsmen. Pottery was a part-time activity for women who made
pots for their own use and for their neighbours. There were some
itinerant shipwrights who built *ngalawas* and *daus* to order out of
mango trunks and other suitable trees. Blacksmithing was an
important specialist industry using imported iron to produce
knives, door fasteners, small hoes, and crowbars (*mtarimbo*)
necessary for cultivation in the coral areas. Peasant households
were self-sufficient in the production of most of the articles of
consumption apart from a few essential imports such as iron and
textiles. Overall, only a few simple tools were used, for the level of
productive forces was low. Needs were restricted.[15]

Nevertheless, a certain amount of surplus was produced. At the
beginning of the nineteenth century Pemba, in particular,
produced a considerable grain surplus for export to Mombasa and
even to Arabia. With the growth of Zanzibar Town and the
plantation economy, this export was apparently diverted to the
internal market. A report in 1901 mentions 'Chillie or copra
merchants, fish hawkers, peddlers, small shopkeepers or traders'
among the peasants, indicating the further development of

Plate 16   The dema *fish traps used extensively in Zanzibar waters.*

Plate 17   An ngalawa *(outrigger) race. The outrigger, which may be of Indonesian origin, is a common fishing boat in Zanzibar waters.*

115

Plate 18 Women weaving baskets and food covers in a doorway. Note the ornately crafted doors.

exchange.[16] Moreover, some surplus was produced for appropriation by the existing social and political hierarchies. The *mvyale*, who controlled the allocation of *uwanda* land and whose office was hereditary in the village senior lineage, was entitled to various offerings which constituted a considerable take. Although the society was quite egalitarian the elders, *watu wanne* (four men), representing the principal kin groups, did exercise some influence and received dues and fines, especially from 'strangers' and tenants, which were supposed to be used for communal functions. However, a more substantial portion of the surplus was appropriated by the political superstructure superimposed by the *Mwinyi Mkuu* (the Great Lord) in the Shirazi area of Unguja, and probably by the *sheha* of Tumbatu and the *diwanis* of Pemba. The *Mwinyi Mkuu* appointed the *shakua* who was charged with the duty of collecting tribute, consisting of millet, mangrove poles and labour. Each *sheha* (locality) had to provide a group of labourers who worked for about a fortnight (*arbataasher*), during which they were given merely their subsistence. Such labour was used in building the *Mwinyi Mkuu's*

116

palace at Dunga which is said to have taken 10 years.[17]

The rule of the Busaidi dynasty was in turn superimposed over the *Mwinyi Mkuu* administration which was used for purposes of indirect rule up until 1865. This deprived the local ruling class of a considerable part of the tribute; the expansion of the clove economy may have increased the demand for labour to help in the harvest on the Sultan's plantations as well as on those of the *Mwinyi Mkuu*. This sharpened the contradiction between the Omani Sultan and the *Mwinyi Mkuu* as a representative of the peasants, resulting in the latter's alleged imprisonment and exile during which, it is claimed, the island suffered from a drought. The tribute was converted into a single poll tax of $2 cash which was shared between the two suzerains. By this compromise the peasants withdrew even further from the clove economy, preferring to produce commodities themselves for exchange to pay the tax. This stimulated surplus production, especially of foodstuffs, for the sizeable urban population of Zanzibar Town. Caught between the expanding Omani political power at the top and changes in the peasant economy which replaced the personal bond of labour service by a monetary tax, the position of the local rulers and of the *Mwinyi Mkuu* became precarious. While some, through landownership and intermarriage with Arab landowners, were assimilated into the ruling landowning class, others were impoverished and sank to the level of the peasants. When the last male heir of the *Mwinyi Mkuu* dynasty died in 1873, rule by this indigenous line lapsed with hardly a ripple. The existing administrative structure was partially absorbed into the Busaidi structure and later into the British colonial state.[18]

2. The poor peasantry: a labour reserve

The abolition of the slave trade in 1873, and of the legal status of slavery in 1897, were turning points in the political economy of Zanzibar. These changes took place at the time British imperialism was establishing its hegemony over Zanzibar. Britain did not want to precipitate a social revolution which would disrupt the economy and destroy the administrative structure it wished to preserve and use for indirect rule, thus cutting the cost of colonial domination. The colonial state, formally established in the 1890s, took it upon itself to ensure continuity in the labour supply required by the landowning class and the clove economy from which derived most of the government revenue.

The produce of the clove tree must be gathered and dried within two relatively short seasons, and under slavery the proprietor had to keep a large enough number of slaves to harvest the crop without recourse to outside labour. The owners could afford to do so only by allowing slaves to produce their own subsistence. This developed into a well recognised custom whereby the slaves had two days of the week to work on their allotted plots and even to sell surplus foodstuffs in the city market. This system diverged considerably from classical slavery, where the whole of a slave's labour was at the disposal of the owner who supplied the slave's means of subsistence, for it contained elements of serfdom which became more pronounced after the emancipation of the slaves.[19]

After abolition, the ex-slaves were 'induced to enter into contracts with their former masters who agreed to give them an allotment of land rent free in return for four days' work a week.' This *burre* (free) system, was in fact a system of labour rent, and it diverged so little from the preceding slave system that in the decade following emancipation only 17,000 individuals were formally freed. However, it proved extremely difficult to get this new type of labour ('squatters') to work for nothing during those four days and the *burre* system had to be abandoned by 1900. Squatters, then, had to be paid a regular wage when picking cloves, and the only obligation that remained was to help pick the landowner's cloves first. Through the cultivation of food crops in between trees the squatters helped keep the plantation free of bush and weeds. They had no security of tenure and were not generally permitted to grow tree crops. Occasionally, old squatters were allowed to plant trees which became the property of the landowner upon the old squatter's death.[20]

After 1900 the number of squatters of slave origin declined drastically. Slaves were said to have suffered from a very high death rate at the height of the slave era, though treatment apparently improved when the external supply of slaves was cut off. Sex ratio imbalance and general lack of security under slavery resulted in a low birth rate. This appears to have persisted after emancipation for many medical authorities commented on the infertility of the detribalised 'Swahili' and ex-slaves. Their numbers were supplemented during this century by new immigrants, largely from the mainland but also from other parts of the islands.[21]

The colonial state, therefore, had to resort to importation of labour. Curiously, its first source of immigrant workers was not nearby. Kirsopp observed that 'many plantation industries both in the East and in the West were only saved from immediate ruin by the extensive importation of Chinese and Indian coolie labour.'[22] In the case of Zanzibar, a certain number of Asians were employed on government plantations in 1897. They proved to be 'too expensive' because of transportation costs, frequent sickness, and their

demand for 'high wages'.[23] The British tapped a closer source of
labour in 1904 when they imported over 500 persons from Kenya on
three-month contracts. Another 3,000 were imported in 1907 from
the same mainland colony at a cost of Rs90,000. It was then argued
that this price was too high for such 'inexperienced and inefficient'
clove pickers, and that the practice of importing labour from
Kenya should be discontinued. There was also pressure from the
mainland administration which wished to control its labour supply.
As a consequence, official recruitment with the offer of a free
passage to Zanzibar was discouraged. Yet mainland labour continued to travel to Zanzibar even after the cost of transportation was
shifted to the shoulders of the immigrant labourers. Likely motives
for emigration were deteriorating conditions in their home areas
and the lower wages paid at mainland plantations. Between 1923
and 1930 a total of 21,699 mainlanders immigrated into Zanzibar, of
whom 3,876 never returned, either because of death or because
they settled down as squatters. In the census of 1924 there were
5,741 adult male 'weeders' from the mainland in Zanzibar, and 7,539
mainlander 'cultivators' who produced food crops.[24]

The demand for labour fluctuated widely from year to year, since
it was dependent on the size of the clove crop which could be
estimated only a few weeks before the harvest. Between 1907 and
1925 the crop varied from 100,000 to 690,000 *frasilas* (= 35 lb). Under
these circumstances, what was needed was a local and fairly elastic
source of cheap seasonal labour which could maintain itself at its
own expense in the off-season. Repeated experience through the
seasons would enable these pickers to become skilled. However,
that potential source was unavailable at the beginning of the
twentieth century, for the peasant economy was still largely self-
sufficient. As one administrator remarked:

> I endeavoured this year [1901] to persuade the Wahadimu
> [Shirazi] to go to the plantations and pick. The result however of
> all our endeavours was that not a single Mhadimu volunteered
> for work. The *Masheha* stated that their people had their
> particular employments and affairs to attend to and had no
> desire to earn money.[25]

A decade later, in 1911, it was reported that clove picking wages
were still not essential to peasant survival. In Pemba some peasants
were prepared to pick cloves on a sharecropping basis, giving the
owner a third to a half of the cloves, but not for wages.[26]

If capital was to penetrate this pre-capitalist formation to create
the required labour, the self-sufficiency and economic autonomy
of the peasantry had to be eliminated. This objective was clear to

colonial authorities who had taken the first steps immediately after the abolition of slavery when they imposed forced labour and taxation upon the peasantry. Regulations were imposed in the Sultan's name in 1899, 'compelling natives not in possession of clove trees to pick cloves for other people' at a fixed rate. 'Valuable assistance was rendered ... in dealing with labour by nearly all the *masheha*,' the local headmen, who were rewarded with an increase in their salaries. The British set up labour bureaus to distribute the clove pickers among the landowners. Over 8,000 Pemba peasants were thus recruited in 1904.

When this new demand for labour met resistance, colonial officials sought to revive the old tribute in labour service formerly extracted by the *Mwinyi Mkuu* and the Sultan. Other means were also used to create wage labour. All 'vagrants' in Unguja were arrested and shipped to Pemba to harvest the clove crop. When the legality of the practice was questioned in 1904, it was proposed to institute Vagrancy Regulations.[27] A senior colonial official confessed that in 1907, 'every possible forcible method was used.' The people were literally driven from their homes, and the *masheha* were suspended or forced to pick cloves themselves till they produced a certain number of labourers.[28] It was not until 1916 that coercion was abandoned, though colonial authorities were authorised by the Secretary of State 'to place at the disposal of natives any information as to where labour is required, and at the disposal of employers information as to sources of labour.'[29]

In addition to these forms of coercion, the colonial government imposed a hut tax or ground rent on peasants and then offered exemption from it to those who went to pick cloves. It was seen as a 'useful weapon in the hands of the government' to obtain labour from the peasantry, though the Collector of Zanzibar argued that the tax was too small to have any influence on clove picking. Moreover, in 1911 the peasants in Zanzibar simply refused to pay ground rent, arguing, with the help of 'native lawyers', that 'they were residing on their own lands.' The revenue from this source declined drastically and the tax was abandoned in 1912.[30]

Colonial authorities, therefore, resorted to financial inducements to draw peasants to work on the plantations. Clove pickers under contract were given 'free' passage on government steamers from Unguja to Pemba. From the plantation owners' perspective, this subsidy, paid out of general revenues of the colony, contributed to a steady labour supply and held down pickers' wages. Return passage, however, was not free and pickers returned to Unguja in 'grossly overcrowded' dhows, sometimes with disastrous results. Many of the pickers refused the free passage because of unacceptable clauses in the contract such as the fixed rate of pay, so they made their own way to Pemba as freelancers. A practice introduced by plantation owners to stabilise the labour supply was the *kopa* (borrowing) system under which cash advances were made to pickers 'to create a tie with labour which turns up year after year for employment on the same estates.' This was quite apart from the practice of making cash advances to those who signed contracts. In this latter case, defaulters were punished under the notorious Masters and Servants Decree, which made the labourer liable to a fine of half a month's wage or imprisonment of up to a month for breach of contract. In 1940 the penal sanction under the decree was abolished for all classes of labour except for clove pickers. In the mid-1940s an average of 83 clove pickers were convicted annually of breach of contract. The government also used its emergency powers during World War II to issue pickers registration cards which were retained by the landowner until the contract was fulfilled, a system analogous to the *kipande* system of the mainland plantations.[31]

In the 1940s the administration introduced a more sophisticated contract based on the piece work system to increase the rate of worker exploitation. Under this contract the rate of pay per unit started at a low level and rose progressively. By 1950, for example, 20 cents per *pishi* (measure of about 4 pounds) was offered for the first third of the contracted number of *pishis*, 30 cents for the second third, and 40 cents for the final third. This procedure was also to discourage the picker from absconding halfway through the contract, which had to be completed within 50 days. The highest rate under the contract was often lower than the prevailing picking rate, so pickers rarely renewed them. The Shirazi Association considered the contract akin to slavery and tried to persuade the Shirazi in 1944 not to sign them.[32]

As a result of these various measures the peasantry contributed a substantial supply of labour to meet the fluctuating seasonal demand of the clove economy. Table 4.1 shows the close correlation between the size of the clove crop and the number of pickers given free passage to Pemba.

These figures do not represent the total size of the clove picking labour force. Excluded from them is the resident squatter population that picked a larger proportion of the smaller crops. Nor do the figures include the many freelancers travelling on their own from Unguja to Pemba. In 1931, apart from the 11,500 who contracted to pick cloves there were about 3,500 freelancers who went to Pemba. Also missing from the table are those clove pickers who remained in their respective islands to pick. In the 1946–1947

Table 4.1 *Number of pickers given free passage to Pemba*

Year	No. of pickers	Clove crop: No. of frasilas
1907	3,694	542,000
1908	4,080	450,000
1909	5,494	300,000
1910	806	139,000
1911	8,139	582,000
1912	301	104,000
1913	806	639,000
1914	732	331,000
1915	8,490	655,000
1916	1,685	303,000
1917	–	234,000
1918	2,290	565,000
1919	508	169,000
1920	253	316,000
1921	48	201,000
1922	5,123	690,000
1923	2,178	237,000
1924	5,528	520,000
1925	3,540	450,000

season, 5,525 Pemba peasants contracted to pick cloves apart from the 11,125 who came from Unguja, but there was probably a larger number of Pemba peasants who did not contract. No reliable estimate is available of the number of peasants who participated in clove picking in Unguja where the clove crop was on average less than a third of the total for the Protectorate. For these reasons, therefore, it is difficult to know the total size of the labour force involved in the clove economy. However, we do know that the government registered all contract and freelance pickers travelling from Unguja to Pemba in 1943, and they totalled 18,662 persons. In Pemba with a smaller total population and large number of small-holder clove producers, the maximum number of peasants normally available for clove picking was perhaps 12,000, giving a total for the Protectorate of about 30,000 in the early 1940s.[34]

It is clear, therefore, that by World War II capitalism had succeeded in shaping approximately half the able-bodied male peasant population of the islands into an elastic source of cheap seasonal labour. This was essentially the poor peasantry which had become a veritable labour reserve. The District Commissioner of Pemba remarked on this development:

122

The most satisfactory aspect of the harvest was the unusual amount of local labour employed therein. For several months the south of the District was denuded of able-bodied persons all of whom had migrated to the north.[35]

They had become dependent on the clove economy for their cash needs which 'caused people largely to abandon the old system of maintenance food crop cultivation in favour of working for wages for the purchase of food and necessities of life.'[36] But clove picking was a spasmodic source of cash income for the peasantry. The poor peasants were on the borderline between a money economy and a subsistence economy. They were neither proletarianised – since under imperialism the monocultural economy of Zanzibar required only seasonal and cheap labour – nor were they self-reliant peasants. They had been transformed into an inexpensive reservoir of labour to facilitate capitalist accumulation.

3. The commercialisation of the peasant economy

The merchant was a further agent for capitalist penetration of the peasantry in Zanzibar. Through his activities local production was reoriented from the satisfaction of internal needs to export production. The pattern of consumption of locally produced goods began to give way to the consumption of foreign goods. The two branches of peasant productive activity, creating means of production and means of consumption, were no longer inter-dependent; now they were linked by foreign production. By eroding the internal structure of the peasant economy, and by exploiting the peasant through moneylending, merchant capital contributed to the flow of labour from the rural village to the plantation.

An important step in integrating the peasantry into the colonial and international economy was the expansion of a transportation system. At the beginning of the colonial period the rural areas were linked to the towns in Zanzibar through a network of land transport, based on animal and human power, and sea travel by dhow. In the name of increased production and circulation of commodities, colonialism began to displace these local sources of power and transportation by foreign ones. Transportation by dhow, which was central to the livelihood of the Tumbatu peasants, began to give way to government steamers which captured much of the passenger traffic between Pemba and Unguja by 1911, while the transport of cloves was lost to dhow owners two decades later when the Clove

Plate 19 Donkey cart transport, here carrying palm frond thatch used to roof huts and houses in Zanzibar.

Growers' Association decided to ship them by steamers.[37]

While the bullock and donkey carts persisted as major means of rural transport, clove production on the island of Unguju was significant enough for an American company to build seven miles of railway from Zanzibar Town to Bububu, at the edge of the plantation belt to the north in 1905–06. In less than a decade, however, the relatively small profit of Rs18,000 became an average loss of the same proportion, so the railway was sold to the Zanzibar government. It continued to be operated until 1928, conveying an average of 1,300 passengers a day, most of them carrying small packages of produce to the town market or imported commodities back to their rural homes.[38]

The most important new form of land transport, however, was 'the ubiquitous omnibus [which] enables cultivators to market their produce.' By 1908 there were 100 miles of roads in Unguja, of which 43 miles were metalled, and there were 42 miles of metalled roads in Pemba by the following year. The primary objective in road construction was to 'bring about the considerable reduction in transport charges' from the plantation belt. Feeder roads were built to the *uwanda* to link up east coast villages with the central road system 'to increase the wealth and productivity of the more isolated places; to permit speedier transport of foodstuffs to outlying areas in time of famine.' The peasantry was expected to contribute labour to build these roads as 'self-help community projects' to facilitate its own integration into the colonial economy.[39]

With such integration, there developed a 'constantly shifting balance between maintenance and cash economy'. Coconuts, a basic food staple and cooking oil, became an item in the peasant 'barter system [for] purchasing their small luxury requirements from rural shops', or 'a small quarterly income between clove picking seasons'. Other subsistence crops such as cassava and sweet potatoes were produced for sale to the towns or to Pemba during the clove season. Isolated rural areas like Micheweni in eastern Pemba were active in the production of food crops for sale elsewhere. It was soon a regular practice for peasants to sell more nutritious foods like chicken, eggs, rice, milk, fish and goats, and to subsist on the less nutritious cassava. Often under financial pressure the peasants oversold their food supplies only to be forced to buy at a higher price later, much to the advantage of the local shopkeeper or merchant. Malnutrition, in the words of the Director of Medical Services, began to affect 'a large proportion of the native population of Zanzibar', a state of affairs, he concluded, 'largely due to the subordination of the interests of food crop production to that of commercial crops for export.'[40]

Many peasant industries were similarly reoriented towards commodity production for export. Fishing, the source of livelihood for an estimated 4,000 fishermen in 1928, had become the principal occupation of some 9,500 men by 1961. It became commercial with the development of a transport system to convey fresh and smoked fish to towns and the plantation belt. Local production of fishing supplies declined as imported lines and nets appeared on the local market, accompanied later by outboard motors which, however, few fishermen could afford to buy. Larger merchants thus began to penetrate the industry. Owning large fleets of boats, they hired these out in return for some control over the catches.[41]

Mangrove poles, a traditional building material, emerged as a source of tannin for export as early as 1903 when a French firm began to exploit the mangrove swamps. Rising demand for the bark during and after World War II, particularly in the United States market, led to wasteful cutting until the market collapsed in 1948 with the resumption of tannin extraction in the Philippines.[42]

The coir rope industry, which had survived in the south of Unguja, found itself hemmed in by commercial monopolies and indebtedness. In 1940, a single merchant contracted to purchase all the rope produced in Makunduchi at a fixed price; when a few 'young bloods' tried to bypass the monopoly, they found all the buses carrying for this merchant alone. At the same time, it was found that 70 per cent of the peasants had mortgaged their few coconut trees to village shopkeepers for small sums to tide them over between clove harvests. The industry revived in the 1950s with the diversion of merchant capital to establish thirteen coir factories which were using diesel and electricity by 1961. The role of the peasant in the industry was reduced to supplying raw fibre and cheap factory labour.[43]

The lime industry expanded in the 1930s with the extension of the road system to more remote parts of the *uwanda*. The centre of production was the extreme north of Unguja where some 5,000 Nungwi peasants supplemented fishing with lime burning on their coralline land. Competition from imported cement caused the price of lime to decline in the 1940s. The more lucrative mainland market was sought out by Zanzibari producers because the price was about three times higher there, but the administration imposed a ban on the export of lime from Zanzibar. It argued that the native industry was denuding the vegetation, although it looked favourably on a proposal by a European to set up a factory in Unguja operating on crude oil to supply the mainland market. The plan was abandoned when the lime industry entered a steep decline.[44]

The peasant economy at the beginning of the twentieth century was at a low level of development; yet it was internally integrated and viable. By the end of the colonial period it had been thoroughly undermined by the penetration of capital with the help of the colonial administration. The peasantry was partially preserved for cheap labour, but its economy was no longer autonomous. Imperialism destroyed peasant self-sufficiency, incorporating them into the national and international economy as a semi-proletarian, semi-peasant group.

4. The rise of the rich peasantry

While the poor peasantry appeared primarily as a colonial labour reserve, it was by no means resolved that plantation production would be the sole basis for the colonial economy. The deep indebtedness of the landowning class, dating back to the mid-nineteenth century and heightened by the 'labour shortage' resulting from the abolition of slavery, raised serious questions about the future of the Zanzibar plantation system. Several colonial officials declared that large landowners were a spent force and that the future lay with peasant smallholders. As early as 1913, it was openly declared that, 'The question of [land] ownership is in a transition stage pending the formation of a new class of owner from the natives of the islands, or alternatively, the introduction of white capital.'[45]

The possibility of landed 'white capital' rescuing the clove economy had been ruled out by the 1920s when colonial administrators concluded that 'this Protectorate can never be a white man's country.'[46] It was argued that African peasant production would be an ideal alternative for Zanzibar's colonial economy:

> [Peasants] are self-supporting as regards labour; secondly they are incomparably the cheapest instrument for the production of agricultural produce on a large scale that has yet been devised, and, thirdly, are capable of a rapidity of expansion and a progressive increase of output that beggar every record of the past.[47]

It was argued, in addition, that self-sufficient in subsistence and labour, simple in their tastes, and with properties too small to serve as security for moneylenders, peasants would be a sound fiscal alternative to the debt-ridden large landholders. While it did not take much time to prove the last assumption incorrect, the other suppositions made a strong case for peasant smallhold production.

Yet the colonial state never entirely abandoned its support of the landowning class. The reason went beyond the platitudes professing a 'sense of obligation to a race upon whom we have imposed our protection,' to the basic fact that to forsake the landowning class would have meant social and political change of unprecedented scope and unpredictable consequences. The British retained faith that the planters were not a spent political force, so they prepared to take the measures necessary to maintain their economic viability. At the same time, steps were taken for the development of clove production by the peasant smallholder.[48]

The background to peasant production of cloves goes back to the last quarter of the nineteenth century. By the time the hurricane wiped out most of the clove plantations on Unguja in 1872, the poorer lands had begun to show sign of exhaustion. The regeneration of the clove economy meant clearing the forests and many of the coconut trees, while greatly expanding production in Pemba where cloves had played a minor role hitherto. Although slaves from Unguja were taken to Pemba to help in the work, the abolition

127

of the slave trade the year following the hurricane created a severe shortage of labour, and the self-sufficient peasants were unwilling to fill the gap. A compromise solution called the 'half-and-half' system was reached in Pemba under which peasants undertook to clear the forest and plant clove trees and food crops on land claimed by others. When the trees reached maturity they were divided equally between the landowner and the peasant. This system, still in vogue at the end of the period, provided an opening for peasant entry into the smallholding of clove trees.[49]

The indebtedness of large landowners also contributed to the rise of the smallholder. In order to reduce their financial burden, debtors with plantations sold off portions to others. Some debtors became smallholders themselves as a result. Other plantations which were hopelessly in debt were foreclosed by moneylenders who then subdivided them for sale in small lots. Larger plantations became fragmented through the Islamic law of inheritance which 'operates to distribute wealth so that a large number of people may have a competence or, at least, a little rather than one or a few should have a large share and the rest nothing.' The smallholder movement grew, therefore, not only through acquisition, but also through the loss and fragmentation of land. Remarking on this phenomenon shortly after World War I, Kirsopp predicted, 'It is not improbable that within the next few generations the further readjustment of our agricultural organization will place the Arabs and Native producers on a common economic level, the Native element largely predominating.'[50]

The smallholder movement gained momentum from measures which, implemented to help the clove industry as a whole, were yet, as Kirsopp argued, 'suited to the needs of peasant rather than plantation cultivation.' One of the first of these was hut tax exemption offered to owners of more than 100 clove trees. This was apparently intended to encourage the emergence of labour-employing rich peasants rather than middle peasants relying solely on family labour. In the Wete district of Pemba, there were 150 exemptions in 1910, a figure that doubled in the next two years. Another measure was the Clove Bonus Scheme instituted in 1922 to encourage regeneration of old plantations and formation of new smallholder *shambas* (agricultural plots). Under this scheme, owners were paid a cash bonus for each clove-bearing tree, and a larger bonus on young plants. Whereas only 7 per cent of the Indian owners claimed the bonus in Pemba, 63 per cent of the Arabs and more than 85 per cent of Africans, most of whom were smallholders, claimed it.[51]

The third and more direct measure was to divide up some of the government plantations and offer parcels to 'native and mainlander' smallholders. This had been suggested as early as 1911, and Kirsopp, foreseeing a shortage of labour as mainland colonial governments sought control of their labour force, argued that existing mainland labourers should be stabilized and settled as smallholders in Zanzibar. In 1934, the 80-acre government plantation at Mahonda was subdivided into 50 plots containing between 100 and 500 clove trees; it was offered to an Indian, several Arabs, and indigenous and mainland Africans. 'Preference was given to manual workers over employers of paid labour.' Few of the new owners actually settled on their plots and 50 per cent remained uncultivated. Most of the smallholders failed to keep up with their payments and those 'hopelessly in debt' were foreclosed in 1941. Although the experiment was repeated in 1948, no substantial class of peasant clove producers was created as a result of direct government intervention.[52]

The smallholder movement grew under its own momentum fairly rapidly after the abolition of slavery. Whereas in 1904 it was reported that 'not many of the Wapemba have clove plantations, and generally a Mpemba clove plantation is a very small one,' by 1913 it was reported that 'many natives possess small plantations'. The first detailed glimpse of the growth of the smallholders comes from the Clove Bonus Scheme of 1922–29 which shows that more than 90 per cent of clove owners on both islands owned less than 500 trees; they owned 58 per cent of the clove trees in Pemba and 45 per cent in Unguja. It reveals a pattern of class stratification which belies the common assumption that race and class coincide in Zanzibar.[53] As Table 4.2 shows, class stratification cut right across racial lines, though somewhat differently between Pemba and Unguja. Thus more than four-fifths of non-African owners on both islands were in fact peasants who owned less than 500 trees. In Pemba, where two-thirds of the clove trees were to be found, the lower strata of the landownership pyramid was almost symmetrical with about as many non-African as African peasants.

In Unguja, on the other hand, class stratification was much sharper and the ethnic tendency was more pronounced. The peasantry was poorer as a whole, and the larger proportion was African, although 81 per cent of the non-African owners were still in this category. What is, in fact, remarkable is the degree of concentration of clove trees in the hands of a very small class of big landowners of all races, with the Arabs predominating. Just over 2 per cent of the clove owners owned 40 per cent and 26 per cent of all the clove trees in Unguja and Pemba respectively. Some of these owners, who owned plantations all over the islands, used to boast

Class Formation

that no rain could fall on Zanzibar without falling on some of their properties. However, as a result of various factors, such as inheritance laws and indebtedness, the plantations continued to be fragmented, and many of their owners sank into the peasant category.

Table 4.2   *Clove Ownership in Zanzibar, 1922–29* [54]

Number of clove trees	Non-Africans: % of owners	% of trees	Africans: % of owners	% of trees	Total % of owners	% of trees
Pemba						
1–99	18.9	4.9	33.1	8.0	52.1	12.9
100–499	20.5	25.1	20.7	20.5	41.2	45.5
500–999	3.5	12.9	0.7	2.6	4.3	15.5
1,000+	2.2	24.2	0.2	1.9	2.4	26.1
TOTAL	45.3	67.1	54.7	32.9	100.0	100.0
Unguja						
1–99	11.4	3.4	67.2	15.2	78.5	18.6
100–499	8.6	15.5	7.5	10.3	16.6	25.9
500–999	2.4	12.9	0.4	2.1	2.8	15.0
1,000+	2.3	39.1	0.1	1.4	2.4	40.6
TOTAL	24.7	70.9	75.2	29.0	99.9	99.9

Although peasant-based clove production had become a reality, the British assumption that this would solve the indebtedness question proved to be unfounded.[55] By the 1930s it became clear that the smallholder was more vulnerable than the large owner to unscrupulous forms of moneylending. Larger landowners could offer more security and thus negotiate lower mortgage interest rates. Smallholders were considered greater security risks and found it difficult to obtain loans at the going rate of interest. Unscrupulous practices by moneylenders were widespread: approximately 10 per cent of smallholders in need of loans in Pemba had to resort to a 'fictitious' or 'conditional' sale (*bei khiyar*) under which they 'sold' their properties and then 'rented' them back at interest rates as high as 50–100 per cent. The sale was conditional in that the owner had the option of buying back property within a specified time. It is clear from Table 4.3 that 'fictitious sales' were particularly prevalent among small debtors. In Pemba, 40 per cent of the revealed indebtedness took that form. Unfortunately indebtedness of less than Rs50 was not recorded, so many of the poor and middle peasants, who must have constituted the vast majority of debtors, have been excluded from the table.[56]

Table 4.3 *Indebtedness in Zanzibar Protectorate, 1933* [57] *(columns 3 to 7 in thousands of rupees)*

Amount of debt	No. of debtors	Mortgages	Fictitious sales	Other debts	Total debts	Total assets (debtors)
More than Rs 4,000	271	1,396	143	256	1,796	2,936
400–3,999	2,458	563	598	438	1,600	2,802
50– 399	2,703	74	22	167	464	518
TOTAL	5,432	2,034	963	862	3,860	6,257

With production individualised on a multitude of small peasant *shambas* there was wide scope for 'the multiplicity of traders and middlemen' to exploit the peasant. In Unguja the great majority of smallholders sent their cloves directly for sale in Zanzibar Town from where they were exported. In Pemba, where the smallholder proliferated, practically the whole of the crop was marketed through Indian middlemen who controlled transport to the export market in Zanzibar Town. By the mid-1920s, there were some 356 clove and copra dealers in Unguja, whereas almost 1,000 merchants were involved in Pemba, nearly half of whom were concentrated at Mkoani. The traders purchased produce, sold general merchandise (often on credit in return for payment in kind), and loaned money.[58]

Smallholders rapidly fell into debt to the merchant-moneylender. It was reported in the early 1930s that 'the Swahili ... are losing their property to Indians and to Arabs more rapidly than the Arabs are losing to Indians.'[59] This was more true for Pemba than for Unguja, as Table 4.4 shows.

Table 4.4 *Net transfer of land, 1926–30 (approx. acres)* [60]

	Unguja	Pemba	Protectorate
Arab to Indian	2,028	825	2,853
Swahili to Indian	272	1,389	1,661
Swahili to Arab	103	135	238

Class Formation

Colonial data like the above present a problem of interpretation since they assume the coincidence of ethnicity and class. Land transfer figures for 1932—34 show that while some Africans sold land worth Rs397,000 to 'other ethnic groups', others bought land worth Rs179,000 from 'other races'. Presumably there were additional purchases made from other Africans which are not recorded. While tendencies are apparent, racially defined colonial statistics only tend to camouflage the complex process of class differentiation even among the Africans.[61]

The international capitalist Depression of the late 1920s and the 1930s hit Zanzibar hard. The price of cloves tumbled from Rs24 in 1929—30 to Rs7.5 in 1933—34. The heavily indebted landowners and peasant smallholders now saw utter ruin staring them in the face, while the government suffered an average 30 per cent loss of revenue in clove duties during 1930—32. The colonial state was determined 'to maintain and if possible to increase production despite a fall in price' by attempting to cut the cost of production and marketing. The first goal called for cooperation between employers to lessen clove picking wages. The second objective was based on the premise that middlemen and moneylenders appropriated too large a proportion of the surplus, so that the colonial state should look towards eliminating them through a centralised marketing organisation.[62]

Thus was born the Clove Growers' Association (CGA) which worked towards both the foregoing objectives. It was simultaneously opposed to labour and the small merchant. It was pro-landowner and big merchant to the extent that their interests coincided with the goal of heightened revenue. There was reason for optimism. While the earliest attempt, in 1913, to form a centralised structure proved a failure, a more recent attempt had been successful in reducing production costs. In 1927 the Arab Agricultural Advisory Committee was created as the sole body representing clove producers and the channel through which clove bonuses were to be paid. The declared objectives of the organisation were (1) to regulate the cost of production by fixing wages, (2) to gain control of the market and (3) to finance the needs of the growers. By 1929 the Director of Agriculture could boast that it had already 'accomplished the reduction in the cost of production of cloves and copra by at least 20 per cent', amounting to nearly Rs500,000 which had been kept out of the clove pickers' pockets. More than 9,000 members joined the Association primarily to receive the clove bonus. When bonus payments were stopped in 1928 active membership declined.[63]

When the effects of the Depression began to be felt acutely in

Zanzibar, the government responded, in 1934, with a whole battery of legislation to deal with these problems. The Alienation of Land Decree prohibited the transfer of agricultural land from Arabs or Africans to Indians, restricted forms of mortgages, and imposed a moratorium on debts. The Moneylenders Decree prohibited compound interest and permitted the courts to reduce excessive interest. The Clove Growers' Association Decree gave that body a virtual monopoly over the internal and external marketing of cloves, 'to deal generally in and export agricultural produce', to do business in agricultural property, and to lend money. The Clove Exporters' Decree limited the number of exporters to be licensed by the CGA, and required each to pay a heavy licence fee. The latter measure affected the big export merchants and provoked a clove boycott organised with the cooperation of the clove merchants in India. It ended in a compromise by which the Zanzibar merchants were given a share in the trade. The measures dealing with the debt question protected property rights of the landowners and rich peasants by reversing the trend of land transfers to Indian merchant-moneylenders. From colonial records based on race rather than class, it appears that both Arabs and Africans recouped their losses at the expense of the Indians.[64] However, a comparison of the 1922–29 data with the survey of landownership in 1943, which unfortunately is available only for Pemba, shows that class differentiation had proceeded apace.

Table 4.5 *Clove ownership in Pemba, 1922–29 and 1943* [65]

Number of trees per owner	Percentage of owners	
	1922–29	1943
1–99	52.1	80.7
100–499	41.2	16.3
500–999	4.3	1.9
1,000+	2.4	1.1

The table shows that the poor peasants, owning less than 100 clove trees, had grown from 52 per cent to 81 per cent, while those owning between 100 and 499 trees had declined from 41 per cent to 16 per cent. There was a similar decline in the proportion of larger landholdings, but this may have been accompanied by a greater concentration of clove trees in the hands of the really big owners.

5. Peasantry as a class

The sizeable class of rich peasants, particularly in Pemba, was composed of Africans and a large number of Arabs. They lived cheek-by-jowl with each other and developed common class interests. Certain privileges enjoyed by Arabs galled the Africans, so the racial ideology that dominated the colonial situation caused initial African demands to be articulated through ethnic associations. It is significant, however, that the maturation of the independence struggle saw the African petty bourgeoisie, of which the rich peasants were a segment, abandon ethnic politics for class alliances.

The Shirazi Association was formed in Pemba in 1940 to represent the interests of 'rural indigenous Africans', since 'urban' Africans were already represented by the African Association formed five years earlier. By 1943 there were between 300 and 400 recorded members, a figure which tripled in the following year. Subsequent continued growth enabled it to become the most influential organ among Pemba Africans. The Vice-President of the Shirazi Association was an ex-*sheha* whose son was a school teacher, and all committee members were 'persons of note in the ... Shirazi community'. One of the first demands of the Association was for representation in the CGA and the Land Alienation Board, and by 1948 it was calling on the government to encourage 'deserving landlords', an argument consistent with the rich peasant's aspiration to become a big landholder. They complained that administration posts were filled only by the Arabs, and demanded that they be opened up to Africans. They resisted attempts to ally with the propertyless urban proletariat. Ultimately they formed the Zanzibar and Pemba People's Party (ZPPP) with a leadership composed of the most influential Shirazi landowners, merchants, shopkeepers, butchers and bus owners. When the chips were down, it was this petty-bourgeois character, with its 'deep-rooted sense of property' dividing it from the proletariat, which broke from its ethnic moorings to form an electoral alliance with the Zanzibar National Party (ZNP) to represent the propertied classes.[66]

The political development of indigenous Africans in Unguja was quite different. The vast majority of them were middle or poor peasants, thoroughly exploited but only semi-proletarianised, still dependent on the peasant economy for much of their subsistence needs. They were capable of spontaneous resistance over specific issues which sometimes turned quite violent. Colonial records contain many examples of boycotts of shopkeepers who cheated and bus owners who increased fares. The most notable was the *Vita vya Ngombe* (Cattle Riot) of 1951. Middle peasants fearing marginalisation

134

and impoverishment resisted government plans to alienate their land for the Kiembe Samaki airport. The breaking point came when the government tried to enforce dipping which seemed to kill their cattle.[67]

Nevertheless, they were incapable of 'enforcing their class interest in their own name' through sustained political struggle. Some of the leaders of the *Vita vya Ngombe* did realise that political struggle was necessary to end colonial oppression and in 1955 they formed the National Party of the Subjects of the Sultan of Zanzibar, with a non-racialist ideology and a demand for universal adult franchise on a common roll. They contacted the Arab Association, then locked in a bitter anti-colonial struggle, with a view to forming a nationalist alliance. The peasant movement, however, was unable to resist a take-over by the educated intellectuals representing the urban petty bourgeoisie and the landowning class.[68]

Other peasants in Unguja, already under the domination of village Koran teachers and a few traders and successful farmers, had looked to the Shirazi Association of Pemba for leadership. In 1941, 55 of them, largely from the southern parts of Unguja, formed the Shirazi Association of Unguja with a Koran teacher for President, and applied for affiliation with the Pemba counterpart. They championed the cause of the semi-proletarian clove pickers by opposing the 'slave' conditions of the 1944 contracts, and of the African proletariat by opening a cooperative shop in Zanzibar Town in 1950. With their economic and social distance from the urban proletariat thus narrowed, it was not difficult for them to join an alliance leading to the formation of the Afro-Shirazi Party (ASP) during the final phase of colonialism.[69]

The peasant base was both a strength and weakness in the forward struggle. As Petras and Merino put it:

> Peasant radicalism is at best an ambiguous phenomenon — expressing both a profound desire to obtain land, including the willingness to use violent means, and a strong sense of property ownership once in a position to exploit it.[70]

The clamour for land, especially strong among the squatters and other poor peasants, contributed to the 1964 Revolution and resulted in a popular programme of land reform. The big landowners were expropriated and a total of 22,210 peasant families were given 3-acre plots between 1965 and 1972. But they were unable to protect their interests as producers against a government monopoly over the marketing of their produce. Forced to accept less than 10 per cent of the international price for their cloves, many could do little more than neglect their cloves and revert to subsistence production.[71]

135

Notes

The following abbreviations are used in the notes. Italicised titles are published; the rest are typescripts in the Zanzibar archives.

ARDA	*Annual Report of the Department of Agriculture*
ARPA	*Annual Report of the Provincial Administration*
	(Published except during World War II. Typescripts for
	these years in the Zanzibar archives)
ARPD	*Annual Report of Pemba District*
ARZD	Annual Report of the Zanzibar District
ARZ(R)D	Annual Report of the Rural District of Zanzibar
DA	Department of Agriculture: Files
ARZP	Annual Report of the Zanzibar Province
MRPD	Monthly Report of the Pemba District
MRZD	Monthly Report of the Zanzibar District
RTCZ	*Report of the Trade and Commerce of Zanzibar*
Z AR	Zanzibar, *Annual Reports*
Z BB	Zanzibar *Blue Books*
ZA: Sec.	Zanzibar Archives: Secretariat Files

1. K. Marx, 'The eighteenth Brumaire of Louis Bonaparte', in K. Marx and F. Engels, *Selected Works*, Vol. I, Moscow, Progress Publishers, 1973, p. 487.
2. F. Engels, 'The peasant question in France and Germany', in *ibid.*, Vol. III, p. 458.
3. Marx, 'The Class Struggles', in *ibid.*, Vol. I, pp. 214, 276.
4. Marx, 'The Class Struggles', *op. cit.*, p. 232.
5. *Ibid.*
6. V.I. Lenin, *The Development of Capitalism in Russia, Collected Works*, Moscow, Foreign Language Publishing House, 1956, Vol. III, p. 155–66.
7. *Ibid.*, p. 27. Super-exploitation occurs when the producer is deprived of not only the surplus value but also part of the necessary value produced by unpaid family labour.
8. J. Banaji, 'Summary of selected parts of Kautsky's *The Agrarian Question*', *Economy and Society*, 5 (1), quoted in H. Bernstein, 'Capital and Peasantry in the Epoch of Imperialism', E.R.B. Seminar Paper, University of Dar es Salaam, November 1976, pp. 7–13.
9. Lenin, *op. cit.*, p. 31.
10. J. Middleton, *Land Tenure in Zanzibar*, London, HMSO, 1961, pp. 11, 42, 62–3; A.H.J. Prins, *The Swahili-Speaking People of Zanzibar and the East African Coast*, London, International African Institute, 1961, p. 61; Loarer, 'Pemba', Archives Nationales: Section Outre-mer, Paris, 'Ocean Indien', 2/10.
11. R.F. Burton, *Zanzibar*, London, Tinsley Brothers, 1872, Vol. I, p. 363; G.E. Tidbury, *The Clove Tree*, London, Lockwood & Son, 1949, pp. 108–9; J.M. Gray, *History of Zanzibar*, London, Oxford University Press, 1962, pp. 167–8; A.M.H. Sheriff, 'The Rise of a Commercial Empire: An

Aspect of the Economic History of Zanzibar, 1770–1873', Ph.D., University of London, 1971, pp. 188–94.

12. Middleton, *op. cit.*, pp. 15–16, 22–3, 28, 33; F.B. Wilson, 'Notes on Peasant Agriculture and Industries in Zanzibar Island', Zanzibar Archives, unpublished monograph, pp. 5, 13, 17, 24–7; R.H.W. Pakenham, *Land Tenure Among the Wahadimu at Chwaka, Zanzibar Island*, Zanzibar, Government Printer, 1947, pp. 6, 8–9, 12, 21; W.R. McGeogh and W. Addis, *Review of the Systems of Land Tenure in the Islands of Zanzibar and Pemba*, Zanzibar, Government Printer, 1945, p. 5; 'Notes on Kiambo', ZA:Sec. 10770; 'Report on Hadimu Land Tenure', ZA:Sec. 12413.

13. J.S. Last, 'Land Tenure', ZA:Sec. 12413; Wilson, *op. cit.*, pp. 5, 7, 12, 25, 30, 32, 34, 36; Middleton, *op. cit.*, pp. 38, 58, 62, 65; McGeagh and Addis, *op. cit.*, p. 11; R.O. Williams, *Useful and Ornamental Plants of Zanzibar and Pemba*, Zanzibar, Goverment Printer, 1949, pp. 393–6; MRZD, 10/1942, appendix; MRPD, 6/1943, p. 2, 12/1943, p. 2.

14. Pakenham, *op. cit.*, pp. 28–9; Middleton, *op. cit.*, pp. 11, 13, 32, 40, 62, 68; Prins, *op. cit.*, pp. 53–4; J.S. Last, *The Economic Fisheries of Zanzibar, 1928*, Zanzibar, Government Printer, 1929, pp. 1–5; MRZD, 4/1936, p. 7, 6–7/1936, p. 8, 3/1937, pp. 3–4, 5/1937, p. 2, 6/1940, p. 3, 10/1940, p. 1; *ARPD*, 1941, p. 9; ARZD, 1938, p. 18; M.H. Jabir, personal communication.

15. M. Abdurahman, 'Anthropological Notes from Zanzibar Protectorate', *Tanganyika Notes and Records*, (hereafter *TNR*) 8 (1939); Prins, *op. cit.*, p. 50, 72–5; W.H. Ingrams, *Zanzibar*, London, H.F. & G. Witherby, 1931, pp. 317–26; Wilson, *op. cit.*, pp. 46–7; Rolleston, 'The Watumbatu', *TNR* 8 (1939); 'Report on the Coir Fibre Industry', DA: 'Coir Fibre' file; 'Interim Report of the Committee on the Pottery Industry', DA: 'Pottery Industry' file; *ARPA*, 1937, p. 3, 1940, p. 5; ARZD, 1934, p. 18; *ARDA*, 1934, p. 13.

16. *ARDA*, 1901, p. 27.

17. Pakenham, *op. cit.*, pp. 14–15.

18. Gray, *op. cit.*, pp. 161–3.

19. R.H. Crofton, *A Pageant of the Spice Islands*, London, John Bale Sons & Danielsson, 1936, p. 95; B. Hindess and P. Hirst, *Pre-Capitalist Modes of Production*, London, Routledge & Kegan Paul, 1975, pp. 126–7.

20. J.E.E. Craster, *Pemba*, London, T. Fisher Unwin, 1913, pp. 141–3; Crofton, *op. cit.*, p. 102; Zanzibar Protectorate, *Report of the Commission on Agriculture, 1923*, (hereafter *Comm. Ag. 1923*), Zanzibar, 1924, p. 38. The last report gives Mathews' 1895–96 estimates of the slave populations of Unguja and Pemba at 140,000 and 65,000 out of total populations of 208,700 and 92,300 respectively. These figures, especially for Unguja, seem to be exaggerated. The first census in 1910 gives the total populations of the two islands as 149,000 and 83,000 respectively. *RTCZ*, 1900, p. 10, 1909/10, pp. 4, 31. Craster gives an estimate of about 140,000 slaves for the two islands put together. O'Sullivan-Beare to Cave, 31/12/1904, ZA: Res. G 13; *ARDA*, 1901, pp. 25–7; Asst. Manager of Plantations to Overseer, 17/9/1941, S.M. Barwani to Asst. Manager, 24/12/1942, pp. 25–7, DA: file 143.

21. Craster, *op. cit.*, p. 141; G.D. Kirsopp, *Memorandum on Certain Aspects of the*

Zanzibar Clove Industry, London, Waterlow & Sons Ltd, 1926, p. 39. Mathews' estimate of 1,000—1,500 slaves annually smuggled into Zanzibar may be as exaggerated as his figures for the slave population of Unguja. See previous footnote.

22. Kirsopp, *op. cit.*, p. 3.

23. *ARDA*, 1897; Z *AR*, 1911, p. 151.

24. Memo, 'Mainland labourers recruited for the 1904/05 clove crop in Pemba', ZA: Res. F8; *RTCZ*, 1904, pp. 7—8, 1907, p. 22; Z *AR*, 1911, p. 151; *ARDA*, 1921, p. 7, 1931, p. 10; *ARPD*, 1926, p. 2; ARZD, 1926, pp. 2—3; Zanzibar Protectorate, *Report on the Native Census, 1924*, Zanzibar, Government Printer, 1924, pp. 8, 11; C.F. Strickland and A. Pim, *Zanzibar, the Land and its Mortgage Debt*, London, Dunstable & Watford, 1932, p. 3; Kirsopp, *op. cit.*, pp. 4, 11; Colonial Reports, *Zanzibar Protectorate, 1931*, London, 1932, p. 7.

25. *ARDA*, 1901, p. 27.

26. Z *AR*, 1911, p. 46; *RTCZ*, 1904, pp. 7—8.

27. Farler to Rogers, 15/8/1904, ZA: Res G 3; *ARDA*, 1901, pp. 27—8; O'Sullivan-Beare to Cave, 18/8/1904, ZA: Res G 8; *RTCZ*, 1904, pp. 7—8, ; Z *AR*, 1911, pp. 30, 51; Rogers to Cave, 29/11/1904, ZA: Res G 13; J.H. Sinclair, *Report on the Zanzibar Protectorate, 1911—1923*, Zanzibar, Government Printer, 1925, p. 15; *Comm. Ag. 1923*, p. 38.

28. Z *AR*, 1911, pp. 30—1.

29. Sinclair, *op. cit.*, p. 15; *Comm. Ag. 1923*, p. 38.

30. Z *AR*, 1911, pp. 31—2, 42—3, 46, 49, 63, 95, and 1912, p. 32.

31. Craster, *op. cit.*, p. 186; MRPD, 3/1942; MRZD, 1/1938, 2/1939, 6 and 8/1943; Provincial Commissioner to Chief Secretary, 17/1/1944, ZA: Sec. 14348; *ARZD*, 1943, p. 6; Zanzibar Protectorate, *Labour Report*, 1947, p. 13; *ARPA*, 1940, p. 6, 1944, p. 4.

32. Senior Commissioner to Chief Secretary, 19/7/1949.

33. Sources: for 1907, Zanzibar, *Annual Report, 1911*; other figures from Kirsopp, *op. cit.*, p. 40.

34. ARZP, 1931, p. 5; ARZD, 1943, pp. 6—7; Zanzibar Protectorate, *Labour Report*, 1947, p. 13; *ARDA*, 1933, p. 5, 1934, p. 2.

35. *ARPD*, 1934, p. 16.

36. *Ibid.*

37. Z *AR*, 1911, pp. 34—5, 97—8, 115; *RTCZ*, 1908, p. 3; MRPD, 5/1942; *ARPD*, 1945, p. 8.

38. *RTCZ*, 1911—12, pp. 8—9; Z *BB*, 1914—28, Section Ze/32.

39. *RTCZ*, 1908, p. 13; ARZD, 1931, 1937, pp. 11, 1938, p. 8; *ARPD*, 1945, p. 8.

40. Wilson, *op. cit.*, pp. 9, 11, 24, 30, 38; ARZD, 1934, p. 19; ARZ(R)D, 1950, p. 7; MRZD, 1/1943; MRPD, 8/1942; *ARPD*, 1939, p. 2, 1940, p. 5, 1942, p. 5; *ARPD*, 1937, p. 3; Zanzibar Protectorate, *Report on the Action which is being taken on the First Report — Part I — of the Committee on Nutrition in the Colonial Empire* (Cmd. 6050), Zanzibar, Government Printer, 1940, p. 22.

41. Last, *op. cit.*, p. 1; Zanzibar Protectorate, *Agricultural Production Programme*, Zanzibar, Government Printer, 1962, p. 21; C. von Bonde, *Report on a Preliminary Survey of the Marine Fisheries of the Zanzibar Protectorate*, Zanzibar, Government Printer, 1929, p. 12.

42. *RTCZ*, 1903, p. 15; MRZD, 5/1938; *ARPD*, 1945, p. 5; *ARPA*, 1939, p. 7; ARZD, 1946, p. 8; *ARDA*, 1946, p. 7, 1948, p. 5; Minutes of the Chwaka Village Council, 17/7/1946, ZA: Sec. 14732.
43. 'Makunduchi Rope Industry', Provincial Commissioner to Colonial Secretary, 2519/1942, 17/1/1944, and District Commissioner (Zanzibar) to Provincial Commissioner, 16/11/1942, ZA: Sec. 14354; 'Report on the Coir Fibre Industry' (1959), DA: 'Coir Fibre'; D.A. to Financial Secretary, 26/8/1961, DA: 'Coconut Industry — General.'
44. Ali b. Juma to Colonial Secretary, 21/1/1953, 9/3/1953, 12/12/1955; Bashasha Adib Ali *et. al.*, to Colonial Secretary, 14/6/1954; Senior Commissioner to Colonial Secretary, 3/7/1954, ZA: Sec. 14470. Provincial Commissioner to Colonial Secretary, 9/10/1944; Executive Officer to Assistant Secretary, 22/7/1949, ZA: Sec. 14470. Development Secretary to Colonial Secretary, 3/9/1953; Colonial Secretary to Attorney General, 8/11/1955, ZA: Sec. 14470.
45. E.M. Dawson, *A Note on Agricultural Indebtedness in the Zanzibar Protectorate*, Zanzibar, Government Printer, 1936, pp. 3–4; J.E. Flint, 'Zanzibar, 1890–1950', in V. Harlow and E.M. Chilver, eds, *History of East Africa*, Vol. II, Oxford, Clarendon Press, 1965, p. 655.
46. *Comm. Ag. 1923*, p. 17.
47. Kirsopp, *op. cit.*, p. 32.
48. *Ibid.*, p. 7; Flint, *op. cit.*, pp. 651–2.
49. Tidbury, *op. cit.*, p. 163.
50. Kirsopp, *op. cit.*, p. 5.
51. *Ibid.*, p. 7; Bartlett and Last, *op. cit.*, Part 2, pp. 1–2; Annual Report, Mkoani, 1933, pp. 3–5; Z *AR*, 1911, p. 50, 1912, p. 36; *Comm. Ag. 1923*, pp. 36–7; Y.E. Jivanjee, *Memorandum on the Report of the Commissioner on Agriculture*, 1923, Puna, Aryabushan Press, 1924, pp. 18–20; *ARDA*, 1926, p. 5.
52. *ARDA*, 1934, p. 21, 1948, p. 26; Colonial Report, *Zanzibar Protectorate*, 1934, pp. 15, 45–6; ARZD, 1937, p. 7; *ARPA*, 1937, pp. 2–3, 1940, p. 4.
53. The Clove Bonus Registers were compiled as part of the payment of the bonus to producers between 1922 and 1929. They were analysed at various times by colonial officials, but using racial categories. See R.S. Troup, *Report on Clove Cultivation in the Zanzibar Protectorate*, Zanzibar, Government Printer, 1932, p. 8, and E. Batson, *Report on Proposals for a Social Survey of Zanzibar*, Zanzibar, Government Printer, 1948, p. 36. Unfortunately, only about half of the voluminous registers have survived, but they seem to be fairly representative.
54. Zanzibar Archives, Clove Bonus Scheme Registers.
55. *Ibid.*
56. Tidbury, *op. cit.*, p. 6; Strickland and Pim, *op. cit.*, pp. 4, 10, 14; Provincial Commissioner to Colonial Secretary, 31/5/1930, ZA: Sec. 12413.
57. Source: Bartlett and Last, *op. cit.*, p. 4.
58. B.E. Ward, 'Cash or credit crops? An examination of some implications of peasant commercial production with special reference to the multiplicity of traders and middlemen', in J.M. Potter, *et. al.*, eds, *Peasant Society*, Boston, Little Brown, 1967, pp. 135–151; Kirsopp, *op. cit.*, pp. 13, 31, 34.

59. Strickland and Pim, *op. cit.*, p. 4.
60. Source: *ibid.*, pp. 4–5.
61. Annual Survey of Sales and Mortgages, 1932–34, ZA: Sec. 10680; Attorney General to Colonial Secretary, 16/5/1930, ZA: Sec. 12413.
62. Flint, *op. cit.*, p. 661; Kirsopp, *op. cit.*, pp. 9, 21, 27–8.
63. *Comm. Ag. 1923*, pp. 12, 55; Strickland, *op. cit.*, p. 10; *ARDA*, 1926, p. 3, 1927, p. 5, 1928, p. 11, 1929, p. 20.
64. Flint, *op. cit.*, p. 661; Pim, *op. cit.*, p. 95; Binder, *op. cit.*, pp. 5–6; Jivanjee, *op. cit.*, p.49; Lofchie, *op. cit*, p. 292; Dawson, *op. cit.*, p. 21; Annual Survey of Sales and Mortgages, 1935–50, ZA: Sec. 10680; Kirsopp, *op. cit.*, p. 56, gives the upper limit for a middle peasant at 30–40 trees. Tidbury, *op. cit*, gives the upper limit for a rich peasant at 500 trees.
65. Tidbury, *op. cit.*, p. 174.
66. Ali Sharifu to District Commissioner, Pemba, 29/8/1940; District Commissioner, Pemba, to Provincial Commissioner, 2/9/1940; Provincial Commissioner to Colonial Secretary, 1/10/1940; Memo IV, 1943, District Commissioner, Pemba, to Provincial Commissioner, 26/10/1943; Juma b. Hasan to British Resident, 22/4/1948; Shirazi Association to British Resident, Welcoming Address, 1948; District Commissioner, Pemba, to Senior Commissioner, 22/6/1948, ZA: Sec. 13831. Suleiman b. Juma to Acting Colonial Secretary, 18/7/1956, ZA: Sec. 16217.
67. ARZD, 1937, pp. 17–18; MRZD, 3/1944, 10/1951; and B.D.Bowles, chapter in this volume.
68. Marx, *Selected Works*, Vol. I, p. 479; Lofchie, *op. cit.*, pp. 147–154; ZNP, *Whither Zanzibar?*, Political Education Pamphlet No. 2, Cairo, n.d., p. 21, photos opposite p. 64.
69. Thabit Kombo to Ali Sharif, 8/10/1941, ZA: Sec. 13831; ARZD, 1943, p. 14; MRZD, 8/1944, 6/1950.
70. J. Petras and H.Z. Merino, *Peasants in Revolt*, Austin, University of Texas, 1972, p. xii.
71. Ministry of Agriculture, Land Distribution Section, File No. 2 of 1973; ASP, *The Afro-Shirazi Party Revolution, 1964–1974*, Zanzibar, Afro-Shirazi Party 1974, p. 45.

Five

The Decline of the Landlords 1873–1963

J.R. MLAHAGWA & A.J. TEMU

Introduction

The history of the landlords in Zanzibar from 1873, the year in which the slave trade was legally abolished on the islands, is a study of the demise of a class anchored in an anachronistic pre-capitalist mode of production.[1] It is an account of a class grounded in slave-cum-feudal relations of production yoked to a dominant capitalist mode of production. As a result of their inability to adapt to the changing circumstances the landlords could only live as a parasitic class, becoming a fetter on the development of productive forces. This does not mean they were absolutely useless to the British. They were the source of administrative personnel and their position in the clove economy served colonial interests: the production of cheap raw materials and the accumulation of revenue in the colonial coffers. Hence, the history of the landlords is also a study of their continued existence. It is this anomaly of the prolonged existence of a decadent class under colonial rule that becomes the subject of investigation in this chapter.

Imperialism penetrated Africa and created the colonial state because of the tendency for the rate of profit to fall at home.[2] In its colonial possessions, the British aimed to increase profits by making colonial labour as cheap as possible. Contributing to that target in Zanzibar was the preservation of elements of the old relationship which permitted the super-exploitation of the labour of plantation workers and peasant producers. The fate of the Zanzibari landlord class can be explained by referring to the theory of dissolution-conservation in the epoch of imperialism.[3] This theory is an aid in analysing colonial social formations resulting from imperialist penetration of the periphery of the world capitalist system.[4] The central thesis is that the expansion of capital through imperialism both destroys and preserves the pre-capitalist modes with which it comes in contact in the regions that are colonised. The traditional relations of production help reduce costs of production in the colonies. Agricultural producers generate surplus value within patriarchal relations which do not make heavy demands on landlords since the producers are not directly confronted by capital. What is dissolved is the independence of the pre-capitalist social formation at both the political and economic levels.

Imperialism superimposes its hegemony in the economic sphere by depriving the traditional pre-capitalist economy of its autonomy and self-sustaining character. Colonial political control becomes the effective form through which monopoly capital is able to exploit its 'economic territories', as Lenin called these possessions.[5] The hitherto autonomous pre-capitalist mode of production is dominated and transformed by the capitalist mode. The dissolution process is simultaneously accompanied by the conservation of those attributes of the pre-capitalist social formation which contribute to the realisation of super-profits by the monopolies. Thus elements of the pre-capitalist mode, but not the mode in its entirety, are retained and articulated with the capitalist mode of production. In the case of the colonial Zanzibar social formation, the landlord class was preserved, while new capitalist entrepreneurs made their appearance. It was in the interest of metropolitan capital, working through the colonial state, to perpetuate the power of the landlords until more productive relations took hold in the colonial agricultural sector.

The argument

Our analytical framework rests on five main points. It is argued, in the first place, that Omani Arab 'colonisation' of Zanzibar in the nineteenth century was an anomaly existing only at the level of appearance. Colonisation in our sense was a product of Western European capitalist development and as such it could only effectively be carried out by the economically dominant classes in the centres of capitalism.[6] It is true that there can be colonisation without industrial capitalism; the epochs before modern imperialism abound with colonial ventures and conquests. What we are saying here is that the early type of colonisation was quite different from that in the epoch of imperialism. In the latter case colonialism was the logical consequence of capitalist growth. We know that the coming of the Arabs from a pre-capitalist social formation in Oman to Zanzibar occurred at a time when the forces of capitalism had already penetrated the Middle East and East Africa. Although the settlement of the Omani Arabs in Zanzibar was related to economic and political upheavals in the Middle East at the time, they were heavily influenced and conditioned by the penetration of merchant capital in the region. Coming from a pre-capitalist social formation, the Omanis could not possibly fulfil the role colonialism plays in the era of monopoly capitalism. Their objective position was akin to a comprador group serving the interests of metropolitan capital.

This brings us to our second point in the argument. The Arab settlers in nineteenth century Zanzibar were an anachronism since they were dependent on a slave mode of production in an era when capitalism was becoming a global force. The Arab landlords could maintain a modicum of dominance, especially at the political level, when merchant capital was predominant in East Africa. But even then, as will be seen, this dominance was more apparent than real. The peculiarity of the Zanzibari landlords is that their political position did not correspond to their economic status. The dictum, 'When [the Arabs] whistle in Zanzibar they dance at the Great Lakes' signified the political pre-eminence of the landlords. But that same class was at the mercy of the Indian moneylenders who held their plantations on mortgage and financed the caravan trade, and the ultimate beneficiaries of the whole trading system were capitalists based in Western Europe.

There is no irony in the fact that the very same external interests which had been profiting from the slave trade system should abolish it in East Africa in the last quarter of the nineteenth century. It emphasises our next point, that the accumulation requirements of industrial capitalism outside the Indian Ocean region led to the abolition of the Zanzibar slave-trading system. The slave mode of production clashed with the interests of capital wishing to establish the more productive system of free labour. The abolition of the slave trade, and later of slavery, was rapidly followed by the economic demise of the landlord class. The argument of British colonisers that Zanzibar was an Arab state was an ideological device used to maintain some of the pre-colonial relations of production. Having undermined the landlords' economic position, the British in a quite characteristic paternalist manner, tried to create an air of credibility by employing the sons of the landlords in the system of indirect rule. For a considerable length of time the landlords indulged the fiction that they were the rulers of the islands, but finally they came to realise that their weak economic position made a mockery of their socio-political status.

The alliance between landlords and British colonisers was based on expediency. It had its limit at the point where the fiction that Zanzibar was an Arab state tended to obstruct capital accumulation. Thus we argue, as our fourth point, that when the British were forced to choose between landlords, moneylenders, and independent producers, they abandoned the fiction and backed the class which facilitated the accumulation process. The administration supported the landlords when they clashed with moneylenders, because the former were controlling the producers while the moneylending community was less interested in actual production. Moreover the landlords had an edge over the Indian moneylenders thanks to their ideological role. But it should be pointed out that the contradictions between the moneylenders and the landlords were not, strictly speaking, the most fundamental.[7]

The basic antagonism lay between peasant producers and their labouring allies in the plantations and towns on the one hand, and capital represented by the colonial state on the other. Indirect rule suppressed this primary contradiction while secondary ones such as that between landlords and moneylenders appeared to be prominent. Ultimately, when the fundamental differences between peasants and landlords came to the fore, the British tended to back the former against the landed class which had become a spent force. The colonial state would support the landlords only as long as they increased production of surplus value. When they ceased to promote that objective, administrators categorically stated that their commitment to Arab landlords was not intended to prejudice the economic interests of the colonial state.

We argue, as our fifth point, that the landlords attempted to close ranks and organise at both economic and political levels to prevent their demise. This was a defensive manoeuvre aimed at recreating a past condition. Sandwiched between the producers and the commercial middlemen, without having any real control, the landlords could only live on borrowed time and money. Economic decline and indebtedness explain their late attempt to control the clove industry at the level of the market in opposition to rich peasants from the Afro-Shirazi community. Political decline led to landlord 'nationalism', essentially another defensive measure by this class to recapture past grandeur and turn fiction into reality. It is against this background that one should place the 1964 Revolution.

We conclude this section with a statement about race and class. It is tempting to equate the two in discussing the Zanzibari social formation. Many writers have done so. This viewpoint arises in part from Zanzibar's peculiar history, as well as from the ideological stance taken by the British. The historian Flint writes on the latter phenomenon:

> The population was labelled by race, and race denoted function: Arabs were landowners and clove-planters, Indians were financiers and traders, and Africans were labourers.[8]

Racist ideology is not peculiar to the British in Zanzibar; racism has always been a basic feature of capitalism. Because class formation cuts across racial boundaries, the ruling bourgeoisie uses ethnicity as an ideology to obscure class contradictions and misdirect the class struggle. Races under capitalism become social as well as biological categories, and an important functional element in the socio-economic formation.[9]

Thus the class approach to every aspect of historical investigation is a decisive methodological principle if one is to avoid the trap of ideological constructs. At a particular point in the colonial history of Zanzibar most of the landlords came from the Arab racial category. But when we refer to 'Arab landlords' we do not mean to say all Arabs were landlords, just as it is naïve to suggest that all Africans were plantation labourers and all Indians financiers. The category of race may be objectively linked with the issue of relations between social classes, but this must be established rather than assumed.

Origin of the landlord class

The history of Zanzibar has been influenced to a considerable extent by developments within the Indian Ocean region. It has been said that the history of Zanzibar was written by the 'wind'. Perhaps that exaggerates the role of the monsoon winds carrying merchants to and from these East African islands. While it is true that Unguja and Pemba have been influenced by people from across the Indian Ocean or from the Arabian Peninsula, it is naïve to treat the history of the islands simply as an appendage of developments in other areas.[10] It is not even true to say that at all times the history of Zanzibar was connected with developments in Arabia.[11]

However, there is little doubt that at particular points in time the impact of foreigners has been strong. They have been in touch with the islands from prehistoric times, but such influence as there had been before the period of the Omani Arab Sultanate was confined to individual initiatives from traders. Some of them settled permanently on the coast and gradually a few Arab families endeavoured to establish quasi-political dominance over coastal settlements and the immediate hinterland. Foreign influence had not yet, however, adversely affected the indigenous social formation in any fundamental way. There had been established a sort of *modus operandi* which, though militating against indigenous African interests in some ways, did not deprive the local communities of their autonomy. The *Mwinyi Mkuu*, for instance, was still the unquestioned ruler in the island of Zanzibar.

It is pertinent to emphasise that many of these travellers permanently settled in the islands and frequently intermarried or became absorbed into the indigenous African communities. As this had been going on for quite a long time, the process of racial diffusion, especially in Pemba, became quite thorough. The result was the appearance of a heterogeneous racial community in the islands. To talk of the indigenous population in Zanzibar on the eve of the Omani Arab Sultanate one has of necessity to take such racially mixed communities into consideration.

The islands had been drawn into the international exchange network long before the establishment of the Omani Arab Sultanate. There was the caravan slave-trading system which became the lifeblood of the landlords after they established themselves in Zanzibar. Many writers give the impression that there was little slave trading going on in Zanzibar before the establishment of the Omani Sultanate. That is erroneous. Slave trading had become a lucrative business before Sultan Said transferred his capital from Muscat to Zanzibar. In 1811, for example, an informed observer in Zanzibar commented that the tribes which supplied the Zanzibar slave markets were too numerous to describe.[12] The volume of trade was definitely smaller compared to later decades. Sheriff has estimated that in the 1830s, some 2,500 slaves were sent to the Persian Gulf annually to be used as domestics.[13]

The situation changed drastically, however, when Sultan Said transferred his capital from dry, domestically troubled Muscat to the fertile and relatively peaceful island of Zanzibar towards the middle of the nineteenth century. Sultan Said was accompanied by a host of others whom he encouraged to settle in Zanzibar. He found it useful and necessary to be surrounded by loyalists who would help him in the event of an attack from the indigenous population as well as from his enemies back in Oman. He set out to make the Arabs the mainstay of the island economy through the establishment of large clove plantations. Sultan Said made it clear to his kinsmen that they could expect royal protection on condition they actively involve themselves in the cultivation of cloves. This was the beginning of the systematic exploitation of Zanzibar and the mainland. The Arabs came to the islands determined to be masters over the local population and they knew very well that they had to employ all possible means to maintain that position.

Plate 20   Picking cloves: men climb the trunk, while women pick the lower branches from the ground.

Plate 21 Picked cloves being weighed. Note the piles of coins on the table as the plantation owner prepares to pay the pickers.

Plate 22 Slave labour stemming cloves on a plantation in the 1890s. The plantation owner is seated in the centre, and a supervisor is standing behind the slaves.

Plate 23   A coconut plantation. The coconuts piled up in front of the farmhouse are husked and broken, the copra removed for drying.

Plate 24   An inside view of an Arab home. Note the chandeliers and the guns hanging on the wall. The owner is in full traditional dress.

The story of the slave trade after Sultan Said's move to Zanzibar can only be outlined here.[14] To create large clove plantations the landlords needed a sizeable labour force. They turned to the mainland as a source and eventually penetrated deep into the heart of Africa. A plantation economy on the islands simply accelerated the slave traffic. Hence the intensification of the caravan trade along well-defined routes. Whole communities were captured and marched from the deep interior under inhuman conditions. Those who reached the coast were auctioned as commodities to be used on the landlords' estates and for domestic purposes. Although the Arabs could not undertake this business without the financial help of the merchant class, they found in the slave trade, slavery and landownership their means of survival. The Zanzibar economy revolved around it.

While the clove plantation economy accelerated the tempo of the slave trade in East Africa, the development of capitalism in Western Europe and North America contributed even more significantly to it. The wealth accumulated in those regions through primitive accumulation brought with it a change in consumption patterns: spices for the food; ivory for billiard balls and piano keys; and jewellery to bedeck the bodies of the ruling classes. That led to a tremendous boost in ivory export, over and above that of cloves. It is estimated that in 1856 some 242,975 pounds of ivory were exported through Zanzibar, three-quarters of this trade going to North America. Three years later the British consul on the island estimated that the volume of ivory export stood at 488,600 pounds.[15] Ironically, at this time the British were trying to put a stop to slave trading along the coast.

The tie between the North American and European capitalist market and the quickening of the ivory and slave trade in East Africa raises serious reservations about the notion of Arab dominance in this region at the political and, more particularly, the economic level. If the magnitude of ivory and clove trading was as high as has been documented, and if the demand for those commodities in the capitalist metropoles was the main stimulus to the slave-trading system in East Africa, then how can one justifiably talk of Arab predominance and control of the economy of the East African littoral and its hinterland? It is our position that the western capitalist nations had begun to dominate the economic scene in East Africa prior to, and concurrently with, the establishment of the Omani Sultanate in Zanzibar. The signing of the Commerce and Amity treaties and the subsequent establishment of consular offices in Zanzibar by Britain, France, and the United States were in effect the crescendo of this economic hegemony. It is a well-known fact that those consulates were backed by the military to ensure that the Sultan did not do anything that hindered the realisation of western commercial interests. It is not a coincidence that most of the British consuls were in fact professionally trained military men: names like Captain Hammerton, Captain Rigby, and General Mathews come easily to mind. This made a mockery of the notion of Arab dominance in the region.

Actually, the Omani Arabs managed to establish themselves in Zanzibar, from where they expanded their influence along the rest of the East African littoral, mainly through European support. After the British had established political control in India, they were content to make local and regional elements appear to be the rulers in the western Indian Ocean while in fact the British were the power lurking in the background. The kind of relationship that developed between the British and the Omani Sultanate is typical of such an arrangement. When the Sultan needed military support in Oman the British would send out Indian troops to maintain the status quo. Pearce makes the point when he notes:

> In 1809 and again in 1820 the government of India assisted Seyyid Said in his military enterprises by sending ships and Indian sepoys to co-operate with the Omani forces against the turbulent tribesmen, who threatened not only the dominions of the Seyyid Said, but the pax Britannica of the northern sea coasts of the Indian Empire.[16]

It is unnecessary to point out that what Pearce refers to as the dominions of Seyyid Said were actually within the ambit of British indirect control. All this boils down to our argument that the Omani rulers could not establish an effective colonial rule on the East African littoral without the British protecting the rear base in Oman. At most they could only act as agents of the British.

The question of land appropriation in Zanzibar needs some attention. In order to sustain and establish themselves the Arab ruling class needed large amounts of land. The Omani settlers indulged in the wholesale alienation of the best land of both islands, a point which cannot be over-emphasised. They took the fertile land on the west and thus displaced the African population to the poor soil of the eastern coast. The absence of widespread violent confrontation between the settlers and the indigenous communities has tempted a number of writers to view the process of change in landownership as peaceful. They argue that while the use of force could not be ruled out, many settlers acquired their estates through purchases from African owners. Other settlers, it is said, were given land free of charge by the host communities.[17]

The weakness of that argument is demonstrated by two points. First, there is the widespread tradition among the indigenous population of forcible expropriation of land by the new settlers as shown by Jabir.[18] Second, the indigenous concept of land tenure was fundamentally different from that held by the immigrant. Sir John Gray explains this point:

> The trouble in many lands between alien immigrants and the indigenous inhabitants is that the parties of these land transactions were not consenting 'ad idem.' Each of the parties was thinking in terms of the law or custom with which he was familiar. The transferor conceived that he was granting nothing more than certain qualified rights of use of the land which he himself enjoyed, whereas the transferee conceived that he was obtaining something in the nature of exclusive rights over the land.[19]

When slavery was abolished most of the ex-slaves became squatters on the landlords' estates. They continued to provide labour for the landowners who in most cases preferred to live in town. From the outset the landlords built a clove economy on slave labour. The landlords mode of life was parasitic. Their use of slave labour apart, they were heavily dependent on the moneylending class of Indian financiers who had come to Zanzibar in Seyyid Said's entourage. Although few of the indigenous Africans of the islands were enslaved, their plight was serious. Those who could not find land in the less arable east were liable to exploitation by the landowners in the form of labour rent.

Such was the position of the landlords towards the last quarter of the nineteenth century when their power in Zanzibar began to decline. Economically, Zanzibar was steadily becoming part of the capitalist world economy. The slave trade had been abolished for the development of industrial capitalism had rendered it anachronistic, much to the dismay of the Arab landlords who had not extricated themselves from the slave mode of production. In the political sphere there was the encroaching tide of the European scramble for colonies. It was becoming apparent that Zanzibar, mainly because of its strategic maritime location, would become central to imperial designs. Thus Zanzibar was poised for a new era. The ruling Arab landowning class could not accommodate themselves to the new situation and lost control of their destiny.

The decline of the landlords

British influence in Zanzibar was paramount by the 1870s on the eve of the European 'scramble for Africa' which began in the following decade. In conformity with the European imperial policy of effective occupation, and faced with the threat of competition from Germany, the British declared Zanzibar a Protectorate in November 1890. It has been argued that the British had no clear policy about the future of Zanzibar.[20] That argument will be reviewed shortly. There is little disagreement that the British planned to leave the Arab aristocracy intact under the Protectorate. It would become the main link between the colonial administration and the mass of the African population. The constitution which established the Protectorate underlined this policy by categorically stating that Zanzibar was to develop as an Arab state.[21]

While the point that the British colonial administrators did not express any coherent future policy for Zanzibar has some validity, it cannot be accepted without reservation. The primary motive in occupying Zanzibar was the exploitation of its resources. To achieve that goal, the British had, of necessity, to use the existing channels open to them, which meant preserving the landowning class. Since Zanzibar had few exploitable materials apart from cloves, the planters had to be given all encouragement to make the economy viable. Moreover, the Arab landlords had hitherto been the ruling class. It was logical for the colonial administrators to back this group to ensure production and sustain the new colonial structures. The quest for wealth compelled the colonialists to use the dominant class in the islands and this coincided with the ideology of racial superiority which served the immediate aims of colonialism. At this initial stage, the existing relations of production had to be maintained as far as possible because the Arab landed intermediaries could not be drawn out of them all at once.

The position of the Arab ruling class created an interesting dichotomy in British colonial administration. Almost immediately after the establishment of the Protectorate both the British colonialists and the Arab slave owners found themselves beset by internal differences. In Britain, the liberal industrialists were demanding that efforts to abolish the slave trade and slavery be carried to their logical conclusion. These goals were reached with the abolition of slavery in the Protectorate in 1897. The British administration had been markedly reluctant to bring slavery to an abrupt end, fearing the social and economic change likely to accompany such a move. This conservatism on the part of the administrators explains the timidity of the emancipation process. The final decree is famous for the numerous constraints which made it difficult for slaves to claim their freedom. The fact that a

153

slave had to obtain freedom from a court which was manned and controlled by the slave-owning aristocracy shows the ambiguous character of the whole 'emancipation' exercise.[22] Still, the 1897 decree is a watershed in the history of landholding in Zanzibar. It added to the worsening position of the landowners whose possession of slaves proved indispensable to the plantation economy.

Landlord indebtedness

The landlord class in the nineteenth century was increasingly reliant on loans from Indian merchant capital. This continued to typify the landlords' mode of life well into this century. To salvage this class from total ruin was one of the principal preoccupations of the colonial administrators in Zanzibar. We now turn to this phenomenon of indebtedness to identify its causes and the British reaction to it.

The British had been aware of the vulnerable position of the Arab landed aristocracy prior to the creation of the Protectorate. In the first few decades of colonial rule they were slow to act and no concrete measures were implemented to make them financially solvent. The colonial administrators were struck by the paradox whereby the abolition of slavery brought an increase in both clove production and landlord debt. It was observed that the habits of a pre-capitalist élite did not die easily. In 1908, for example, the British Agent and Consul-General reported:

> A great deal of difficulty ... has been experienced in securing the proper and systematic cultivation of the Arab plantations and even, in some cases getting the crops picked at harvest time. [This] has been due to the absolute want of thrift and business like habits among the Arab planters.[23]

Yet the administration had taken no concrete steps to remedy this situation by the time of the outbreak of World War I.

The first serious attempt to cope with planter indebtedness and thus ensure their continued control of clove production was made after the war. In 1923 a Commission on Agriculture was created and charged with the task of making recommendations to relieve the indebtedness of the Arab landowners. The Commission's report, issued the following year, spoke in favour of government loans to landowners, but otherwise made no tangible recommendations for tackling the problem of debt.[24] It concluded that the Arab landlord had been unable to accommodate himself to the changed conditions of labour arising from the abolition of slavery in 1897. But the scapegoat for the 'labour problem' was the ex-slave who now allegedly 'found it possible to live without the necessity of work', thereby causing an acute plantation labour shortage.

The failure of the Commission on Agriculture to provide guidelines for the resolution of landlord indebtedness prompted the administration to appoint G.D. Kirsopp to probe into the problems of the Arab landed aristocracy and the Zanzibar agricultural system in general.

Kirsopp's analysis, which appeared in 1926, completely contradicted that of the 1922 Commission on Agriculture. In his view, neither the abolition of slavery nor the growing burden of debt was really the root of planter decline. He argued that a principal cause of the landowner's plight was the subdivision of Arab properties from generation to generation resulting in the fragmentation of estates. More important was his observation that, in contrast to the decline of the large plantation owner, the rural African population was steadily becoming 'prosperous' without any government help. The pace had been set, in his opinion, by mainland Africans who, having come essentially as labourers, acquired land and settled down to become smallholders. Kirsopp contended that the enterprising smallholder should henceforth be the key to a new agricultural policy in the Protectorate:

> Our agricultural problem is not the regeneration of the original plantation system so unsuited to modern conditions, but the building up of a system of smallholdings on lines best adapted to economic conditions.[25]

He supported his argument with statistics showing that African peasant smallholders had increased the clove trees they owned over the past decade, whereas the Arab landholdings were in decline.

Kirsopp provided arguments for a different perspective on colonial agricultural policy. Increased production could profitably be achieved by making sure that Africans got involved as independent producers.[26] Yet, though there was increasing apprehension about the cost involved in continuing to maintain a parasitic landed class, the administration was slow to forsake the landlords in favour of independent smallhold peasant production. It was a dilemma that was not quickly acted upon.

Kirsopp took a moderate position and spoke in favour of supporting both classes. He argued the need to uphold landlord interests while in the same breath he castigated this class for its lack of enterprise:

> Our obligation to do everything possible to further Arab interests must remain. Any measures devised for the expansion of Native

production are calculated to serve the best interests of the Arab community.[27]

He did not see the interests of the African peasantry as being opposed to those of the Arab landowners. The British colonial administrators were unwilling to accept that the Arab landowners' position had deteriorated beyond recovery. Overall, Kirsopp's position and that of the administration can be explained by one simple fact: the African producers had not yet become the central force in production, hence their interests were not a priority in agricultural policy.

In spite of the pledge and assurance of continued sympathy towards the Arab landlords' cause, Kirsopp's memorandum disturbed the colonial administration. It acknowledged a new element which they wanted to ignore. They had been preoccupied with the status of the Arab landlords. Now they were told that it might be worthwhile to encourage the African peasantry, which had appeared through its own enterprise. In response to Kirsopp's report, the Director of Agriculture wrote a memorandum to spell out the administration's agricultural policy. It said:

> The first duty of the department of agriculture must ... be to examine the financial position of the producers and exercise its efforts to the correction of anything found amiss with the financing of the industry...[28]

This statement succinctly reflects the sympathies of the colonial administration with respect to the problem of agriculture in Zanzibar: the Arab landowners would continue to be regarded as the producers to be salvaged from debt.

The Protectorate administrators probed further into the issue of indebtedness through various commissions in the 1930s. When the Director of Agriculture was writing the above memorandum in 1931, the Colonial Office commissioned C.F. Strickland to examine planter indebtedness on the islands. He recommended that Arab planters should get substantial financial help from the government to settle their outstanding debts to the Indian financiers.[29]

The following year, Sir Alan Pim wrote a report on the question in which he observed that larger estate owners were more heavily in debt than smaller ones; he estimated that about a third of the Arab landowners were unable to meet their liabilities. Pim maintained that the case for 'protecting the Arab against himself' rested on grounds which had very little to do with economics. His argument can be summarised as follows: the state of Zanzibar is Arab both in origin and in constitution; the British government had undermined the Arab landlords by destroying the institution of slavery, without taking steps to enable the former slaveholders to meet the conditions of the post-slave era; hence the government was responsible for the injury caused.[30]

Quite a different viewpoint was offered in 1934 by Sir Ernest Dawson, a well-known expert on colonial administration. He criticised previous reports, especially the 1923 Commission findings, for being shortsighted and naïve. He was closer to Kirsopp in many of his observations. Dawson recommended that government efforts should not be restricted to propping up Arab landlord interests alone; attention should be given to small landholders as well as the big landowners. Dawson reasoned in this manner:

> Since economic progress cannot be barred out, it must be assimilated if healthy conditions are to be established, but such assimilation demands a suitable development of local economy, not its suppression. And the first step towards promoting this development is to endeavour to understand the current motives and actions of the agricultural population more fully.[31]

Such arguments for modification in colonial agricultural policy generally fell on deaf ears within the Protectorate administration which was obsessed with the idea of protecting the Arab planters. They argued that their primary obligation of saving the landlords from ruin had still to be honoured. The situation, they hoped, had not yet deteriorated beyond salvation. We will now examine the various measures taken by the government to boost the landowners.

Steps to save the landlords

After the end of World War I, the Protectorate government introduced a bonus scheme. It was to encourage landowners to take greater care of their estates. Those who planted new seedlings were given cash bonuses, the size of which depended on the number of plants and clove-bearing trees. In addition they were given financial advances by the government during harvest to help meet labour costs. All this was intended to enable the landowners to undertake clove production without recourse to the Indian moneylenders. It aimed to keep the landed class intact and to discourage members from abandoning their estates. However, the bonus system was stopped in 1928 because it had become too much of a burden to the government. In the absence of a thorough survey of land titles it was difficult to establish the exact size of the estate, let alone the number of clove-bearing trees. Many of the landowners had several disjointed estates which had no marked physical boundaries. Fraudulent claims for bonuses were common.

Class Formation

Administrative experience in the 1920s led to the conclusion that steps to improve the position of big landowners were being compromised by a lack of unity and organisation among the planters. One of the difficulties faced in the bonus scheme was the impossible administrative burden of dealing with individual landowners. To promote the interests of the clove planters as a group the Clove Growers' Association (CGA) was formed in 1927. Its main objectives were a standard wage for clove pickers, the provision of storage and marketing facilities, and government loans to meet overhead production costs. If these objectives were reached the landowners would be less vulnerable to the dictates and whims of moneylenders. When the CGA was formed its membership was in theory open to all clove growers, but in practice the Association came to represent the interests of the big landowners. In spite of the existence of the CGA, however, moneylenders continued to dish out loans to individual growers. The number of planters who came up for such loans increased while many of those who borrowed failed to repay loans. As a result, more estates were being mortgaged to Indian merchants and bankers who had very little interest in becoming rural planters.

The suspicion of increasing indebtedness in the clove industry was confirmed by the report prepared in 1933 by Bartlett and Last.[32] The authors observed that the clove industry was passing into the hands of a non-agricultural class, the Indian commercial group, through mortgages. Acting on these fears the government issued the Alienation of Land Decree of 1934, which forbade the sale or transfer of Arab or African land without the approval of the British Resident. The move was to prevent the Indian commercial class from acquiring landed property as a result of the Arab landowners' failure to pay outstanding loans. While the argument that the deterioration of the clove industry was mainly due to Indian traders acquiring land is debatable, the magnitude of the transfer of land property from the Arab landowners to the Indian commercial bourgeoisie could hardly be refuted. This is testified by the Registrar of Documents' Report of 1934 which showed that during the period 1923 to 1933 Indians in the two islands acquired about 490,000 out of a total of 2 million clove trees. A report by the Commission on Agricultural Indebtedness published in 1935 estimated that in the same decade Indians had increased their clove holding from 152,000 to 502,000 trees.[33]

The administration also moved to restrict and control the marketing of the clove produce. This was the activity in which the commercial class was firmly established. In the same year as it issued the Land Alienation Degree, 1934, the government passed the

158

Clove Exporters Decree which gave the British Resident power to limit the number of marketing licences and made the CGA the 'licensing authority'. The decree aimed to reduce the number of clove dealers at the marketing level, and by giving the CGA power to issue licences it hoped to show that the interest of the clove plantation owners was being upheld.

The landlords achieved their goal of marketing their cloves at international level in 1937 with the proclamation of the Clove Purchase and Exportation Decree. The decree gave the CGA a purchasing and exporting monopoly. The move was primarily a response to a 1936 report by H.H. Binder, an acclaimed British chartered accountant who had been hired by the Zanzibar government to probe into the problems of the clove industry. He recommended that all competitors to the CGA in the field of clove purchase and exportation should be eliminated.[34] This, it was argued, was the only way to get rid of Indian hegemony in the clove industry and boost the morale of the landowners.

The Clove Decree naturally inflamed the Indian financiers as it fundamentally undermined their main source of income and livelihood. They had not been very worried by previous measures which left them in control of the purchasing and marketing of cloves. The Zanzibar commercial class appealed to their kinsmen in India who, in solidarity, responded by boycotting Zanzibar's clove exports. Since India was the leading importer of the island's cloves the boycott had a serious adverse effect on the economy of the Protectorate. In the following year the CGA's marketing monopoly was relaxed by the appointment of a new British Resident who was more favourable to Indian financial interests. Moreover, the colonial administration was anxious to accommodate the movement against British power in India which was gaining momentum on the eve of World War II.[35]

The position of the landlords from 1939 to the end of British rule neither recovered nor deteriorated. The most notable feature was the diminishing size of the landlord class due to a number of factors. The Protectorate administrators relaxed their unqualified support of plantation production of cloves by Arab landowners incapable of maintaining their estates. Indians came to acquire estates so long as the British Resident was satisfied that they would take care of their acquisitions.[36] There was a growing number of smallholders, many of whom acquired their holdings from impoverished Arab landowners. Although these smallholders were not getting the kind of government support that had hitherto been accorded to big landlords, their efforts to organise and advance their class interests could not be ignored.[37] Furthermore, this was a

period when the Zanzibar clove industry was facing stiff competition from other clove producing countries like Madagascar.
All these factors had the effect of reducing the number of landlords and increasing the number of African peasant smallholders.
Increasingly, landlords were reduced to becoming smallholders
and permanent residents of the towns.

Conclusion

The fate of the landlords in Zanzibar was summed up by Dawson
when he observed:

> It is one of the clearest lessons of history that no landed aristocra-
> cy can long maintain substantial privileges after loss of economic
> independence, however this may have been occasioned.[38]

In his view, the landlords lost their economic independence when
slavery was abolished in the final decade of the nineteenth century.
But we have argued that the landlords had already lost that 'economic independence' a half-century earlier when western capitalist
countries created economic ties with Zanzibar through the treaties
of the 1830s and 1840s. We have also indicated that the decline of
the landlords in Zanzibar is a representative example of a ruling
class unable to transcend outmoded relations of production. In the
case of Zanzibar, the landlords were steeped in relations which had
feudal and slave features. In the nineteenth century, the landlord
bought and owned a slave just as he did any other commodity. He
used them to produce on his clove or coconut plantation and what
they produced was his to enjoy. When slavery was abolished the
landlord tried to retain this relationship with labour as far as he
could. The ex-slaves who now assumed the status of squatters
continued to maintain the landlord's plantation at the price of
being allowed to cultivate annual crops. Landlords permitted
squatters to settle on the land, build houses, and cultivate crops
such as bananas or cassava. The squatters paid no direct tax for
their stay on the landlord's estate, but the work they did for the
landowner can be considered labour rent. The arrangement continued to benefit the landlords so long as the squatters lived at
subsistence level and did not cultivate cash crops. When peasant
agriculture began to be commercialised, leading to the emergence
of a rich peasantry, the old class of big landlords began to diminish
in number and to disintegrate.

Notes

1. For the concept of mode of production see B. Hindess and P.Q. Hirst,
   Pre-capitalist Modes of Production, London, Routledge & Kegan Paul, 1975,

and H. Bernstein and J. Depelchin, 'A Materialist History', History Seminar Paper, University of Dar es Salaam, 1977.

2. The law of the tendency of the rate of profit to fall is developed in K. Marx, *Capital*, Moscow, Progress Publishers, 1974, Vol. III, Part III. See also D. Wadada Nabudere, *The Political Economy of Imperialism*, Dar es Salaam, Tanzania Publishing House, 1977, Part 2.

3. Lenin's *Imperialism, The Highest Stage of Capitalism*, Moscow, Progress Publishers, 1974, stands as the basic analysis of imperialism. Formulation of the dissolution-conservation theory is found in Appendix I of A. Emmanuel, *Unequal Exchange*, New York, Monthly Review Press, 1972.

4. For the concept of periphery, see S. Amin, *Accumulation on a World Scale*, Volume One, New York, Monthly Review Press, 1974.

5. Lenin, *Imperialism*, and Jack Woddis, *Africa, The Lion Awakes*, London, Lawrence & Wishart, 1961.

6. See Marx, 'The modern theory of colonisation' in *Capital*, Vol. 1.

7. On the concept of contradictions see Mao Tse-tung, 'On Contradictions', in *Four Philosophical Essays*, Peking, Foreign Languages Press, 1964.

8. J.E. Flint, 'Zanzibar, 1890−1950' in Vincent Harlow & E.M. Chilver, eds, *History of East Africa*, Vol. II, Oxford, Clarendon Press, 1965, p. 651.

9. See articles in *World Marxist Review*, Vol. 20, No. 8, August 1977.

10. R. Coupland, *East Africa and its Invaders*, Oxford, Oxford University Press, 1938, and W.H. Ingrams, *Zanzibar, Its History and Its People*, London, H.F. & G. Witherby, 1931.

11. As stated by F.B. Pearce, *Zanzibar, The Island Metropolis of Eastern Africa*, London, T. Fisher Unwin, 1920, p. 18: 'No matter in which epoch of history the name of Zanzibar appears, we find the island closely connected with the history of Arabia'.

12. See E.A. Alpers, *Ivory and Slaves in East Central Africa, Changing Patterns of International Trade to the later 19th Century*, London, Heinemann, 1975, pp. 209−263. The best early account of the slave trade in East Africa is found in Richard Burton, *Zanzibar; City, Island and Coast*, 2 vols, London, Tinsley Brothers, 1872.

13. Abdul M.H. Sheriff, 'The Rise of a Commercial Empire: An Aspect of the Economic History of Zanzibar, 1770−1873', Ph.D. Thesis, University of London, 1971.

14. For a useful discussion of the slave trade in East Africa, see Edward Alpers, *East African Slave Trade* (Historical Association of Tanzania, Paper No. 19), Dar es Salaam, Tanzania Publishing House, 1967, and for a wider treatment see R. Gray and D. Birmingham, *Pre-Colonial African Trade*, London, Oxford University Press, 1970.

15. Alpers, *Ivory and Slaves in East Africa*, p. 234. See also E.D. Moore, *Ivory Scourge of Africa*, New York, Harper & Brothers, 1931.

16. F.B. Pearce, *op. cit.*, p. 116.

17. Within this group of writers should be included D.D. McCarthy, 'Report of the Zanzibar Research Unit, June 1934 − Sept. 1937', Zanzibar, 1941; William Addis, 'Review on the system of land tenure in the island of Pemba', Zanzibar, 1934. Both are in Zanzibar Archives, hereafter cited as ZA.

161

Class Formation

18. Mahmoud Hemeid Jabir, 'The Plantation Economy During the Protectorate Period in Zanzibar', M.A. Dissertation, University of Dar es Salaam, 1977, pp. 32–9.

19. John Gray, *Report on the Inquiry into claims to certain land at or near Ngezi... in the Mudiria of Chake Chake, Pemba,* Zanzibar, Government Printer, 1956.

20. See Flint, in Harlow and Chilver, *op. cit.,* p. 642.

21. L.W. Hollingsworth, *Zanzibar Under the Foreign Office, 1890–1913,* London, Macmillan & Co., 1953.

22. For details of the emancipation decree, see Hollingsworth, *op. cit.*

23. Colonial Office, *Annual Report on Zanzibar Protectorate, 1908,* London, 1909.

24. Zanzibar Protectorate, *Report of the Commission on Agriculture 1923,* Zanzibar, Government Printer, 1924.

25. G.D. Kirsopp, *Memorandum on Certain Aspects of the Zanzibar Clove Industry,* London, Waterlow & Sons Ltd., 1926.

26. It is significant that this was the period when Governor Donald Cameron was implementing the policy of indirect rule in the mainland British possession of Tanganyika. In Kenya there had been the Devonshire Declaration (1923) which theoretically and flatteringly claimed to be upholding African interests (1923).

27. Kirsopp, *loc. cit.*

28. V.H. Kirkham, *Memorandum on the Functions of a Department of Agriculture with Special Reference to Zanzibar,* Zanzibar, Government Printer, 1931.

29. C.F. Strickland, *Report on Co-operation and Certain Aspects of the Economic Condition of Agriculture in Zanzibar,* London, Crown Agents, 1932.

30. Sir Alan Pim, *Report of the Commission appointed by Secretary of State for the Colonies to consider and report on the Financial Position and Policy of the Zanzibar Government in Relation to its Economic Resources,* London, Crown Agents, 1932.

31. Sir Ernest Dawson, *A Note on Agricultural Indebtedness in the Zanzibar Protectorate,* Zanzibar, Government Printer, 1936.

32. C.A. Bartlett and J.S. Last, *Report on the Indebtedness of Agricultural Classes, 1933,* Zanzibar, Government Printer, 1934.

33. Zanzibar Protectorate, *Report of the Commission on Agricultural Indebtedness,* Zanzibar, Government Printer, 1935.

34. H.H. Binder, *Report on the Zanzibar Clove Industry,* Zanzibar, Government Printer, 1936.

35. In India this had taken the form of the 'Quit India' movement organised by the Congress Party.

36. Indian traders also gained access to the CGA Board and Advisory Committee, the two organs which were empowered to fix prices.

37. The Agricultural Department's March 1938 Bulletin spelled out the government's shift of policy towards the landlords: 'The ultimate prosperity of any agricultural country depends eventually on the condition of its peasantry and the seasonal nature of employment in the clove and coconut plantations of Zanzibar Protectorate emphasises the imperative necessity of making the agricultural labouring classes and smallholders independent of the importation of large proportions of their food supplies.' Secretariat File No. 13454, Vol. I, ZA.

38. Dawson, *loc.cit.*

Six

The Contradictions
of Merchant Capital
1840–1939

ZINNAT BADER

Merchant capital, when it holds a position of dominance, stands everywhere for a system of robbery, so that it is directly connected with plundering, piracy, kidnapping slaves and colonial conquest.

Karl Marx, *Capital*, Volume III

In this chapter we will examine the development of exploitative exchange relations in Zanzibar. Imperialism began to get a foothold in East African territories in the nineteenth century as schemes to forge advantageous trade relations became the prime activity of colonising powers. The year 1840 opened the way to a period of struggle between various industrial capitals and merchant capital which was gradually subjugated. Before examining the period, we will describe the pre-nineteenth century phase of primitive accumulation through the triangular Indian Ocean trade between the East Coast of Africa, the Arabian Coast and the West Coast of India, at the height of which Zanzibar emerged as a key link in the commercial chain.

One of the earliest records of this maritime commerce is to be found in the *Periplus of the Erythraean Sea* which details the ventures undertaken to amass merchant wealth in this part of the Indian Ocean around the first century A.D.[1] The development of sea routes led to the planting of settlements of appropriating classes — Indian, Arab and Persian merchants — along the east coast of Africa. This encroachment on foreign soils was required for more efficient exploitation of the trade which they sought to control.[2] It also eliminated extensive rake-offs by their agents. Markets began to appear along the coast, becoming the hub of merchant transactions.

163

It was these markets which in the nineteenth century formed the nuclei for the advance of capitalism disguised as 'legitimate commerce' into the region as a whole.[3] Zanzibar formed the entry point: it was from there that slave-hunting expeditions were mounted and the profits split among the beneficiaries of the slave trade.

The Indian merchant class appeared to be the dominant group in the trade network. With their maritime experience and knowledge of various media of exchange, they extended their influence through alliances with other appropriating groups in the pre-capitalist orders. They controlled most forms of commerce. By the eighteenth century, Bombay had become the grand storehouse of East African, Arabian and Persian commerce.

This explains why Bombay became the political seat from which British imperialism aimed its policy of controlling the Indian Ocean trade to East Africa via Zanzibar.[4] When Captain Smee visited Zanzibar in 1811 as a Bombay Government representative to investigate trade possibilities, he noted that wealthy Hindu traders 'held the best part of the trade in their hands', much to the envy of the Omani Arabs who were vying for economic control.[5] So long as this trade could be harnessed to serve the needs of industrial capitalism, by directing British goods to potential markets and initiating a cash economy, Indian trading concerns would be sanctioned and protected.[6] That would be their privilege as British 'subjects'. In the 1820s, this policy of granting political support to Indian merchants engaged in 'legitimate commerce' clearly demonstrated imperialist aims, even though they wore the gloss of anti-slavery sentiments.[7]

Another party which had a long-established stake in the Indian Ocean trade and specifically the slave operations was the Busaidi ruling class in Oman. In Muscat as well as the Arabian coast, Indian merchants were established and recognised as customs collectors prior to the nineteenth century. The Busaidis, upon annexing Zanzibar as part of the 'new dominions', promoted these merchants whilst ensuring that they extracted a fixed income from them.[8] In the 1830s, for example, the Indian merchants dominated most forms of commerce and operated as creditors and customs collectors in Zanzibar. The Arab and Swahili traders operated principally as caravan leaders who hunted the mainland for slaves. Their missions were equipped and financed by the Indian merchants who supplied them with goods on credit. These were exchanged for slaves, ivory and other produce whilst they travelled under the protection of the Busaidi Sultan's flag. On their return, all exchangeable goods would pass through the hands of their creditors who would settle accounts and proceed to load outgoing ships. Towards the late 1830s, the returns from the slave trade alone was 60 per cent.[9] Indian merchant capital appeared to be well entrenched and unthreatened.

This was the composition of forces engaged in appropriation in the sphere of exchange in the early nineteenth century. Now we will outline the major trends which transformed this condition in the periods 1840–1890 and 1890–1939. In each phase, we will identify the role of merchant capital in the exchange economy. This is the necessary background to understanding colonial rule in Zanzibar.

1840–1890

This is the period when merchant capital loses its independence in the territories joined by the Indian Ocean trade. It is no longer allowed to operate solely on its own account but is forced to become an agent of industrial capital. In Zanzibar, this is marked by the opening of the British Agency under the control of the Bombay Government and the East India Company in 1841. A prime interest of the British Consul in Zanzibar up to the eve of the Partition in the late 1880s was to reinforce the use of Indian merchants for 'legitimate commerce', hence the increasing jurisdiction over them as British Indian subjects. Under this policy they captured the bulk of the trade in the leading markets of the western Indian Ocean, which included those ports on the west coast of India which commanded the largest part of the trade with East Africa.[10] But it was clear that if they were to achieve the same dominance in Zanzibar, key to the East African trade, they would have to channel their influence via the existing slave trade framework.[11]

The Omani Sultan of the Busaidi dynasty, Seyyid Said, declared Zanzibar his second capital in 1840. He had drawn up his economic programme on the basis of the slave trade and plantation production of cloves through slave labour. Plans were made to extend the trade in captives. Cloves as a rare luxury spice could not only increase his revenue but feature as a much-needed commodity in exchange transactions with foreign goods, thus attracting a greater volume of trade to Zanzibar.[12] In these schemes, he contracted the support of the principal Indian merchants. With their finance, the caravan routes into the interior would proliferate, drawing out more and more slaves and produce (gum copal, ivory, etc.) whilst channelling in foreign commodities on which he could pick up a proportion of the levied taxes.[13] The role of Indian merchant capital in these activities was prominent. In the inseparability of the legitimate trade and the slave trade lay the

Class Formation

concrete fact of pillage of humans and their environment.

With the Indian agencies acting like efficient suction pumps in both directions even before Said's arrival, the role of the Sultan as the ally of imperialism was decided. In the late 1830s an alliance had been struck between the leading trade and customs-collecting firm of Jairam Sewji — also Said's financial adviser and creditor — and the trading firm represented by the American consul, R.P. Waters. When the British consul, Hamerton, arrived, he was quick to perceive that this near monopoly in import-export trade, and the increasing quantity of American goods, would not serve British interests. By a series of diplomatic moves, he connived to gain the support of the Sultan by accusing his authorities of harbouring feelings against English merchants, and finally managed to break the alliance by 1841.[14] To a great extent, he had achieved this through the British claim of jurisdiction over the Indians in East Africa. It was not surprising that the gut reaction of some Indian merchants was to repudiate British 'protection' and opt for that of the Sultan — underestimating his own subservience to British interests. The shrewder merchants saw the profit margin which British protection offered and bided their time. It now became crucial for British imperialism to use Indian merchant capital to expand 'legitimate' trade over the slave trade.

The first serious British attempt to curb the slave trade in 1846 led to losses in revenue as well as in foreign trade, much as the Sultan had forecast in his earlier protestations to the British Government.[15] The 'mistake' was rectified; foreign trade began to pick up. Zanzibar was becoming the commercial emporium of the East African coast, and only with the thriving of the slave trade could other forms of foreign trade gain a foothold in the area.

But whilst imperialism could use the slave trade to carve out new corridors into the interior of the continent with the aid of merchant capital, local trade and production amongst the indigenous population was being seriously undermined. With the outflow of the able-bodied section of the population as slaves, total production was bound to fall. Again, since merchant capital principally stimulated production of exportable commodities, the demands to be satisfied were not intra-communal but external. Hence merchant capital accumulation left in its wake a distorted social production, which it further augmented by creating 'artificial wants' for foreign goods from advanced capitalist countries.

Though it is difficult to give reliable figures on the numbers of slaves exported in the 1840s and 1850s, it can be estimated roughly that between 10,000 and 20,000 were reaching the coast. A large number, in fact, ended up in Zanzibar and the coast of Kenya where they were used in the production of cloves and food grains. By 1870 the number had increased to about 95,000, with most of the slaves coming from the mainland.[16] The revenue to the Sultan was one dollar per slave in 1846, a figure which doubled in 1871. A strong suggestion that sizeable profits accrued to Indian customs collectors can be found in the total assets held by Jairam Sewji's firm which stood in the region of 4 million dollars in 1844. Besides being a leading trading firm, Sewji could release supplies of cash as large as 10,000 dollars at short notice.[17] It is reasonable to assume that at the time when 'legitimate commerce' had not made significant strides, most of this lucrative wealth resulted from the slave trade.

By the mid-1850s, British and Indian goods had begun to constitute the bulk of those imported into Zanzibar, though the island still had no direct trade with Britain. Between 1855 and 1859, only twelve British ships called at Zanzibar in comparison to 154 from America, 97 from Hamburg, 89 from France and 30 from Portugal, Germany, and other nations.[18] But British manufactured goods were being channelled indirectly from India, Singapore and Hamburg by Indian merchants who had become instrumental in the spread of British commerce. British cotton was now in hot competition with American cotton (*merikani*) as well as the Indian cottons which had been so popular in previous centuries. British iron goods and weaponry were gaining markets. In effect, Indian merchant capital could no longer select freely to its own exclusive advantage. This does not necessarily imply constraint as much as a certain adaptability on the part of this dominant class.

During the following decade, direct trade between Zanzibar and England grew rapidly. Having successfully countered the American threat during the US Civil War, British interest pegged down the French to a comfortable size by 1862. Though British legal efforts seemed to militate against the slave trade by calling it 'wasteful and unnatural', their continued reliance on it is borne out by the fact that a leading English firm by the name of Fraser and Company, a most vocal champion of British imperialism, was one of the largest slaveholders in the 1860s.[19] Legitimate trade as it grew in volume was part and parcel of the traffic in slaves. And whilst slaves continued to feature as an important exchange commodity, the imperialist powers were ready to supply arms and ammunition not only to capture the slaves, but to facilitate the flow of their own commodities along the caravan routes into the interior. It is not hard to see why the various treaties signed between 'Her Majesty and the Sultan of Zanzibar for the Suppression of the Slave Trade' were proving to be ineffectual.[20]

British interests in Zanzibar during this period were asserted more decisively at the political level. After the succession crisis within the Busaidi regime in 1859, the British military presence in the Indian Ocean could no longer be defined simply as a patrol force against slave trafficking.[21] The new Sultan now owed his right to rule in Zanzibar to the British who had virtually blocked off Muscat's influence. But whilst they sought to eliminate adversary interests, the British recognised the importance of the Busaidi regime in Zanzibar. In conformity with their principle of 'indirect rule', they propped up the regime to administer the economy and establish the 'peace and order' necessary for their own commercial expansion. The Sultan's claims over much of the East African mainland would also be of great value. Thus both the Indian merchant bourgeoisie and the Busaidi regime were tools for imperialist penetration as it unfolded through the colonisation process towards the end of the century.

The Indian merchant bourgeoisie experienced little difficulty adjusting to the Busaidi regime under which it had come to wield important influence in both financial and civil administration. In contrast, they became progressively more ambivalent towards the British as they became hegemonic over the commerical economy in the ensuing years. British presence became more burdensome as it went beyond commerce to the social existence of the Indian community on the pretext of Britain's right of jurisdiction over 'British Indians'. With respect to education, religious observance, and right to appeal, Indians as a whole were intentionally isolated to form a separate community under the imperial policy of divide and rule. Under this scheme, it was possible to divide the local appropriating classes along racial lines whereby 'community denoted function', a policy which paid off for the British in the years of colonial rule. Between 1860 and 1869, it was declared unlawful for 'members of the Indian community' to hold domestic slaves, although slaves continued to be held legally by the Arab landowners. As a result, some Indians repudiated British citizenship but they were soon to find out that policy-making was no longer the sovereign right of the Sultan in actual practice. The next decade demonstrated this amply.

The British wanted important positions such as Customs Master in the hands of Indian merchant firms, as this was the biggest revenue-earning monopoly in Zanzibar.[22] The firm of Jairam Sewji enjoyed cordial relations with the British consulate and Indian business firms assisted the mainland expeditions of British explorers by acting as their bankers and suppliers. It is significant that when the first British consul died in 1857, it was a prominent member from the customs-holding firm of Jairam Sewji who took care of the consulate for as long as a year. Through the convergence of interests, the merchant class was nurtured under the wings of British interests for a very specific task.

There is little information about capital accumulation by the merchant class being used outside of reinvestment and expansion of trade, loans and mortgages.[23] In most cases, the leading firms had parent companies in India which suggests that capital repatriation did occur. There is no indication that the merchants invested in production in Zanzibar.

So far reference has been confined mainly to the dominant Indian section of the merchant class, but it must be pointed out that there was an important section of Arab and Swahili traders who operated extensively on the mainland from a base in Zanzibar. These were the caravan leaders who hunted slaves and ivory. Amongst these was the infamous Tippu Tip who opened up the interior for imperialist expansion in the second half of the nineteenth century.[24] Because of the wealth and influence which he commanded right up to the Congo, he was relied upon by the Busaidi Sultan to protect his dominions from imperialist threats. Tippu Tip would borrow goods worth up to 8,000 pounds from the leading Indian merchants in Zanzibar. Some of them, such as Tharia Topan of the customs-controlling firm in the late 1870s, would supply him with porters, arms and goods upon instructions from the Sultan. The Indian financiers were also his bankers but, unlike them, Tippu Tip possessed landed property in Zanzibar as well as plantations worked by slave labour. Like all merchants, however, he could not hold his own against the forces of imperialism which came to dominate independent merchant spheres of influence.

During the 1870s the stage for the take-over was set. By 1871, British shipping to and from Zanzibar was greater than that of any other nation. Zanzibar's entrepôt role had grown with the re-export, or transshipment, trade which had reached the value of 2 million pounds, doubling within the previous decade. Coinciding with this advance, there followed prohibitive measures against the slave trade as the bulk of trade in other commodities increased. The Sultan was forced to close the biggest slave market in Zanzibar and to protect the emancipated slaves. The crux was that production and trade in cloves had become paramount and free enterprise dictated that output would receive a stimulus only under free labour conditions.[25] So it was necessary for the export of living labour to cease and social production to be reorganised. Under such circumstances it was only logical that the activities of the dominant merchant class should be brought in line with the changing situation. Consequently, the 1871 Select Committee on the Slave Trade was followed quickly by the 1872–73 Frere Mission, half the cost of which was met, ironically enough, by the Indian Government.[26] In investigating the 'complicity' of Indian merchants in the continuing slave trade, the Mission in effect absolved them of guilt, accusing them of having only an 'indirect' hand in it. Whilst this meant that the Indian merchant bourgeoisie would continue to serve the needs of metropolitan trade, their role would become increasingly circumscribed. Although the slave trade did not die out till the end of the century, this period marked the reorientation of the dominant merchant class in the exchange economy. It is significant that members of this class joined the British anti-slavery efforts in the 1880s, and that Tharia Topan, one of its most prominent members, was knighted for his contribution in that effort.

Whilst the merchant class was quick to adjust to these changes, the Arab landowning class was weakened as the slave basis of the plantation economy diminished. Mortgaging to Indian merchants became a more frequent practice leading to Arab indebtedness whilst the total capital investment of the merchant class began to expand.[27] This issue was to define the terms of the colonial state's relationship to the merchants in the period after 1890.

The Busaidi Sultanate, whose social base had been seriously weakened by the British since 1873, faced invasion by the Khedive of Egypt in 1875.[28] In the interim, the Sultan toyed with the idea of offering Zanzibar to the Germans for 'protection', but the choice was eliminated for him by the British who employed military force to defend his title late in the year, thus reinforcing his dependence upon the imperial monopoly of violence. Because of this subordination, the Sultan lacked an independent political voice in this period when other imperialist powers were seeking to establish their influence over his mainland dominions. Though the British did provide him with the basis for an army in 1878, it was clear whose battle it would be fighting.

In 1883, the right of jurisdiction over 'British Indians' was transferred from the Indian Government to the Imperial Government. This shift foreshadows the end of the first phase of policy in which the Indian merchant bourgeoisie had been groomed to channel British interests to East Africa via the strategic markets in the Indian Ocean. Now the British began to redefine their policy, a process which was reflected in their relationship with the Busaidi regime. The latter in turn revised its own policy towards the merchant class by revoking the practice of hiring out the post of

170

customs-collection which had in the past few years become highly competitive. Reaction was expressed immediately in India by the merchant bourgeoisie's counterparts there who called upon the British to protect the trading interests of Indian communities resident in Zanzibar. It was this same voice of class affiliation which argued that wealth would henceforth 'accumulate ... for the natives of the British Isles', which was an accurate assessment in the aftermath of the Partition of East Africa in 1886.[29]

The British attempted to minimise the Indian merchants' role through the formation of the Imperial British East Africa Company (IBEAC), which was granted a royal charter in 1888. This move implicitly recognised that, with the declaration of a German protectorate in Tanganyika, the British could no longer control that area of the mainland through Zanzibar. This policy failed to pay off, leading to a short period of reaccommodation to the Indian merchant class, for the British were worried that the Germans would utilise the latter to build up their commercial economy.[30] There was a basis to this fear in the years after the Partition, when many Indian merchants emigrated to the mainland to extend their activities. To strengthen its position in Zanzibar and maintain its commercial value, Britain declared Zanzibar a protectorate in 1890. In intra-imperialist rivalry, this was a device to prevent other powers from securing control.

Thus the 'harnessing' of the merchant bourgeoisie had effectively started before the colonial period. Without this class, British imperialism would have had greater difficulty gaining a foothold in East Africa as a whole.[31] With the declaration of a protectorate, merchant capital was reduced to a secondary position.

1890—1939

The impact of British imperialism in Zanzibar at the end of the nineteenth century is marked by accelerated attempts to pattern local production and consumption to the needs of the metropolitan ruling class through the establishment of colonial capitalism. In this process there was a redefinition of the relations of domination of appropriators over producers, as well as those within the appropriating classes. In respect to the latter, British imperialism had decisively supplanted Arab hegemony during the Partition years and had begun to recast the role of the Busaidi regime. The trading firms of other imperialist nations in Europe and North America, variously referred to as 'enemy' or 'non-enemy' importers, would be allowed to carry-on as long as they did not threaten British interests.[32] The crucial relation to be redefined was that of merchant capital

171

Class Formation

residing in Zanzibar. As long as the preponderating influence, if not monopoly' of the big Indian merchants continued, capitalist accumulation outside the Indian Ocean could not proceed smoothly.[33] That influence was bound to be reduced and made amenable to British industrial capital whose rule was mediated through the Zanzibari state. The Indian merchant class did not concede this loss of power tamely in the following decades.

The main reason why the IBEAC failed was that it lacked the experience as well as the capital of the Indian merchants. By 1892, the latter were called upon by the British Resident to make Zanzibar a great commercial 'depot' with the launching of the free port policy. In reality, colonial commitment to free trade was more apparent than real. It was conceived as a device to counter German attempts to divert the trade from Zanzibar to the mainland ports and as such would be upheld for as long as it paid dividends. The Zanzibar Chamber of Commerce was also formed to serve the same end six months later. But whereas the free port policy was abandoned in 1899 it had by then become quite clear to the imperial policy-makers that a new basis for the exchange economy would have to be created.

Relations between the British and Indian merchants in Zanzibar were defined by problems of clove production in the 1890s. The abolition of slavery in 1897 led to a shortage of labour on the plantations. The British worked through resident Indian merchants to import labour from India to harvest cloves.[34] This source of labour did not continue for long, as labour from the mainland came to supplant it.

More serious was the growing indebtedness of the Arab plantation owners to the Indian merchants. Such capital 'incapacitation' was said to hold back the production of cloves, the importance of which had been registered by the introduction of the clove tax of 25 per cent in 1887. The Indians for their part were basically a merchant class and as such they were not inclined to reinvest and advance production. In fact Arab indebtedness was clear evidence of the 'fettering' of production by merchant capital. The merchants drew profits primarily from the sphere of exchange by undervaluing the products they bought and overvaluing the ones they sold. Indeed the origin of such profits lay in the sphere of production as the 'unrewarded product of labour'.[35] But for the moment the Arab landed class seemed to be the safer candidate compared to the non-entrepreneurial Indian merchants.

As the clove economy became the chief source of colonial surplus extraction, the limitations of backing the Arab plantation owners began to be felt. In 1915, the British Resident, in rejecting the idea of introducing a European landowning class to salvage plantation production, had this to say:

> What is required is for someone to devise a scheme to *regenerate the clove plantations* of those Arabs who, ruined by the abolition of slavery, have got deeper and deeper into the hands of the Indian money-lender until, unable to redeem their mortgaged properties or pay their labour, they have relinquished all interest in their plantations. The Indian mortgagee who was probably long ago repaid his initial loans by charging exorbitant interest does nothing to replace the dead clove trees with young ones. Hence the *danger of reduced clove output* in the future. I cannot but realize that the advent of Europeans as shamba-owners would inevitably lead to the financial crippling of Zanzibar eventually (sic), because I can conceive of no European settlers tolerating for any length of time *the payment of the 25% duty of cloves.* I do not necessarily uphold this heavy burden on the clove producer (sic) but the fact remains that *it is one of our main sources of revenue* and it is evident to me that with the advent of the European landowner, the tax is doomed. It would be of benefit to Zanzibar that a Chartered Company or any other Company should obtain a controlling interest either in the clove or copra industry, more particularly in the former. Several attempts have been made in the past by syndicates to secure a position which would enable them to control the clove market. These attempts have so far been frustrated by the fact that the Government is always in possession of nearly 30 per cent of the total crops which are realized from *duty and from its own plantations.* (All emphasis added.)[36]

Imperialism seemed to have grasped the main drawbacks as well as the assets in its favour. It was decided what form the exploitation of the producing classes would take and through what mechanism it would be achieved. More importantly, the secondary contradiction at the level of consumption, between merchant and industrial capital, was beginning to emerge. But since this was a non-antagonistic contradiction there were possibilities for temporary alliances or 'partnerships'.

Control of landed property by Indian moneylenders became more widespread with the decline of Zanzibar as the great East African entrepôt after 1905. Just as the colonial rulers were putting emphasis on the cash crop economy so too the Indian merchants began to extend their network in siphoning out surplus through commercial and usurious transactions. As early as the 1880s, approximately two-thirds of the clove plantations had been mortgaged to Indian creditors. The practice had become more pronounced with the abolition of the legal status of slavery in 1897, as the Arab landowner increasingly borrowed money to hire free labour. The Indians could secure almost the whole clove crop before harvest, either in repayment for a loan or through purchases at ridiculously low prices. That the continuation of this relationship would lead to falling production whilst the major benefits accrued to the moneylender-cum-mortgagee was becoming quite apparent to the British colonial rulers.

Serious difficulties are encountered when trying to assess the extent of benefits accruing from this complex mortgagor-mortgagee relationship, for the actual details of the transactions were seldom recorded. This is especially true when both the mortgagee and mortgagor were Muslims, since interest on loans was denounced as *haraam* (unlawful), but this was easily circumvented in practice. It is difficult to establish the extent of crop underpricing required to determine the profit margin of the merchant when he either exported to India or resold to other European firms in Zanzibar. Indian accounting was done almost entirely in Gujarati, while a rather informalised system of 'promissory notes' was evolved, much to the annoyance of the British rulers.

As their monopoly of Zanzibar's transshipment trade gradually decreased in the post-Partition years, some of the leading Indian firms like those of Sewa Hajee Paroo and Alidina Visram moved to the mainland German colony where they hoped to find profitable new opportunities. But as far as Zanzibar was concerned, it had become quite clear by 1913 that Indian merchants could no longer rely on the threadbare coat of British protection to grow prosperous. Customs collection was no longer the monopoly of Indian firms and major changes in the method of accounting were being considered.[37] The 50 per cent increase in customs duty in 1908 was borne entirely by Indian traders and in the following year a series of decrees had been passed *inter alia* to end their right to trial by jury, and of appeal to the Bombay High Court. The constitution of 1913 contained no proviso for Indian representation.[38] Along with the loss of rights and privileges in the 'Indian community', their 'commitment to the country' was now questioned.[39] What is more ironic is that in 1910 the British Consul castigated them for remitting their savings to India when a high proportion of Zanzibar funds were being invested in Government of India securities by the colonial state as a matter of routine practice![40] By the new definition, accumulation was solely an imperial right, while the trading activities of the Indian merchants would be tolerated as a 'necessary evil' in the colonial economy.

One activity the British particularly encouraged was the

expansion of small shopkeeping and retail trade in the countryside, while they deplored the 'over-concentration' of Indian shops in the urban areas. The spread of small shops throughout the Protectorate was a necessary adjunct to production for cash exchange, since money was fast becoming the only means for acquiring imported goods many of which had become basic means of subsistence. At a higher level, the Clove Growers' Association was conceived in the 1920s by the colonial rulers to perform precisely this function of 'increasing the demand for goods, thus stimulating imports' by paying 'good prices' to the producers. The ideal was expressed in one informal report from the colonial administration in the late 1930s which suggested that:

> Traders, of whom there are 850 of all nationalities, are experiencing a boom that has no precedent in Zanzibar, and are continually replenishing their stocks by cash payments rather than by means of barter or loans as heretofore. It is particularly gratifying to note that the Indian district shopkeeper is obtaining his full share of the prosperity.[41]

Although the picture painted is intentionally rosy, it outlines the specific character of the colonial economy. The small-scale trader or shopkeeper was an inexpensive and necessary agent in the expansion of commodity production and consumption. But the bigger wholesaler-exporter, or the commercial bourgeoisie proper, raked off a sizeable portion of the surplus and was thus regarded as a threat. More importantly, by employing his capital in usury and mortgaging, he had a certain leverage on production. It was his capital which in effect financed clove picking and preparation. It was primarily his lorries and dhows which transported the produce to the market, packed and sewn in gunny bags which he supplied. The processing and marketing of cloves were also carried out by him. To clip the wings of merchant capital – or, much better, to replace its functions by a state agency – were to become items of crucial importance on the colonial agenda.

Resistance to this objective was strong. The Indian Merchants' Association had been formed in 1905, and it later became the political organ of the upper crust of the commercial bourgeoisie. In the first two decades of the century they pursued a two-pronged struggle. At one level, they attempted to recapture the former alliance with the British in Zanzibar, and at another they sought an independent political voice at the level of the state in order to secure their class interests. In the former instance, the struggle became a campaign to seek 'protection for the rights of Indians in the British Empire', hence pleas were made to the British Foreign

Plates 25 and 26   *The old and new markets of Zanzibar.*

Plate 27   A bazaar in Zanzibar Town. The narrow shops are stacked high with bundles of textiles. Note the overhanging balconies typical of Indian homes above their shops.

177

Plate 28   The Ithnaasheri Dispensary, Zanzibar Town. Built in the 1890s by Tharia Topan, a prominent Indian merchant, it exhibits the refinements of colonial Indian architecture.

Office and Indian National Congress.[42] In the latter instance, they clamoured for the establishment of a legislative council on which they would be represented. This struggle gained strength through association with that waged by their counterparts on the mainland, especially after 1920. The demand was for 'equal treatment' to that accorded to white settlers.[43] However, the demand was ignored and the 'paramountcy' of African interests was proclaimed by the British in 1923.[44] By that measure the British placed the Indian bourgeoisie, as it were, on 'the proper rung of the Empire ladder'.[45] The only way for them to survive under the racially segregated colonial system would be to adhere to the 'middle position' in commerce, industry and administration. In essential terms, this meant that the primary right to exploit would be that of metropolitan capital.

Throughout World War I the British were preoccupied with the liquidation and control of German commercial interests. Smith Mackenzie & Co., which was the major British firm operating in Zanzibar, was given the go-ahead to 'take over trade of non-enemy importers formerly in the hands of the enemy'.[46] But Indian merchants still continued to play the role of agent for the European firms, and be the all-pervasive 'middleman' of the clove trade. After the war the scope for moneylending and petty commercial transactions by smaller capital began to expand with increased peasant production. Cloves would be purchased through exchange for imported consumer and producer goods or in repayment of debt as the merchants penetrated the countryside. By the 1920s it was becoming quite clear to the colonial state that something had to be done to curtail this expansive network of merchant capital. Cloves were important not only as a source of revenue but also as raw material for the vanillin industry in the West which took more than half the clove output up to the mid-1920s.[47] Accumulation at the higher level could only continue apace if the colonial state could effectively reduce costs of production and gain control of the clove market. This meant taking care of the growers' needs, as merchant capital had hitherto done to its overwhelming advantage. Wherever the activities of merchant capital collided with the interests of advanced capitalism, it would be the latter which would prevail. But before the British could rip away the ties which merchant capital had created with the landed class and later the peasant producers, the colonial state would have to evolve its own agencies of control. Quite typically the path was paved with opportunism.

In 1922, a Clove Bonus Scheme was launched with one of its aims being to lessen reliance on local moneylenders. But the colonial state could not prohibit the practice altogether because it fulfilled the necessary role of enabling the plantation owners to hire labour and the peasant producers to carry out production. In 1927, the colonial state institutionalised further controls on moneylending whilst stating that the 'local moneylending business does not correspond entirely with English ideas.'[48] Interest rates were to be more closely scrutinised and irregular dealings reduced by threat of court charges. When the financial depression in western capitalism hit Zanzibar shortly thereafter, the scheme was abandoned with the consequence that the growers fell back even more heavily on the moneylenders.

Another scheme which had failed to take root up to this time was the Clove Growers' Association (CGA). It was conceived as an instrument which would bring both production and marketing under the control of the colonial state. The lure of the clove bonus and cheaper labour arrangements in the 1920s had made it appear that the CGA would be in a position to oust the moneylender and the merchant, but this did not become a reality for another decade. In fact, throughout the 1920s and early 1930s, the state-owned plantations continued to auction their clove crop to Indian merchants with long-established connections in the Indian sub-continent. These trade channels became particularly important towards the late 1920s, as the demand for cloves in the metropole declined.

When the pinch of depression grew sharper in 1929, amidst talk of 'establishing a balance between receipts and expenditure as an ideal of state economy', it was recorded that revenue had fallen by £18,750 in clove duties and by £33,750 in import duties.[49] To increase the revenues, the agricultural economy would have to be restructured in a manner that would take into account the growing indebtedness of the smallhold producer as well as the big land-holders.

The early 1930s were marked by the hectic activity of various teams of British 'experts' trying to find solutions to regenerate the economy. One report in 1933 stated that the Indian merchants had 'used agriculture as a milch cow which they had now milked almost dry.'[50] The Indian National Association (INA) queued up to defend its leadership by making counter-charges. In its memo-randum to the Colonial Office in 1933 following a high-level enquiry into the financial position of the Protectorate, it claimed that the island's surplus balances had fallen from £253,000 in 1913, to £192,000 in 1939. It advanced as a primary reason for the decline the sharp rise in salaries to European officials from £155,000 in 1913 to £384,000 in 1929.[51]

The INA then argued against the administration's 1927 austerity measure of abandoning the free port policy and the reimposition of 15 per cent import levies. It alleged that taxation had reached its maximum level and the time had come for the government to intro-duce economies elsewhere rather than 'halt the engine of free enterprise'. It was, after all, through the latter that Indian merchants had 'raised the standard of life of the natives (by) popularization of the modern necessities of life.' Further, by acting as bankers they had helped 'to market the produce of the agriculturists'. In all this protestation, the commercial bourgeoisie were up against the basic fact that it was not in imperial interests to promote the much-acclaimed policy of free trade in a colony when it hindered rather than facilitated accumulation by the metropolitan bourgeoisie.

The time for wielding the big stick seemed to have arrived in 1934 when five successive decrees were passed to withdraw the clove trade from the grip of Indian merchants. The Alienation of Land (Restriction and Evidence) Decree was passed to liquidate the mortgagor-mortgagee relationship. It ended the 'fictitious sale' and transfer of land to Indians by African or Arab owners unless sanctioned by the British Resident. A moratorium was imposed on debts to Indian moneylenders. Secondly, the Clove Growers' Association Decree was to give the CGA a monopoly over the clove industry 'aimed at eliminating ruinous private speculations and securing stable markets abroad.' The CGA was to be financed by a levy on all clove exports and, henceforth, all agricultural produce, property and finance were to become the business of the CGA. Thirdly, the Clove Exporters' Decree dictated that nobody could export cloves unless a licence costing up to Rs5,000 per annum was obtained from the CGA. The British Resident could restrict the number of licences granted, and accounts of transactions were to be available to the CGA. Fourthly, the Adulteration of Produce Decree was to ensure the marketable quality of exports. And fifthly, the Agricultural Produce Export Decree instituted a system of grading cloves which *inter alia* empowered government inspectors to enter premises for the purpose of examining produce and removing it if necessary. Failure to comply would mean court proceedings. In sum, no tool was to be spared in chipping away at the structure of merchant enterprise and replacing it with one which would serve metropolitan interests more faithfully and rigorously.

The commercial bourgeoisie was struck with panic. In its endeavours to seek redress against what it termed 'anti-Indian legislation', the INA galvanised the support of its business counterparts and class allies in India. The latter through the Congress Working Committee, the Imperial Indian Citizenship Association, and the Federation of Indian Chambers of Commerce and Industry, were able to force the colonial government in India to send a deputy to enquire into the Zanzibar situation. His findings revealed that, if implemented, the new export levy would have the effect of making Indian exporters contribute to the running of the rival CGA. The CGA would, in fact, be in a position to undersell the Indian exporters. A year after the decrees were implemented in mid-1934, the effects were apparent. As many as 80 Indian businesses folded up and 20 others were declared insolvent, whilst a minor exodus seemed underway.[52] But the British stuck to their guns and all pleas to repeal the decrees were rejected.[53] The colonial government in India would not be moved either. It was up to the merchants themselves to join forces and launch a counter-offensive in what appeared to be a sharp class struggle. When diplomacy fails to contain the destructive drive of the enemy, the placing of strategic boulders is often the only way of retarding its advance and paving the way towards compromise. In what they termed as 'passive resistance', the INA called upon all Indian clove exporters to stop buying further licences and have nothing to do with the CGA. In India, the various merchant associations started an unofficial embargo of Zanzibar cloves on the principle that 'any attempt to injure Indian interests for the advancement of British Imperialism' ought to be bitterly opposed.[54]

The clove boycott imposed serious strains on the exchange economy and its effects were felt on both sides within six months. Since cloves could not be channelled to South Asia through the Indian markets, clove revenue dropped dramatically as the trade circuit withered. The estimated collection for the year fell short by £26,000 in spite of the bumper crop.[55] In the previous year 72,678 cwt had been exported at a revenue of £40,699 while only 22,153 cwt were exported in 1937, bringing the revenue down by approximately 30 per cent.[56] The Indian merchants, for their part, caught their toes under the boulders which they had successfully propped up. Some merchants were recording daily losses of up to Rs15,000. There was also fear of a counter-boycott against Indian business by Arab plantation owners and African smallholders in support of the CGA policies. In his address to the Legislative Council meeting on 12 February 1937, the British Resident reasserted the CGA claim that 'the material prosperity of Arab and African communities' was a result of the new clove scheme 'which the Indian merchants had impeded by fostering a sterile movement.' It was said there was still the possibility for future gain for the merchants if cooperation could be achieved 'without impairing the essential working of the new Decree.'

The British were unwilling to alter the clove marketing scheme except as to detail, even if the Indian export trade were to be resumed. The import trade had already grown in bulk under the aegis of the colonial state and it could not continue to thrive unless the exporting of cloves continued. A colonial spokesman explained:

> It is of course commonplace that the whole economy of Zanzibar rests on cloves. The export duty represents an important element in the public revenues, and the customs duties which are *an even more important element* are entirely dependent on the people getting money from their clove exports to pay for their imports. (Emphasis added.)[57]

The trend in Zanzibar's exchange economy was towards a surplus of imports, the bulk of which came from Britain and the Empire. The reason for the surfeit of imports lay in the failure of the colonial state to find other export commodities to serve the accumulation needs of the metropolitan economy. While the major productive effort was channelled into cloves at the expense of food crops, a reliance had developed on imported food items like rice and sugar.

These commodities bore the brunt of heavy taxation whenever the need arose.[58]

The trade connection with India, controlled by the Indian merchants, formed a central component in this import-export nexus, for India remained indisputably the biggest importer of dried cloves from Zanzibar in the pre-boycott years. For this reason, it was important to forge an alliance with the Indian merchants in order to break the nine-month old embargo. By mid-1938, an agreement had been worked out between the British Resident and INA in which the export trade in cloves was returned to the Indian merchants while their hold over the clove economy was to be phased out in the following manner. First, the colonial state adopted a more thorough programme to pay off debts incurred by landowners and smallholding peasants to Indian moneylenders and traders, though there was room still for 'legitimate' moneylending.[59] Second, the CGA now controlled the local clove market through the power to decide minimum prices, while the Indian merchants themselves were to purchase part of their cloves from the CGA.[60] Earlier, a certain Lord Dufferin summed up the new situation in a letter to the Colonial Office:

> The plain truth is that even with the proposed changes in the original scheme, there remains very little scope for Indian enterprise or capital in the Island. The CGA system is too well-known now for the ordinary trader to have very much chance of even a reasonable turnover in the clove trade. The grower will squeeze him too hard as long as there are CGA buying depots accessible to almost everyone.[61]

The foregoing measures contributed to the decline of smaller merchants in the clove trade. Only the bigger ones with capital to branch out into other enterprises could hope to survive. The CGA itself in the following decades became a ruthless commercial arm of the colonial state, an unpopular body which could neither be squeezed nor elbowed out. With its discretionary control over clove prices and its free hand in other export crops and processing industries, the CGA became the most powerful agency in the clove business.

As World War II began, the main concern of the colonial state was to ensure a steady flow of revenue and the marketing of CGA's large stock of cloves in the face of increasing competition from Madagascar.[62] The Indian merchants voiced the fear that 'the clove trade will never be what it was in the past.' It was the lament of a dependent commercial bourgeoisie, caught in the interstices of colonial capitalism.

Notes

1. The author was a Greek pilot who wrote towards the end of the first century A.D. He described a flourishing Indian commerce with East Africa, Rome, Egypt, Axum, the Red Sea, Cape Guardafui and Azania. See R.G. Gregory, *India and East Africa 1890—1939*, Oxford, Clarendon Press, 1971, pp. 9—10.

2. Products such as ivory, cloves (classified as 'human cargo'), gold dust, gum copal, beeswax, tortoise and cowrie shells were traded for Indian cottons, rice and muslins, dates from Arabia, salt and ghee from Socotra. There was a barter economy along the caravan routes.

3. Early reference to merchant connections with slave markets can be found in the *Periplus*. During the tenth century, Zanzibar, Sofala and Mozambique were thriving slave-trading centres.

4. In the words of H. Luthy, 'India and East Africa: Imperial partnership at the end of the First World War', *Journal of Contemporary History*, Vol. 6, No. 2, 1971, pp. 55—85: 'British Imperialism did not speak with one voice, but as a perplexing bunch of different imperialisms and sub-imperialisms, among which British-Indian Imperialism was the oldest and best-established, the imperialism of a ruling corporation (East India Company) which had taken possession of India, and substantially autonomous, pursued its imperial policies and aspirations in a perspective of British-Indian paramountcy over all southern Asia and the Indian Ocean area.'

5. A Governor Yakut, appointee of the Imam of Muscat, wanted to raise customs dues on Indian merchants. Smee, as the representative of a superior force, was able to intervene on behalf of the Indian merchants and thus enhance their position *vis-à-vis* the Omani interests. See W. Hollingsworth, *Zanzibar Under the Foreign Office, 1890—1913*, London, Macmillan, 1953.

6. Maria Theresa Dollars (thalers) were progressively replaced by the Indian rupee and pice in the nineteenth century through this import-export economy which was becoming highly internationalised.

7. This is well argued in L. Sakkarai, 'Indian Merchants in East Africa', mimeograph, 1976.

8. See J.S. Mangat, *Asians in East Africa, 1886—1945*, Oxford, Clarendon Press, 1969, pp. 2—3, where he mentions the appointment of the firm of Wat Bhima as customs collectors in Zanzibar in 1833. It has been recorded that the Busaidi Sultan came to Zanzibar with a whole company of Indian financiers in the hope of enlarging his own coffers through their services in his dominions.

9. According to R. Coupland, *East Africa and its Invaders*, Oxford, Clarendon Press, 1938, quoted in Sakkarai, *op. cit.*

10. Between 1830 and 1835, the value of imports from East Africa to Bombay increased from Rs322,584 to Rs635,106 according to Bird, as quoted in Sakkarai, *op. cit.*

11. Despite the supposed injunctions against the slave trade imposed by the

British starting from 1807, followed by the Moresby Treaty of 1822 and Hamerton Treaty in 1845. Slaves continued to be exported to India between 1840 and 1860 despite slavery being outlawed there as well.

12. According to Rigby, writing of this period, Arabs had 'neither goods nor money to give in exchange for foreign goods ... almost the only trade carried on was the export in slaves....' It was for this reason that cloves had been introduced in Zanzibar as early as 1810 from La Reunion since it had favourable climatic and soil conditions. In Sakkarai, *op. cit.*

13. The Sultan had signed 'Amity and Commercial Treaties' with the United States in 1833, Britain in 1839, and France and Germany (Prussia) in 1844. A special clause stated that a levy of only 5 per cent would be charged on imported goods. But it is crucial to point out that Indian merchant capital mediated the passage of their commerce and that they often borrowed from the big Indian firms; see Mangat, *op. cit.*, pp. 10–11, where he quotes a report from the British Consul, Kirk, in 1872.

14. See Mangat, *op. cit.*, pp. 4 and 16.

15. See in Sakkarai, *op. cit.*, 'Instructions from his Envoy to the Queen of Great Britain', February 1842. He warned that if slaves were prohibited the revenue would entirely disappear, trade in ivory would be lost and, worse still, there would no longer be purchasers for European goods, e.g. cotton. The point was made persuasively.

16. A.M.H. Sheriff, 'The Rise of a Commercial Empire: An Aspect of the Economic History of Zanzibar, 1770–1873', unpublished Ph.D. thesis, University of London, 1971, pp. 438–40.

17. According to Hamerton in Outward Letter No. 12, Serial E. 11 of 1849 to Bombay, quoted in Mangat *op. cit.*, p. 10. The customs rental rose as its extractive capacity increased with the bulk of trade.

18. See Sakkarai, *op. cit.*

19. Fraser (1860–62) is quoted at length in Sakkarai, *op. cit.* A leading imperialist, he argued that all trade that would absorb manufactured goods and furnish raw materials would be important to Britain. His interest, therefore, lay in expanding production in tropical Africa and teaching the natives to have 'new wants'.

20. From Public Record Office (hereafter called PRO), London, FO 84/1426 (The Slave Trade), especially in reference to the Treaty signed on 5 June 1873, which stated that 'the export of slaves from the coast of the mainland of Africa, whether destined for transport from one part of the Sultan's dominions to another or for conveyance to foreign parts, shall entirely cease.' In fact the Sultan was told the British navy would blockade Zanzibar if he did not implement the instructions in the Treaty.

21. See Coupland, *op. cit.*, pp. 17–25. British Consul Rigby's military intervention was later justified because it 'threatened British property and prospective annihilation of British trade', in the words of the Secretary of State for India.

22. See Mangat, *op. cit.*, pp. 18–19. In 1880, the customs rental was itself worth £500,000 and the leading Indian firms were in competition for it.

23. From the PRO, FO 84/1391. Frere refers to one firm (possibly Jairam Sewji's) whose books showed capital of about £434,000 invested in loans and mortgages in East Africa; see Mangat, *op. cit.*, p. 19.
24. L. Farrant, *Tippu Tip and the East African Slave Trade*, London, Hamish Hamilton, 1975.
25. After the 1872 hurricane in Zanzibar, Pemba was the biggest clove producer. In 1879, the clove trade brought in £170,000 and the ivory trade £160,000 as the two major export commodities out of the total of £900,000. Another commodity which hastened the prohibition of the slave trade by the imperialists was 'India rubber' which brought in £250,000 in 1879. Figures from Coupland, *op. cit.*, p. 320.
26. The Bombay organ of the Indian bourgeoisie, *Native Opinion*, defended the firm of Jairam Sewji and asked why India was required to pay half the costs of the Frere Mission. See Gregory, *op. cit.*, p. 140 and pp. 23–6.
27. Estimated at approximately £160,000 by Kirk in 1873 on Zanzibar island alone, PRO, FO 84/1391, Frere to Granville.
28. In J. Flint, 'The wider background to partition and colonial occupation', in R. Oliver and G. Mathew, eds, *History of East Africa*, Vol. 1, Oxford, Clarendon Press, 1963.
29. In Gregory, *op. cit.*, p. 140.
30. Such fears were expressed by Kirk in PRO, FO 84/1774.
31. In 'Report of the Committee on Emigration from India to the Crown Colonies and Protectorates', when Kirk said in his evidence to the Sanderson Committee: 'It was entirely through the Indian merchants that we were enabled to build up the influence that resulted in our position (in East Africa)', in Mangat, *op. cit.*, p. 5.
32. PRO, CO 618/11.
33. Frere to Granville, 27 February 1873, correspondence in Coupland, *op. cit.*
34. 'Report of the Committee on Emigration from India to the Crown Colonies and Protectorates', Part II, Minutes of Evidence as cited in Mangat, *op. cit.*
35. See Geoffrey Kay, *Development and Underdevelopment: A Marxist Analysis*, London, Macmillan, 1975, chapter on Productive and Circulation Capital.
36. PRO, CO 618/11, correspondence of 16/12/1915, in relation to a Mr Wilson Fox aspiring to purchase the *shamba* of Tundana in Pemba Island.
37. PRO, CO 618/47/8, 'Method of Accounting for Refund of Customs Duties.'
38. See Gregory, *op. cit.*, p. 117.
39. From the Indian Office Emigration Proceedings of February 1911, quoted in Mangat, *op. cit.*
40. PRO, File No. 23383 of 1930, Estimates for 1931 on the Question of Investment of Surplus Balances.
41. PRO, CO 689/31, British Resident's address to Legislative Council meeting on 2/12/37.
42. H. Luthy, *op. cit.*

43. Letter from the British East Africa Indian Association to Sir Horace Byatt, quoted in Luthy, *ibid.*

44. The Devonshire Declaration of 1923 as cited in Mangat, *op. cit.*

45. Letter by an English settler in Kenya writing to the *East African Standard* of 26 June 1921, as quoted in Hollingsworth, *op. cit.*

46. PRO, CO 618/11, March 1916.

47. PRO, CO 618/44/25, File No. 23116, the Moneylenders Decree, 1928 (Amendment of 1927).

48. *Ibid.*

49. PRO, CO 618/44/25, File No. 23141 of 1928.

50. Report by C.A. Bartlett and J.S. Last, *The Indebtedness of the Agricultural Classes, 1933,* Zanzibar, Government Printer, 1934.

51. PRO, CO 618/56, File No. 3840 of 1933 on Enquiry into the Financial Position of the Protectorate, report by Sir Alan Pim, containing a memorandum by the INA.

52. Report on the effect of the recent legislation passed by the Government of Zanzibar on Indian interests, by K.P.S. Menon, 1934.

53. PRO, CO 618/56, File No. 23815/34.

54. From *Indian Review* of October 1937 as quoted in Gregory, *op. cit.*

55. PRO, CO 689/31, British Resident's address to the Legislative Council meeting on 2/12/37.

56. PRO, CO 618/70, File No. 41159 of 1937 on the Financial Position. Basis of Calculation of Revenue from Clove Duty in Estimates for 1938.

57. PRO, CO 618/72, File No. 41159 of 1938 on the Financial Position.

58. One instance of this is recorded at the beginning of World War II as revenue earnings fell; PRO, CO 618/75, File No. 41159 of 1939 on the Financial Position.

59. Land Protection (Debts Settlement) Decree of February, 1938.

60. Under the 'Heads of Agreement', May 1938.

61. PRO, CO 618/72, File No. 41159 on Administration of Zanzibar: Impressions of Lord Dufferin to Ormsby, Government, 21/2/32.

62. PRO, CO 618/75, File No. 41159 of 1939 on the Financial Position.

Seven

The Development of a Colonial Working Class

GEORGE HADJIVAYANIS
& ED FERGUSON

Formation of the working class

The origin of the working class in Zanzibar can be traced back to the nineteenth century and the labour needs of the plantation economy. Alongside the unfree labour force of slaves, there appeared a small number of free labourers as a result of accords reached between the Arab rulers and indigenous chiefs, as explained in this colonial report:

> During the reigns of the first Sultans of the Albusaid Dynasty and down to the year 1897, when slavery was abolished, labour in Zanzibar was of two kinds, slave and free, the latter being that provided by the Wahadimu and Wapemba in accordance with agreements made with the Sultans.[1]

Two features distinguished this nineteenth-century form of free labour. First, labourers kept hold of their land, although they were increasingly forced to the less fertile areas with the expansion of the plantations. Second, no payment was made to the individual; labour was taken as tribute without monetary compensation. This particular arrangement disappeared with the loss of power by indigenous chiefs prior to the end of the century. Abolition of the slave trade and slavery in Zanzibar by degrees in the last quarter of the nineteenth century weakened planter control of the slave labour force. An administrator explained it this way:

> With each successive measure adopted for the abolition of slavery, labour troubles increased, the freed slaves being disinclined to do more than was necessary for a bare subsistence....[2]

188

When slavery was formally abolished in 1897, most of the ex-slaves remained as squatters on the plantations where 'hidden slavery and semi-slavery continued to exist ... for some time and unpaid labour ... remained a prevalent social institution.'[3] True wage labour made its appearance by 1900 when the colonial state introduced immigrant labour from the mainland colonies.[4]

Composition of the working class

The colonial export economy was based on clove and coconut production, processing and transportation. The nucleus of the working class was associated with these activities. Five types of workers appeared: casual labourers, dockworkers, plantation labourers, domestic servants, and industrial workers. In this section we will identify the composition and distribution of this work force. In the next section we will trace the development of each type of worker and the formation of trade unions. Unique work experience in each category led to different levels of working-class consciousness, which explains why some occupations organised themselves into trade unions earlier, and were more militant, than others.

Casual labourers

Casual labourers were found in many sectors of the economy, but they predominated in transport and construction. The former, *wachukuzi*, appeared in commercial activities which required transfer of goods. There were casual labourers throughout the trading centres of the Protectorate, but the most sizeable concentration was found at the main port in Zanzibar Town. They carried imports and exports between the port, warehouses, wholesalers, and retailers. The 1955 Labour Report gives the following information on these workers:

> The largest group of casual labourers is employed in transportation services in the towns. Most of those in the town of Zanzibar belong to an association which is a registered trade union. They use handcarts in teams of four or five and are paid at piece rates. They are known to earn up to Shs10/- in a day, but their work is so irregular that they may remain unemployed for several days when there is a dearth of ships in the harbour.[5]

Uncertainty of employment was only one trait that made this work particularly insecure. The handcarts required for transport — *hamali* carts or *rikwama* — were not owned by the transport workers. Petty Arab traders would hire them out for a fixed fee to a team

189

Plate 29 Hamali *(porters) carrying cloves on a hand cart* (rikwama) *to the port.*

of *wachukuzi.* The fee was paid whether or not the team found work. These teams were organised by a *chepe,* an experienced worker having enterprising contacts with the important merchants of the town. After payment of the fee, any remaining earnings would be distributed by the *chepe* who would take the largest share for himself. It was this category of casual labourer, the *wachukuzi,* that organised the first trade union in Zanzibar.

The construction industry was controlled by Indian contractors who employed Indian artisans and African unskilled casual labour. These contractors were artisans who used their accumulated wealth to open a private workshop for carpentry, smithing, masonry and so on. The influx of new artisans from India was so great that it was restricted by the colonial government in 1954. The unskilled casual labour for construction came primarily from the mainland. This was considered one of the lowest forms of manual labour. Viewed as a temporary source of livelihood by those who hoped to find employment in other occupations, these casual labourers in construction tended to be transient.

Dockworkers
All the dockworkers were concentrated at Zanzibar port. The

Plate 30   A street in Ngambo, the working class quarter in Zanzibar at the end of the nineteenth century.

significant feature of this type of work was specialisation of task. There were stevedores, boatmen, baggage porters and produce packers.

Stevedores included dockers, tugmasters, and winchmen employed by the African Wharfage Company. Boatmen were employed by a syndicate of Asian merchants. They were fewer in number — perhaps 50 — and were organised in teams on the pattern of transport workers. Their earnings were distributed between themselves and the syndicate owners. Baggage porters were licensed to carry luggage in teams and share the earnings among themselves. They, too, numbered around 50 workers. Produce packers were organised into teams to do the final packing of exports. They were linked with the transport workers who received the packed goods from them.

Each type of work had its particular specialisation, which made overall unity difficult. Stevedores, the most radical group among them, made an attempt to organise all these specialists into one dockworkers' union, but it was unsuccessful in the face of manoeuvres by the African Wharfage Company which offered free meals and overtime work to the stevedores. The latter were 'bought off' and dropped the idea of a common union. They formed their own narrow union which had some 600 members by the late 1950s.

Class Formation

Plantation workers

The agricultural sector of clove and coconut production depended on three sources of labour: plantation squatters, migrant labour from the mainland, and segments of the Protectorate peasantry. Since the latter are covered elsewhere in this book, we will concentrate on the role of squatters and migrant labour.

The category of the rural workforce called squatters were freed slaves who remained on the plantation. One authority on Zanzibar agriculture described them in these words:

> On large plantations the populace lives principally as squatters who are there on sufferance and have no direct rights to the land. Permission to cultivate open pieces of land and rice valleys is given generally on the understanding that labour will be given at clove harvest.[6]

Squatters were an important source of labour after the termination of slavery in 1897. Land was allocated to them on the plantation between the clove and coconut trees, or outside the planted area altogether. Following abolition they had to pay rent in kind, called *jizia*, to the landlords. This tax was a characteristic feature of serfdom introduced in the transition period from slave labour to wage labour. It was only when the landed class depended entirely on surplus from the export of cloves and coconuts that *jizia* lost its significance. Then squatters agreed to provide wage labour during harvest in return for continued use of the land.

Immigrant workers arrived from the mainland as wage labour developed in Zanzibar. Most came from Tanganyika, Kenya, Uganda, Nyasaland and Mozambique, where the colonial state had created labour reserves through the alienation of land and imposition of taxes. They were viewed as an essential source of labour power by the Zanzibar authorities:

> The mainland African is beyond doubt the hardiest and the most adaptable worker in the Protectorate and he is to be found in practically every occupation but he still looks to the mainland as his home. No steps are being taken to restrict the entry of these mainlanders although in lean years they aggravate the unemployment problem.[7]

This description does require qualification. While the migrant labourer was essentially a seasonal labourer, some settled permanently in Zanzibar, especially those who worked on government-owned plantations. Their work was confined to weeding, bush clearing and general cultivation, while the harvesting of cloves was left to indigenous labourers since it required experience. Mainlanders were affected by the contract system introduced by the

Plate 31   The msewe *dance, with the musician playing a* zumari.

Plate 32   A Swahili women's dance at the beginning of the twentieth century. Note the elaborate costume.

Plate 33 The Manyema *dance by immigrants from eastern Zaire. Note the painted white faces of the women dancers.*

Protectorate authorities. This included cash advances and free passage to Pemba Island. Breach of contract was met with punishments varying from fines to imprisonment. Most labourers preferred freelance picking to contract work.

Domestic servants

Numerically, domestic servants composed the largest group of labourers in the Protectorate. They worked for the Arab landed class, the Asian merchant class and the Europeans. There were both male and female domestics. Not all worked for a wage. Clearly, this was an occupation shaped by precapitalist relations. The administration, for example, made this observation in its 1948 Labour Report about the recruitment of servants:

> No reduction was discovered … in the employment in urban areas as domestic servants of children, especially Watumbatu from country homes, with or without the consent of their parents, although efforts have been made by the Administration to stop this practice. This employment is sometimes disguised as 'adoption', which although lacking in legal form is regarded by the public as benign, and makes administrative action more difficult.[8]

194

The so-called 'adoption' of youth for domestic service, and as concubines (*Masuria*), was a pre-capitalist practice that concealed a slave relationship. It was justified on the basis of Islamic ideology which encourages adoption of the poor. Originally it appeared within Islam to provide for those without adult kin; in the colonial era it was used as a means for wealthy individuals to obtain offspring and cheap servile labour. The element of domination and paternalism in the master-servant relationship was quite apparent from the names given domestics: they were called by the Swahili word for child, or boy, regardless of whether they were actually children, adults, or elders.

The Asian merchant and commercial class had the largest number of domestic servants in the Protectorate by World War II. This reflected the financial prosperity of the merchants, as well as a pre-capitalist outlook. The administration's 1958 Labour Report noted the role of domestic servitude within this class:

> Many children leave their villages with parental consent and live in towns where they obtain employment with Asian households. It is generally believed that these children become victims of low wages, long working hours, bad housing and inadequate feeding, but with the connivance of both the parents and the employers, these evils are not easy to detect.[9]

Domestic servants employed by Europeans were paid wages in contrast to the general practice among the Arabs. They tended to be adults, the majority of whom were males employed as *shamba* 'boys', laundry 'boys', house cleaners and cooks. It was only these domestic servants that attained a degree of class consciousness resulting in the European Domestic Servants Union. In 1947 the union had a total of 165 members, of whom 45 were women. Cooks, however, would not join it. They received higher pay and lived in servant's quarters provided behind the employer's house. Material benefits — used clothing, shoes, food — led them to disassociate themselves from trade union activity.

Industrial workers

No industry was encouraged or permitted to compete with that in Britain, so there was very little manufacturing in Zanzibar during the colonial era. The result of this policy was the primacy of agricultural production as reported in 1955 by the official responsible for labour on the islands: 'This country being mainly an agricultural one, industrial expansion is slow and consequently only a few factories are constructed each year.'[10]

Workshops and small firms were scattered about Zanzibar Town, and there was a concentration at Saateni on the town fringe. The most important of them prepared raw materials for export. By the 1950s the were 17 of these establishments converting coconuts into copra and oil for the foreign market, while soap and cakes were made for the domestic market. Some 300–400 workers were employed in coconut oil and soap firms, the total number depending on the size of the harvest. The latter, too, determined the length of employment: it varied from seasonal to year-round. Labour tended to be migratory or semi-proletarianised. The other enterprises which contributed to the formation of an embryonic industrial proletariat included the following, each of which employed less than a hundred persons: an oil depot; a clove distillation plant; a half-dozen flour mills; quite a few bakeries; two soda factories; five coir rope factories; more than a dozen carpentry and furniture shops; mechanics' workshops; garages; and a number of small printing presses. Independent artisans in gold, silver, copper, and tinsmithing usually employed a few assistants. Much of the skilled and artisanal labour tended to migrate to mainland colonies where, it was often said, higher wages were obtainable, so there was a turnover in certain occupations.[11]

While factory workers were few in number and appeared relatively late in the colonial era, they came to play a decisive role in the struggle for proletarian class interests, and the general anti-colonial movement for national independence.

Organisation of the working class

Working-class consciousness develops from common experience in production and seeks organisational expression. John Iliffe has observed this phenomenon in his study of Dar es Salaam dock-workers in colonial Tanganyika:

> Men work together, share common experiences, and realise that they have common interests. By acting together to advance these interests, they learn their need for unity. This growing consciousness enables them to act more effectively and shared experience of successful action in turn intensifies group consciousness. This is how a nation creates itself, through common action by the people who form it. It is also how a working class creates itself.[12]

This leads to a number of important distinctions we must make to grasp the evolution of working class organisation in Zanzibar.

Labourers are brought together in a common activity or occupation to work for a wage. Through identical work experience they develop an awareness of mutual interests as wage labourers within the particular occupation. That awakening leads to demands to advance themselves against private employers or the colonial state. These may be put forward in many different ways. They are most effectively expressed as an occupational strike. The likelihood of success increases when workers have organised into a trade union.

Working-class consciousness solidifies when labourers think beyond their own occupation to see themselves as members of the working class in general. They view themselves not only as dockworkers, domestics, or labourers in a soap factory, but as members of the whole working class. This deeper understanding may be expressed, for example, through the general strike, or by uniting many independent trade unions into a federation.

These higher levels of working-class consciousness and organisation are achieved through class struggle. The progression was neither smooth nor made solely through working-class initiative in Zanzibar. New organisational structures for the working class were initiated both by labour to advance the struggle and by the colonial state to contain it. The latter had greater experience in class struggle and it was used to block and retard collective action by workers. A trade union or federation, for example, should advance working-class interests, but in practice it may be controlled by other class interests to blunt worker initiative. A common tactic of the colonial state was to try and co-opt a union and use it to control wage labour in the interest of capital.

Working-class organisation advanced through five stages in colonial Zanzibar. The earliest covered the years of the Depression and World War II, 1930—45, when the first decrees were passed by the colonial state to permit formation of trade unions. The second stage, 1946—48, had three distinctive features: the first large strike in 1946; the first general strike in 1948; and the initial formation of trade unions. The third stage, 1949—55, was marked by a lull in working-class organisation. Activity resumed to give a distinct imprint to our fourth period, 1956—58. It had these features: the proliferation of trade unions along occupational lines; the active role of nationalist parties; and an unsuccessful effort to create a trade union federation. Early in the fifth stage, 1959—63, two large federations had appeared and the majority of unions joined one or the other body. After the formation of the Umma Party in July 1963, and its alliance with the Afro-Shirazi Party (ASP), leadership in both federations joined this opposition force to create the broad base for the 1964 Revolution.

1930—1945

The first legislative act in Zanzibar legalising trade unions was the 1931 Trade Union Decree. The fact that it was not passed in response to demands advanced by workers, and that no trade union was registered until after World War II, raises the intriguing question of why Britain prepared the way for trade union development in the Protectorate. Since we are hard put to find the answer locally, we must look for our answer at the international level.

Working-class activity in the metropolitan capitalist state had forced Britain to formulate a domestic policy on trade unions by World War I. But it had no coherent policy for its overseas possessions. In the 1920s, considerable strike activity leading to trade union formation took place in the Caribbean, India, Kenya, and elsewhere in the British Empire. This led the Colonial Office to develop a uniform policy on colonial trade unions:

> In 1930 the Labour government appointed a Colonial Office Labour Committee ... to consider 'the basic formulation of a Colonial Office labour policy, the drafting of model laws and the effects on dependencies of some of the international labour conventions of the period.' A conference of colonial administrators and governors was also held in the same year, and this paid some attention to labour questions. To back the exhortations of the conference and the work of the Labour Committee, the Secretary of State (for the Colonies), Sidney Webb, circulated a Dispatch in September 1930 to all colonial governors, urging the passage of legislation to give trade unions formal legislative rights.[13]

The object was to move rapidly to restrain the colonial working-class struggle, both where it was taking clear organisational form, and where it was bound to appear with the impact of the capitalist Depression.

The trade union guidelines had the purpose of restricting activities to narrow economic demands. This is explained by Meynaud and Bey in their study of trade unionism in Africa:

> The aim of British policy on trade unions was to keep economic and political demands separate and to ensure that trade unionism did not reinforce the nationalist movement. The Colonial Office ... had seen at a very early date the dangers involved if trade unionism became a weapon for the political leaders.[14]

Close supervision would be necessary to achieve that objective. A warning was issued in the September 1930 Dispatch of the Secretary of State for the Colonies:

> I recognize that there is a danger that without supervision and guidance, organisations of labourers without experience of

combination for any social or economic purpose may fall under the domination of disaffected persons, by whom their activities may be diverted to improper or mischievous ends.[15]

The response in Zanzibar to the Secretary's communication was the 1931 Trade Union Decree. It required formalities far beyond those enforced in the metropolitan country. Ioan Davies describes the measures:

> Trade unions throughout Africa were registered and closely supervised by the labour departments: accounts were scrutinised, political affiliation was discouraged, union offices were closed, and, in practice, the right to strike was severely circumscribed by the 'emergency' actions of Governors....[16]

Widespread intervention by the colonial administration into trade union activities was made possible by this legislation.

The impact of the international capitalist Depression of the 1930s on the colonial world led to a general decline in standards of living. Wages were cut and production was increased, causing intensified exploitation of the labour force. There was widespread strike activity by workers in India, the West Indies and Africa. The year 1939 in East Africa, for example, witnessed the first sizeable dockworkers' strike in Dar es Salaam and a general strike in Mombasa.[17] Such militancy throughout the empire had caused the Colonial Office to take further steps to control the developing proletariat by the end of the decade:

> From 1938 the Colonial Office ... [would] insist on the introduction of labour legislation, the creation of labour departments, the appointment of inspectors and the establishment of industrial disputes machinery.[18]

The Colonial Development and Welfare Act passed in Britain in 1940 had the stipulation that 'no territory might receive aid ... unless it had in force legislation protecting the rights of trade unions.'[19] When those conditions were met, and technical aid programmes were established, 'trade unionists seconded from the [British] TUC were sent overseas to help establish and administer African trade unions.'[20]

A second Zanzibar Trade Union Decree was passed in 1941, outlining registration formalities and conditions for recognition. All unions were to keep accounts of finances, officers, and clerks employed, to be submitted annually for audit and review by the Registrar of Trade Unions. The administration used these reports to grant, deny, or withdraw recognition. It was a convenient means to harass and intimidate on a daily basis those attempting to organise in their class interests (see Appendices A and B).

Class Formation

In 1942, a Colonial Labour Advisory Committee was formed in Britain to supervise trade union development overseas. To this committee were appointed representatives of metropolitan employers and the Trades Union Council (TUC) to supervise the colonial unions. We might expect employer representatives to be loyal to their class interests; it is perhaps more surprising that the representatives of the British TUC collaborated with the colonial regime as well. This is explained by Ioan Davies in his study of African trade unions:

> The effect of this alliance − between metropolitan labour and colonial administration − was to devise a system ... for ensuring that [colonial workers] were controlled in the interests of the administration.... One of the areas of compromise reached with colonial administrations was TUC insistence that trade unionism in the colonies should be 'non-political', hardly itself a marked feature of British trade union affairs.[21]

This well-defined structure of control over the colonial labour movement anticipated by many years the development of workers' self-organisation in Zanzibar. During the decade and a half after the enactment of the 1931 Trade Union Decree in the Protectorate, no group of workers had come forth to register. They had, however, taken other steps to defend their class interests. Mutual protection and self-help organisations had been formed along ethnic and class lines. They aided members and their families with expenses arising from sickness, death and repatriation to the mainland. These groups were working-class microcosms of the larger multi-class ethnic associations organised in Zanzibar from 1900 to 1939 by leaders of the Arab, Indian, Shirazi and mainland African communities.

While Britain correctly anticipated increased labour militancy in the colonies by the end of World War II, the dynamic was not predictable. Immediately the situation in Zanzibar was altered profoundly by the spontaneous strike of 1946 which ushered in one of the most militant phases in the Protectorate's post-war history.

1946−1948

The outburst of working-class activity in Zanzibar was caused primarily by economic decline. External trade links disrupted by the war were not quickly rebuilt. Clove exports were in sharp decline to pre-war markets in Malaya and Indonesia, while rice imports from South-east Asia were slow to recover to pre-war levels. The price rise for consumer goods was not accompanied by an increase in wages. Food shortages led to famine during the 1946 drought. The rural population sought additional income by

200

stripping mangrove bark to sell to merchants. Heightened unemployment benefited government and employers who profited from the resulting labour surpus:

> The number of casual labourers increased. Even the government administration which was the greatest employer [hired] more casual labourers than permanent ones. Wages were low: shillings 1/30 per day. Owners of soap and coconut mills took advantage [of unemployment] and forced their workers to toil in long night shifts.[22]

The colonial economy was in 'crisis. The working-class response was militant labour action and trade union formation. This laid the groundwork for post-war class struggle.

The 1946 strike began spontaneously in late March. It was the work of the *wachukuzi* who transported commodities in Zanzibar harbour. Most of the port workers were of mainland origin. They had been hit hard by the slump in external trade and sought to protect their jobs. The spark which ignited the strike was the shift away from *wachukuzi* labour by 'one merchant [who] was said to be using members of a dhow crew to pack cloves in his godown.'[23] They moved decisively through unified class action to defend their jobs, as acknowledged in this Labour Report:

> The *Wachukuzi* obeyed the strike almost to a man, and not only the [clove] industry became involved but also copra marketing and distribution of goods between wholesalers and retailers.[24]

The strike lasted four months and involved some 2,000 workers, paralysing economic transactions in the main port in defiance of repressive measures taken by the state to break it.

The outcome was disappointing in one respect, because strikers won few concessions from the administration and employers. In another respect, the achievements were impressive. Working-class leadership and heightened class consciousness created by the strike became the base from which the Zanzibar labour movement would arise. In October 1946, only a few months after it was over, the Labour Association was recognised as the first trade union in Zanzibar. It had a founding membership of 179 *wachukuzi.*

To contain such outbreaks of working-class militancy in the post-war empire, the British introduced further measures to regiment colonial unions. For example, the position of Labour Officer was introduced to the colonies. Sharon Stichter's remark that the Labour Officer in Kenya had 'the duty of fostering "responsible" African unionism', applies equally well to Zanzibar.[25] Under the 1946 Labour Decree, this role was shared by many individuals in the Zanzibar administration: District Commissioners,

Assistant District Officers, and the Welfare Officer, who also served as Registrar of Trade Unions. By 1953, a single individual had been given the sole responsibility of Labour Officer and expenditure was authorised to establish a Labour Office in the Protectorate.[26]

The Labour Officer fostered 'responsible' trade unionism by enforcing strict registration procedures and intervening to 'mediate' working-class struggles against capital. Employers were encouraged to form associations as well. How better to blunt the workers' struggle than to organise their class oppressors? The first of these was the United Agriculturalists' Organisation, formed in 1946 to represent clove plantation owners. Subsequently, employers in the coconut industry came together as the Oil and Soap Manufacturers' Association, and a Schooner Captains and Owners Association was recognised.[27] This plan to organise the propertied class proved to be a failure in the long run, however, for the only group to survive more than a few years was the Oil and Soap Manufacturers' Association which had only five members in 1961.[28]

The evidence for trade union formation during this period reveals opposing class forces in combat, each side aiming to establish the content, direction, and pace of working-class organisation. The challenge to the historian is that of identifying the initiatives of labour and capital throughout the post-war era. It is argued here that the momentum in East Africa as a whole lay with the working class in the 1946–48 period when three general strikes occurred in rapid succession. Those of 1947 in Kenya and Tanganyika foreshadowed that of 1948 in Zanzibar.

Both external and internal forces contributed to the Zanzibar General Strike which began on August 20, 1948, shutting down activity in the main port for three weeks. Economic issues unresolved by the spontaneous strike two years earlier were the principal cause. Job security was among the grievances:

> The 1948 strike arose out of insecurity of employment among dock workers. Because of availability of abundant labour in town, the African Wharfage Company, operating on the Zanzibar docks, decided to place almost all workers on daily paid service. The feeling of insecurity among workers became unbearable and they rose in a strike...[29]

The claim for a higher wage, like that won by dockworkers in Mombasa and Dar es Salaam the previous year, was not the only demand; the other was expressed in the slogan, 'Reduction in the cost of living!'

The administration tended to play down these economic grievances as the cause of the strike. Rather, it stressed the role of 'outside agitators' who stirred up workers:

A particularly unfortunate feature of this strike was the clearly evidenced inspiration by agitators not normally resident in the Protectorate. It is not clear to what extent cooperation in the general strike was voluntary or induced by threats of violence, but it was apparent that a number of African workers came out on strike for no better reason than mistaken sense of loyalty to their own race; this is a Protectorate in which the cordial relations between races has always been notable.[30]

Since the advanced level of unity reached in the strike went beyond 'agitators' and 'race', the administration's argument is both superficial and misleading. To account for the success and accomplishments of the 1948 General Strike, it is best to contrast it with the 1946 spontaneous strike. The fact that the two were initiated by dockworkers is a similarity easily overshadowed by their differences.

Whereas the earlier strike was a spontanous action by *wachukuzi*, the 1948 work stoppage was carefully planned by their union, the Labour Association. Unity was limited to one occupation in the first strike, while a much higher level of consciousness was attained in the 1948 action when working class solidarity transcended occupational boundaries to become general. Port workers were joined by domestic servants, office messengers, casual labourers and others who withdrew their labour power from employers.

There is further compelling evidence for greater unity in 1948. A personal plea by the Sultan could not persuade workers to return to their jobs and the government was unable to recruit strikebreakers.[31] Women gave their support to strikers by refusing to purchase cloth from merchants.[32] Squatters and peasants in the countryside gave their approval by refusing to send food to the central market in Stone Town, the residential area of the ruling class in the capital.[33] Finally, material gains were won by workers in 1948: the dockworker wage was increased from Sh1/30 to 2/- per day. A Price Control Committee was also created to regulate the cost of consumer goods, but prices rose in spite of it.

1949–1955

Post-war political change was echoing throughout the colonial world by the 1950s. Britain's loss of India and Pakistan in 1947, the independence of Burma and Ceylon in 1948, and China's socialist revolution in 1949, all made a strong impact on East Africans. Nationalist struggles of the early 1950s in North, North-east, and East Africa were close enough to be known firsthand by many Zanzibaris. Each of these struggles reflected the changing international order in which anti-colonial movements for national independence were the dynamic element. This was not lost on the Protectorate, for the decade of the 1950s became the dawn of the nationalist advance against British rule. Although the major parties did not appear until 1956–57, this political action tended to over-shadow independent working-class activity from 1949–55.[34]

The price of cloves was at a record high level throughout this period. That might have contributed to the lull in trade unionism, assuming workers had more to spend. But the assumption is questionable because the price of consumer goods continued to go up, and it was not until 1954 that the administration introduced the first wage increase since that won in the General Strike of 1948.[35] The minimum daily wage for unskilled labourers rose from Shs2/- to 3/30, although workers outside government employment generally received less. A more likely reason for labour inactivity was manipulation by the Zanzibar Labour Office. A broad colonial manoeuvre was underway in British East Africa whereby unions were controlled more closely so that they would be excluded from the political struggle.[36] Each was to restrict itself to narrow economic issues of a particular trade and not make attempts to federate. Department Labour Councils were formed to regulate disputes and thereby restrict workers' demands against capital. In Zanzibar, the position of Labour Officer was introduced to centralise the work done by many administrators previously. This offensive seems to have contributed to the inertia which had hit the Zanzibar labour movement by 1954, according to that year's Labour Report:

A few men who returned to the country from abroad made sporadic attempts to infuse life into the existing unions and to convert other workers to become unionists but their efforts failed on account of apathy amongst workers.[37]

Yet, the inaction was only temporary, much to the dismay of the administration. It had disappeared within two years when a new wave of activism hit the Protectorate in 1956.

1956–1958

This brief period was remarkable for the scope of organisational work which laid the foundations for trade unions and political parties. In 1956 over twenty unions sought recognition. Although only twelve were recognised by the Registrar of Trade Unions the total was three times that for the previous decade (see Appendix C). In the same year, the Zanzibar National Party (ZNP) was created as the first nationalist party, to be followed in 1957 by the launching of the Afro-Shirazi Party (ASP).

Here were the elements of a broad anti-colonial movement. What caused them to appear in this period? While party formation has received considerable attention, the forces shaping trade unionism have not been scrutinised. We have isolated for investigation five components of the resurgent workers' movement. These are the nationalist parties, individual workers, the collective working class, the colonial state, and the International Confederation of Free Trade Unions (ICFTU). Different class forces made for a complex dynamic. Nevertheless, an initial assessment will be made of the impact of each of these on the course of trade union evolution during this final decade of colonial rule.

To grasp the influence of the nationalist parties on the trade union movement, it is necessary to explain the class differences between the two bodies. A trade union has the objective of advancing a single class, that of the exploited class of workers against the exploiting class of capitalists. In contrast, a nationalist party in the colonial setting has the goal of mobilising all classes as a nation against foreign rule. Historically, trade unions were founded by propertyless, class-conscious workers, while nationalist parties were created by propertied individuals, large and small, with a bourgeois class position. Leadership of nationalist movements in Africa has been in the hands of the petty bourgeoisie. That of trade unions has fluctuated, for there are times when workers have lost control of union leadership to the petty bourgeoisie. The principal distinction between the union and party remains, however, one of class: in terms of origin, composition, aims, and leadership.

The history of the Zanzibar trade union movement during the decade 1946–56, was one in which leadership grew out of the rank and file of the working class. In this early period, the colonial administration blocked the maturation of working-class power by banning trade unions from political activity. The working class was not yet strong enough to challenge the state through independent political action on the scale required to end colonial rule. When the political offensive broke out and matured in the 1950s, therefore, it was led by nationalist parties with petty-bourgeois leadership.

The ZNP was founded by petty-bourgeois Arabs and Shirazi, while the ASP had petty-bourgeois African leadership of mainland origin. Both parties needed the support of peasants and workers. To the extent that the latter were already organised, a firm tie was sought with the union. When workers were unorganised, parties tried to bring them together.

Ties between parties and unions tended to develop along ethnic lines. The ASP had greater success where workers from the mainland predominated. Totalling perhaps a quarter of the Protectorate population, they were a sizeable portion of the wage labour force in Zanzibar Town and the main port. This is reflected in the names of some of the unions which were allied with the ASP by 1959: the Labour Association, Dock Workers' Union, Zanzibar Seamen's Union, Boat Builders' Union, Transport and Allied Workers' Union, and the Building and Construction Workers' Union.

The ZNP used its possession of property to recruit as well. Ownership of dhows enabled it to influence dhow crews and the Maritime and Allied Workers' Union, while land ownership enabled it to use employment as a leverage to sway workers in the clove and coconut industries. These attempts to forge alliances between parties and unions created divisions in the labour movement as well, for broad class unity was ruled out as each party bid for worker loyalty.

The process of trade union formation in Tanganyika showed similarities and differences with that in Zanzibar. Following a lull in the working class movement from 1950–53, 'during which trade union activity was at its lowest ebb', there was a burst of trade unionism immediately following the founding of TANU in 1954.[38] Where TANU was banned, as in Mwanza, unions were formed in its absence by party members.[39] Created along occupational lines, they were brought together in 1955 by 'white collar' leadership as the Tanganyika Federation of Labour which was the organised working class component of the mass nationalist party. The absence of an organised opposition to TANU made for early party-union unity on the mainland. A strong alliance between parties and unions did not crystallise until 1960 in Zanzibar.

Additional research is required to shed light on the second formative force which is the contribution by individuals to the development of the workers' movement in the Protectorate. The activity of some persons is known, but that of others remains to be discovered. Jamal Ramadhani Nasib and Sheikh Manga Said Kharusi, for example, were early trade union organisers. They both returned to Zanzibar in the mid-1950s with organisational experience acquired abroad. Soon after they reappeared in the Protectorate they began to edit the first labour newspaper, *The Voice of the Workers*. In 1956, Nasib organised the Agricultural Workers' Union, while Kharusi formed the Unguja & Pemba Transport Workers' Union. Administrative opposition caused both to be shut down the following year. Nevertheless, they were persistent; by 1959 Nasib had created the Agricultural & Allied Workers' Union, and Kharusi the Transport & Allied Workers' Union. Both men were active in forming the first trade union federation in 1957, an initiative rejected by the administration (see Appendix B). Undaunted, they proposed it again the following year when it was rejected once more. These were nevertheless key struggles that prepared the ground for ultimate recognition of the Zanzibar and Pemba Federation of Labour (ZPFL) in 1959.

Pioneering work by advanced workers must be acknowledged, but caution must be exercised to avoid isolating them from the collective in which they worked. Leaders were the medium through which the rank and file expressed a unified outlook. It was this class action which was the third force moulding the trade union movement in this period. There were many means of collective expression. For example, petitions were submitted to the administration and other bodies. One such appeal in Zanzibar was the list of grievances submitted by 'members of Union experience' to a visiting British TUC delegation in 1957 (see Appendix A). It was a careful inventory of workplace abuses and a strong assertion of workers' rights which reflected heightened awareness of class interests.

Petitions presented in an orderly and peaceful manner often gave way to more direct action. Numerous disputes, or workers' grievances, were taken for arbitration at the Labour Office: 329 in 1956, 292 in 1957, and 244 in 1958.[40] In the rural sector, eviction of plantation squatters following the June 1957 elections led to the boycott as an effective tool for change, although this was essentially a party, rather than worker, initiative by the ASP. Workers joined other classes to boycott stores and bus companies owned by ZNP supporters. Party mobilisation of the working class was crucial for the success of these boycotts.

The colonial state, the fourth force influencing trade union development, used a number of tactics to try and arrest the workers' movement. One of the most effective was to deny or cancel union registration. Technical excuses were common: five of the more militant unions were cancelled in 1957 because they had 'failed to submit the audited annual accounts' for the previous year.[41] A more important reason for cancellation was that officials in at least two unions were champions of federation.[42] The façade of technicalities was blown away in the annual Labour Report that year:

> When the registration of some Unions, whose leadership happened to be the principal advocates for the federation of small Unions, was cancelled, the campaign for closer alliance which was not without its potential dangers came to an end.[43]

Beyond these formative forces internal to the Protectorate, the International Confederation of Free Trade Unions (ICFTU) influenced the workers' movement in Zanzibar. A brief account of its origin will clarify why it reached out to colonial trade unions.

A World Federation of Trade Unions (WFTU) whose members included the USA and USSR, as well as the European colonial powers and their possessions, had been founded immediately after World War II. One of its objectives was to create an international framework for trade union development. Unity soon broke down. The reason, according to Ioan Davies' analysis of international trade unionism, was because 'the Americans were less concerned to develop a labour movement than to recruit troops for an anti-communist crusade.'[44] Thus the United States led an exodus of trade unions from the WFTU in 1949 and with CIA assistance set up the ICFTU as a rival body.[45]

To understand fully the purpose of the ICFTU, it must be recalled that the European allies of the USA suffered staggering losses in World War II. They were replaced at the peak of the world capitalist structure by the North American giant which coveted the wealth of their colonies. But capitalist supremacy in the post-war world faced a serious challenge from socialism which was proving to be resilient and strong. Much to the dismay of the West, the Soviet Union was not defeated by the Nazis in World War II, and yet another large socialist state was created in China by the 1949 Revolution. To gain access to the colonies, the United States had to draw them away from its allies, and prevent them from taking the socialist path to freedom. To reach that goal the ICFTU had a dual role in US foreign policy: it was to coax the colonial trade unions out from under their metropolitan masters, and keep them isolated from the working class ideologies of Marxism and socialism.

The relatively progressive position of the ICFTU *vis-à-vis* the colonial powers on the question of colonial freedom helped to attain the first objective. Support was expressed for self-determination. In its 1952 'General Declaration on Non-Self Governing Territories', the ICFTU proclaimed:

> Free trade unionism is by its very essence opposed to all forms of oppression. It condemns colonialism. It proclaims the right of all peoples to self-government.... The role of the ICFTU will be to propose effective measures which will lead to rapid self-government....[46]

This argument appealed to both the trade unions and the independence movements of which they were a component. Of course there were objections from the colonial powers and there was tension between them and the USA on this issue, but they deferred for two reasons. The Western European governments were dependent on US capital for post-war recovery and were fearful of the appeal of socialism to the colonised.

The ICFTU pursued the second objective of isolating the colonised from socialism by supporting and financing moderate organisers and trade unions who would not question capitalism as the basis for the post-colonial order. The organiser in East Africa who became the ICFTU 'man on the spot' was Tom Mboya. Progressive trade union leadership was opposed wherever it appeared. Feared by the ICFTU were Pan-African bodies such as the All-African Trade Union Federation, and the African Trade Union Confederation which were unreliable in the anti-communist crusade.[47]

By the late 1950s, when the CIA had become heavily involved in its activities, the ICFTU was active in all British East African possessions.[48] An ICFTU publication claims it was instrumental in introducing unions to Zanzibar in this period:

> Impetus to trade union organisation (in Zanzibar) was given by a visit of free trade union representatives in 1956 and ten unions were registered in that year.[49]

Trade union federations in Kenya, Tanganyika and Uganda affiliated with the ICFTU, and the ZPFL had joined it by November 1959. However, it was not long before the ICFTU came to be seen differently and the ZPFL voted at its general convention in July 1962 to disaffiliate.[50] Trade union federations in Tanzania, Uganda and Kenya followed the ZPFL and withdrew by the mid-1960s.

1959–1963

A high point in workers' protest and extra-parliamentary forms of struggle was reached in Zanzibar by 1960–61. Impressive labour militancy in 1960 led to strikes in many industries as workers advanced demands pertaining to wages, overtime, leave, and improved work conditions. The following year, dhow workers staged a strike of 84 days, the longest in Zanzibar's history, and ended it successfully by achieving practically all of their demands.[51] The 1961 election results, as well as a poor clove and coconut harvest, pushed labour militancy to its zenith and hastened the end of the colonial order: the *Vita vya Mawe* Riots, organised by competing factions of the nationalist parties, included widespread rural squatter violence against landlords, and strike activity by urban workers.

It was in this period that trade union federation was realised by the working class. Opposed by the state when it was first proposed in 1957, the administration had to acknowledge the growing pressure for federation the following year:

> There was a definite revival of enthusiasm in trade unionism and three new unions were formed [in 1958]. Even some cancelled unions reorganised themselves with a view to re-registration. A notable feature in the trade union movement was the combination of seven of the most progressive unions in matters of policy, and there was evidence of these unions forming themselves into a federation.[52]

The federation was rejected on the argument that it functioned illegally according to the 1958 Trade Union Decree.

Trade union federation became a reality in 1959 with the formation of the Zanzibar and Pemba Federation of Labour (ZPFL). Although the majority of its unions tended to be aligned with the ASP, there were differences within the rank and file and leadership that tended to reflect party lines. This led to an open split at the time of the 1960 Constitution Commission headed by Sir Hilary Blood. A memo had been submitted to it by the ZPFL demanding 'Self-Government Now', and 'Immediate *Uhuru*', which was consistent with the position of the ZNP. But it was withdrawn under ASP pressure. The ZPFL position, as a result, was to support *uhuru* by stages, which was consistent with the ASP platform. Those in the ZPFL who continued to demand immediate independence withdrew and formed the Federation of Progressive Trade Unions (FPTU).[53] The majority of workers and unions, however, remained in the ZPFL. By 1962, its membership of approximately 10,000, organised into 13 unions, was roughly five times greater than that of the five affiliates of the FPTU (see Appendix D).[54]

The advance from independent to federated trade unions both unified and split the labour movement. It was not long, however, before a more profound level of working-class unity was reached in 1963. The formation of the Umma Party shortly before the July elections caused the leadership of the FPTU to defect from the ZNP to it. The Umma-ASP alliance after the elections then drew together the FPTU and ZPFL leadership as the National Labour Committee. It worked closely with the All Zanzibar Journalist Organisation to build a formidable anti-government front. It was this unity that made the organised working class a vital force in the final stage of colonial rule and laid the basis for a single Federation of Revolutionary Trade Unions shortly thereafter.

Notes

1. Great Britain, Colonial Office, *Annual Report on Zanzibar Protectorate, 1927*, London, HMSO, 1928, p. 15.
2. *Ibid.*
3. Michael Lofchie, *Zanzibar: Background to Revolution*, Princeton, Princeton University Press, 1965, p. 61.
4. J.W. Tritton in Memorandum, 26 March 1901, Mombasa, opposed Sir Lloyd Mathews' proposed scheme of recruiting labour from the mainland, arguing that the mainlanders would take it as disguised slavery and would oppose colonialism.
5. Zanzibar Protectorate, *Labour Report for the Year 1955*, Zanzibar, Government Printer, 1956, p. 4. (Hereafter, all references to this annual publication will be abbreviated as, for example, *Labour Report 1955*.)
6. F.B. Wilson, 'Notes on Peasant Agriculture and Industries in Zanzibar Island', unpublished monograph, 1939, p. 12. Wilson records that squatters were ex-slaves and their descendants were joined by immigrant labourers from the mainland who came to work on the plantations.
7. *Labour Report 1954*, p. 7.
8. *Labour Report 1948*, p. 8.
9. *Labour Report 1958*, p. 8.
10. *Labour Report 1955*, p. 6.
11. *Labour Report 1949*, p. 7.
12. John Iliffe, 'The Creation of Group Consciousness among the Dockworkers of Dar es Salaam 1929–1950', in Richard Sandbrook and Robin Cohen, eds, *The Development of an African Working Class*, London, Longman, 1975, p. 50.
13. Ioan Davies, *African Trade Unions*, Harmondsworth, Penguin, 1966, p. 38.
14. Jean Meynaud and Anisse Salah Bey, *Trade Unionism in Africa: a Study of its Growth and Orientation*, London, Methuen, 1967, p. 26.
15. *Ibid.*
16. Davies, *op. cit.*, p. 42.
17. John Iliffe, *op. cit.*, pp. 55–7, and Makhan Singh, *History of Kenya's Trade Union Movement to 1952*, Nairobi, East African Publishing House, 1969, Chap. 10.
18. Davies, *op. cit.*, pp. 38–9.
19. *Ibid.*
20. Meynaud and Salah Bey, *op. cit.*, p. 22.
21. Davies, *op. cit.*, p. 40.
22. Mahmoud Hemeid Jabir, 'The Plantation Economy during the Protectorate Period in Zanzibar (1890–1964)', M.A. dissertation, University of Dar es Salaam, 1977, p. 192.
23. *Labour Report 1946*, p. 2.
24. *Ibid.*
25. Sharon Stichter, 'Trade Unionism in Kenya, 1947-1952: the Militant Phase', in P.C.W. Gutkind, R. Cohen, and J. Copans, eds, *African Labour History*, Beverly Hills, Sage, 1978, p. 159.
26. *Labour Report 1953*, p. 2.
27. Jabir, *op. cit.*, p. 193; and *Labour Report 1950*, p. 18.

28. *Labour Reports 1960 & 1961*, pp. 5, 25.
29. Jabir, *op. cit.*, p. 195.
30. *Labour Report 1948*, p. 3.
31. Anthony Clayton, 'The General Strike in Zanzibar, 1948', *Journal of African History*, XVII, 3 (1976), pp. 427–429.
32. *Ibid.*, p. 431.
33. Jabir, *op. cit.*, p. 196.
34. For an account of these early years of the nationalist movement see Lofchie, *op. cit.*, Chapters 5 & 6.
35. See *Labour Reports* for 1948 through 1955 for statistics on price of consumer goods.
36. See Davies, *op. cit.*, p. 194; and Stichter, *op. cit.*, p. 160.
37. *Labour Report 1954*, p. 3.
38. Issa G. Shivji, 'Working Class Struggles and Organisation in Tanzania, 1939–1975', *Mawazo*, Vol. 5, No. 2, December 1983, pp. 8–10.
39. *Ibid.*
40. *Labour Report 1956*, p. 25; *Labour Report 1958*, p. 27.
41. *Labour Report 1957*, p. 26.
42. The two unions were the Agricultural Workers' Union and the Unguja and Pemba Transport Workers' Union.
43. *Labour Report 1957*, p. 3.
44. Davies, *op. cit.*, p. 189.
45. 'The International Confederation of Free Trade Unions (ICFTU): Labour centre set up and controlled by the CIA to oppose the World Federation of Trade Unions (WFTU)'. Philip Agee, *Inside the Company: CIA Diary*, New York, Stonehill Publishing Company, 1975, p. 611. Agee was a CIA secret operations officer for twelve years. Also see Barry Cohen, 'The CIA and African Trade Unions', in Ellen Ray, *et al.*, *Dirty Work 2: The CIA in Africa*, Secaucus, New Jersey, Lyle Stuart Inc., 1979, and Ronald Radosh, *American Labor and United States Foreign Policy*, New York, Vintage, 1969.
46. See Document 4 in Documentary Appendix to Meynaud and Bey, *op. cit.*, pp. 189–91.
47. See Meynaud and Bey, *op. cit.*, and Davies, *op. cit.*, for accounts of the ICFTU opposition to Pan African trade unions.
48. Davies, *op. cit.*, p. 201; see Shivji, *op. cit.*, for ICFTU in Tanganyika.
49. Julius Braunthal and A.J. Forrest, eds, *Yearbook of the International Free Trade Union Movement, Vol. 2, 1961–1962*, Lincolns-Prager International Yearbook (under the auspices of the ICFTU), 1963, p. 393.
50. United States Department of Labor, Bureau of Labor Statistics, *Directory of Labor Organizations: Africa*, Washington DC, US Gov't Printing Office, 1962.
51. Information supplied by Mr Ahmed A. Quallatein, former FPTU Committee Member and editor of its publications, *Kibarua* (daily), and *Worker* (weekly).
52. *Labour Report 1958*, p. 4.
53. Information supplied by Mr Ahmed A. Quallatein.
54. United States Department of Labor, Bureau of Labor Statistics, *op. cit.*, p. 49.1.

Appendix A

Zanzibar
11.2.57

The Visiting Members of the Trade Union Congress,
The Labour Officer, Zanzibar.

Sir,
   We beg to submit the following grievances with members of Union experience in their service. We hope these grievances will be adjusted correctly:

1. There is no equal pay for equal work.
2. The standard of living of the workers is very low.
3. Therefore expatriate workers from overseas get better pay and more consideration for the same type of work.
4. There is no arrangement for the housing or housing guarantees for the number of employees. Workers of higher grade receive better privilege inspite the heavy salaries they draw. The underpaid workers get no such facilities.
5. No children under fifteen years of age should be allowed to work.
6. The education and health facilities for the children of workers should be encouraged.
7. There is no arrangement for the pension both to daily workers and workers employed in the mercantile companies.
8. There is no wearing of shoes or any other garments for the workers such as sweepers and those working in gas station and Electricity Department.
9. We do not know why we are being discouraged in amalgamating with overseas Trade Unions.
10. That there is no written agreements between the workers and the employers in all services, nearly, outside the government.
11. The members of Trade Unions here are victimised when they know that they associate with Trade Unions.
12. That there are some members who were sacked from service and we beg that these should be reinstated.
13. As the workers receive lower salaries, canteen should be opened to relieve this great need.
14. Workers who put more than 8 hours daily should be paid overtime allowance.

We beg to remain, Sirs,

Class Formation

Appendix B

c/o Welfare Office
P.O. Box 344
ZANZIBAR
17th May 1957

Sir,

Proposed Zanzibar Federation of Trade Unions

1. I have the honour to refer to your letter dated 9th April 1957, which has been delivered by hand by Sheikh Manga Said Kharusi on 8th May 1957.
2. You state in your para 3(a) that you are enclosing a copy of the minute of the General Meeting, authorizing application for the registration of a Zanzibar Federation of Trade Unions, but no copy of the minute was enclosed. A list of names of members cannot be accepted as a clear record of the decision of the meeting and it is presumed that no reliable record is available.
3. In your para 3(b) you write 'Also enclosed'. From this I presume that I was intended to understand that a copy of the constitution of the proposed Federation was enclosed. None was in fact enclosed and I must therefore presume that no constitution for the proposed Federation has in fact been examined and approved by a General Meeting of your Trade Union.
4. I cannot consider the application of your Trade Union without your compliance with all of the requirements of para 3 of my letter of 3rd April 1957 and I would therefore suggest that if you wish to proceed further in this matter that you should convene a General Meeting of your Trade Union. Should you wish to invite the Labour Officer to be present or represented at this meeting I have no doubt that he would be able to give you every assistance in complying with my requirements.
5. I should however inform you that I am unable to entertain your Trade Union's application for registration of a Federation of Trade Unions until such time as your Trade Union has complied with all requirements of the Trade Union Decree 1941. In this connecton I would invite attention to your failure to submit audited annual accounts for the year 1956 before 31st January 1957 and to the fact that the accounts have still not been presented to me fully vouchered.

I have the honour to be,
Sir,
(signed) Your obedient servant.
Registrar of Trade Unions

The Secretary,
Agricultural Workers' Union,
PO Box No. 389, ZANZIBAR.

Appendix C

Trade Unions Registered in Zanzibar, 1946–61[1]

Name of Trade Union	Registered	Maximum No. Members
Labour Association	1946–	700 (1956)
Zanzibar Carpenters Association	1946 only	36 (1946)
European Servants Union/		
(1955) Domestic Workers' Union/	1947–1960	253 (1947)
(1959) Zanzibar Domestic Workers' Union	1947–1957	80 (1955)
Shop Assistants Association	1949–	261 (1958)
Zanzibar Seamen's Union	1952–1955	32 (1955)
Zanzibar Port Checkers Union	1955–1961	40 (1957)
Gold & Silver Smith Workers' Union/		
(1961) Z&P Commercial, Industrial and Allied Workers' Union[3]	1956–1957	430 (1956)
Unguja & Pemba Transport Workers' Union	1956–1957	150 (1956)
Agricultural Workers' Union	1956–1957	60 (1956)
Bakery Workers' Union	1956–1959	208 (1957)
Oil Factory Workers' Union		
Chake PWD Workers' Union/		
(1956) Pemba PWD Workers' Union	1956–	1,219 (1960)
Dock Workers' Union/		
(1959) Z&P Dock Workers' & Stevedores' Union	1956–	654 (1960)
Medical Workers' Union/		
(1961) Government Workers' Union[2]	1956–1961	684 (1959)
Office Messengers' Union/		
(1961) Government Workers' Union[2]	1956–1961	96 (1958)

Appendix C *continued*

Name of Trade Union	Registered	Maximum No. Members
Tailors' Union	1956–1959	39 (1957)
Carpenters' Union	1956–1959	107 (1958)
Boat Builders' Union	1956–	45 (1961)
Building & Construction Workers' Union/ (1959) Z&P Building & Construction Workers' Union/ (1961) Z&P Commercial, Industrial & Allied Workers' Union[3]	1956–1961	1,020 (1959)
Dairy Workers' Union	1957 only	140 (1957)
Printing Press Workers' Union/ (1961) Z&P Commercial, Industrial & Allied Workers' Union[3]	1957–1961	35 (1957)
Painters' Union	1958–1959	40 (1958)
Coconut Huskers' Union/ (1959) Coconut Huskers' & Allied Workers' Union/ (1961) Z&P Commercial, Industrial & Allied Workers' Union[3]	1958–1961	159 (1959)
Zanzibar Skippers' Union	1958–1959	28 (1958)
Transport & Allied Workers' Union	1959–	222 (1961)
Agricultural & Allied Workers' Union	1959–	1,529 (1961)
Zanzibar Government Agricultural Staff Union	1959–	73 (1960)
Zanzibar PWD Workers' Union/ (1960) Government Workers' Union[2]	1960–	2,694 (1961)
Government Teachers' Union	1960–	436 (1961)
Maritime & Allied Workers' Union	1960–	422 (1961)
Pemba Electricity Board Workers' Union	1960–	32 (1960)
Zanzibar and Pemba Commercial, Industrial & Allied Workers' Union[3]	1961–	1,220 (1961)

Appendix C *continued*

Name of Trade Union	Registered	Maximum No. Members
Zanzibar Electricity Board Workers' Union	1961 –	131 (1961)
Masonry, Wood & Allied Workers' Union	1961 –	84 (1961)
Cable & Wireless Zanzibar Staff Union	1961 –	67 (1961)
Pemba Union of Public Employees	1961 –	135 (1961)
Health Workers' Union	1961 –	62 (1961)
Metal, Engineering & Allied Workers' Union	1961 –	21 (1961)
Hotel, Domestic & Allied Workers' Union	1961 –	36 (1961)
Printing Press & Allied Workers' Union	1961 –	42 (1961)

1. Unions were registered beyond 1961 unless a date is given for registration refused or cancelled. A change in original union name is indicated by a slash, date of change, and new name.
2. Zanzibar PWD Workers' Union changes name to Government Workers' Union immediately after registration in 1960. The Medical Workers' Union, and the Office Messengers' Union merged with it within a year.
3. Zanzibar and Pemba Commercial, Industrial and Allied Workers' Union formed by merger of Z&P Building and Construction Workers' Union; Coconut Huskers' and Allied Workers' Union; Gold & Silver Smith Workers' Union; and Printing Press Workers' Union.

217

Appendix D

Labour Federations & Independent Unions, 1962

Zanzibar and Pemba Federation of Labour (ZPFL) Affiliates

Name*	President	Maximum No. Members
Labour Association (1946)	Kesi Juma Hassan	556 (1960)
Zanzibar Seamen's Union (1949)	Kombo Ahmed Mwinyjuma	171 (1961)
Pemba PWD Workers' Union (1956)	Ahmed Omar Skekh	482 (1961)
Z&P Dockworkers' & Stevedores' Union (1956)	Ismail Saleh Ismail	654 (1962)
Boat Builders' Union (1956)	Suleiman Sena Farijala	45 (1961)
Transport & Allied Workers' Union (1959)	Ramadhan Kirebu Makungu	228 (1962)
Z&P Government Workers' Union (1960)	Chum Omar Suleiman	6,000 (1962)
Z&P Commercial, Industrial & Allied Workers' Union (1961)	Abdi Baraka Mchenga	2,200 (1962)
Z&P Clove Growers Association Workers' Union (1962)	Hassan Juma Hassan	200 (1962)

Federation of Progressive Trade Unions (FPTU) Affiliates

Name	President	Maximum No. Members
Agricultural & Allied Workers' Union (1959)	Mabrouk Mbarak Hassan	1,529 (1961)
Maritime & Allied Workers' Union (1960)	Saleh Hashim Saleh	422 (1961)
Masonry, Wood & Allied Workers' Union (1961)	Suleiman M. Suleiman	84 (1961)
Metal, Engineering & Allied Workers' Union (1961)	Ashur Ahmed Suleiman	21 (1961)
Hotel, Domestic & Allied Workers' Union (1961)	Tajiri Shafi Abdulla	36 (1961)

Appendix D *continued*

Independent Unions

Name	President	Maximum No. Members
Zanzibar Government Agricultural Staff Union (1959)	Yusuf Mzee Yusuf	71 (1961)
Government Teachers' Union (1960)	Juma Himidi Juma	436 (1961)
Pemba Electricity Board Workers' Union (1960)	Abdulla Mohamed Rashid	19 (1961)
Zanzibar Electricity Board Workers' Union (1960)	Ali Yusuf Ali	131 (1961)
Cable & Wireless Zanzibar Staff Union (1961)	Ferdoon M. Mehta	67 (1961)
Pemba Union of Public Employees (1961)	Fakih Thabit Ahmed	135 (1961)
Health Workers' Union (1961)	Tahir Rashid Haji	62 (1961)
Printing Press & Allied Workers' Union (1961)	Salim Abdulla Khamis	42 (1961)

* Union name followed by year it was formed. First date of registration/recognition may be later.

Eight

The 1964 Revolution: Lumpen or Vanguard?

A.M. BABU[1]

The Zanzibar Revolution of January 12, 1964 took Africa by storm and shook the entire imperialist camp as a devastating blow to their well-planned post-colonial strategy for East Africa. The Revolution at once heralded a new era in African politics with far-reaching possibilities. It had the potential of the single spark that starts a prairie fire.

Both friends and foes were stunned by the efficacy of the event, the proficiency that had sustained it for as long as it lasted, and the resolute firmness of the revolutionaries themselves which inspired the people of the two tiny islands to take a bold stand against imperialist arrogance and bullying tactics. Moreover, it inspired the masses of the oppressed not only in East and Central Africa but practically throughout Africa and beyond, who regarded the Zanzibar Revolution as the beginning of their own revolution.

The Revolution was the culmination of a people's struggle against more than two centuries of aggression and oppression by foreigners, by slave traders, by Omani colonialism, and by seventy years of British colonialism. This struggle sometimes expressed itself positively and sometimes negatively depending on the prevailing leadership. The only consistent element throughout all those years was the people's perseverance and resolute determination to achieve a genuinely free society — free from the shackles of slavery, of feudal landlordism and of colonial humiliation.

This struggle expressed itself negatively, as we shall see, when it had a weak and reactionary leadership which created divisions among the people to the advantage of oppressive forces. On the other hand, it expressed itself positively when it was headed by

220

progressive and revolutionary leadership which strove to unite the people in a solid front against oppression. These ups and downs, advances and retreats, are the substance of the political evolution that culminated dramatically in the Revolution.

Vita vya Ngombe

For the purpose of this concluding chapter it is not necessary to trace the course of the struggle over the years as this is discussed elsewhere. It will be enough to capture the spirit of modern political struggle in Zanzibar by locating its 'beginning' with what one might call the 'Anthrax Revolt', or *Vita vya Ngombe* (Cattle Riot) of 1951.[2] This uprising first shattered the colonialists' self-confidence, marked the beginning of mass organisation and ushered in the era of 'party politics'. More importantly, it initiated the revolutionary alliance of workers, peasants and revolutionary petty bourgeoisie which made Zanzibar's political experience so unique in East Africa.

Vita vya Ngombe was epoch-making because for the first time the peasants of Unguja rose in revolt against the British administration; it was a move which, also for the first time, took a definite class character overriding all the ethnic differentiations which were being nurtured by colonialism. The consequences of this revolt have had a decisive impact on the body politic of the country in a way that no other event prior to it ever had. It is thus important to understand the circumstances that led to it and its after-effects.

The peasants revolted in opposition to a government project to inoculate all the country's cattle against rinderpest, anthrax, and foot and mouth disease. Word got around that the colonialists' real objective was not to save the cattle but to kill them off at a time when the price of cattle was at its highest peak due to the 'Korean boom'. From 1950 onward this boom had sent the price of cloves, the country's main export crop, soaring to unprecedented levels. The price of one hundred pounds of cloves in 1948–49 before the Korean War was only Shs64/-; it soared to more than Shs900/- in 1952–53.[3] This brought a lot of prosperity to the country and the price of cattle went up accordingly. A threat to the survival of the peasants' cattle, therefore, was a real threat to their own standard of living.

However, the revolt was only the last straw. Long before this incident the peasants were becoming restless as a result of colonial oppression and arbitrary rule which destabilised their lives. They did not understand the cause of their frustration and the instability of their earnings. They were not well organised nor did they have a formal leadership that could identify and articulate their smouldering discontent. But suddenly the perceived collective threat brought them together; they provided their own leadership and went into action.

As usual when confronted with historically new situations, the colonialists tended to panic and resort to retaliatory measures, often violently. Accordingly, when the revolt erupted the colonialists employed draconian measures to suppress it, resulting in several deaths and a number of peasant leaders being taken into custody.

In retaliation, the peasants decided to storm the central prison at Kiinua Miguu to secure the release of their leaders. They broke in, overpowered the guards and took away their leaders. When the revolt was subsequently suppressed by massive use of force, the leaders were rearrested, charged with 'inciting riot' and sentenced to imprisonment. They immediately became martyrs and authentic leaders of the ensuing peasant movement.

Prominent among these leaders were Maalim Zaidi, Miraj Shaalab, Haji Husein and others. As soon as they were released, following massive popular pressure, they decided to organise a political movement for independence as the only permanent solution to their problems.

Although this was not the first peasant movement on such a massive scale, it was the first out-and-out anti-colonial political movement. A few years earlier there was another peasant movement known as 'Ittihadil Watany', National Unity Movement. While it took the country by storm, its objectives were purely economic: a cooperative movement intended to get rid of the middlemen. In spite of its early vigour, it died out only a few years later largely because the urban petty bourgeoisie ignored it and did not provide it with leadership.

The new movement was not only political; it was fighting foreign occupation as well, and was therefore immediately embraced by the urban petty bourgoisie who saw in it the potential for their own liberation. The peasant leaders decided to call their movement 'Hizbul Watan li Riaia Sultan', the 'National Party of the Sultan's Subjects'. The emphasis on the 'Sultan's subjects' was significant. It was the only political categorisation which could unite the hitherto ethnically divided population, which was the primary aim of these awakened peasants in their long struggle for independence. The second reason for the emphasis on 'subjects' was to give the movement a much wider appeal, embracing Pemba Island as well as the people of the Kenya coast who were then officially categorised as the Sultan's subjects.[4] The third objective was to distinguish

222

between themselves and the immigrants from the mainland who identified politically with Tanganyika, at that time a rather alien country to many Zanzibaris.

Fourthly, a lot of the peasants, rightly or wrongly, genuinely were for the monarchy and saw nothing wrong in being ruled by the Sultan. In fact there are several stories in Zanziba. among the peasants which claim that it was their forefathers who travelled to Oman to seek the assistance of the Sultan in their struggle against Portuguese colonialism. The Omanis had earlier fought and defeated the Portuguese in Muscat, and this victory was widely celebrated on the East African coast where the Portuguese still reigned supreme. Partly for this reason and also because the 'royal family' had already ceased to be purely Arab, having become part-Swahili through years of intermarriage, these peasants did not consider the Sultan to be alien, and they took him and his family to be 'their own'. To the average peasant, therefore, the grandiose name of 'Party of National Unity of the Sultan's Subjects' did not sound at all awkward and many were quite proud to be identified as such.[5]

To the sophisticated urban petty bourgeoisie, however, any identity with the royal family seemed both embarrassing and wrong. They liked the idea of national unity but they did not approve of associating it with the monarchy. So they suggested to the peasants' leaders the more politically acceptable name of the Zanzibar Nationalist Party (ZNP), which then became the official name of the party until its dissolution after the 1964 Revolution.

A side-line development, but equally significant and arising directly from *Vita vya Ngombe* was the involvement of the radical young members of the Arab Association in the nascent independence struggle. The official weekly paper of the Association, *Al-Falaq* (The Dawn) came out strongly on the side of the peasants' uprising and accused the British colonialists of barbarism and brutality. In 1954 the British reacted to strong nationalist demands by charging the paper, its editor Ahmed Lemky, and the entire central committee of the Association with sedition.

Lemky came from the landlord class. But his education in Egypt where he was imprisoned for political activities (he is said to have been in prison with the then rebel Anwar Sadat) and his experience in London turned him into a radical nationalist and an advocate of Zanzibar independence.[6]

This trial for sedition marked a turning point in Zanzibar politics. It radicalised the hitherto conservative Arab Association which decided to boycott all links with the colonial government. They withdrew all their representatives from the Legislative Council, and when one of them defied the boycott he was immediately assassinated.[7]

At this time every citizen was identified with an ethnic association. There were about 23 such associations. Thus the Arab Association was composed of those who claimed their origin from Oman, while other Arabs, mostly from southern Yemen originally, had their own separate association with their own leadership. Ethnic distinctions thus became part of the popular consciousness which was bound to influence the country's politics.

Most of the leaders of the Arab Association came from the landlord class, although rank and file members included petty landowners, government clerks, school teachers, the working class, peasants, and petty-bourgeois intellectuals. The vast majority of them had long ago ceased to be Arabs. Most of these 'Arabs' descended from ex-slave mothers or grandmothers. After generations of intermarriage it was impossible to make out the difference between what passed for an Arab and those referred to as Africans.

Thus over time ethnic distinctions became irrelevant and many urban petty-bourgeois intellectuals refused to be identified by ethnic tags. They preferred to refer to themselves simply as Zanzibaris. Some organised themselves into a 'Zanzibar Association' headed by Maalim Zam-Ali Abbas; and there was a weekly called *Mzanzibari*, edited by one Khalil.

But none of these efforts lasted long enough to attract a popular following, partly because the intellectuals who led them did not reflect the aspirations of any social class; they expressed their own individual visions or wishful thinking. Secondly, they did not have any coherent political or economic policy and their notions of Zanzibari nationalism were mostly abstract. They made no effort to start any form of serious organisation such as study groups, discussion circles or actual political parties. Moreover, they did not attempt to raise the question of colonialism or imperialism; they only quarrelled with some of the outrageous manifestations of colonialism which to them appeared unjust.

However, although these pioneers of Zanzibar nationalism did not enjoy a popular mass following, they nevertheless succeeded in implanting in the minds of the emerging educated stratum the notions of nationalism and the hopelessness of attempting to achieve anything through ethnic organisations and pressure groups. A more lasting solution, they argued, lay in the entire people of Zanzibar coming together as one and demanding their rights from that united position.

Thus when the Anthrax Revolt erupted with its anti-colonial stance, it immediately enjoyed the support of the urban petty bourgeoisie, the radical members of the Arab Association, the urban working people and urban poor, the small craftsmen and so on.

The most outstanding of these Arab radicals was Ali Muhsin who later became the leader of the ZNP. The influx of intellectuals into the peasant movement was welcomed. The peasants needed the intellectuals to articulate their frustrations as well as their aspirations. On the other hand, the intellectuals needed the peasants to provide them with a mass social base, which now also included the tiny but emerging proletariat and the vast lumpen proletariat.

This was the earliest social composition of the Zanzibar Nationalist Party; it contained all the necessary ingredients for a full-blooded national liberation movement.

Zama za Siasa [8]

The British colonialists soon realised that a new political force with dangerous potential to eliminate colonial rule had emerged. The ZNP at once demanded universal adult suffrage, a new constitution committing the British government to early independence for Zanzibar, and the immediate abolition of all racial or ethnic representation.

Typically, the colonialists responded by first opposing the whole idea of independence on the ground that the country was not yet ready for it; and secondly by actively trying to create an opposition to these demands from local stooges, or better still, from dissident elements with some national credibility.

To create a favourable atmosphere for this kind of game, the colonialists got busy invoking all sorts of bogies against the new movement. To the Arab landowners they depicted the movement as a direct threat to their traditional privileges and to their position in the economy. To the Indian merchants they said the movement was essentially anti-Indian, designed to get rid of them as soon as the British left. To the African and Shirazi petty bourgeoisie they presented the movement as a skilful Arab 'front' organisation designed to get rid of the British and expose the masses of the Africans to the mercy of the Arabs. Were not the British the real protectors of the Africans? Who abolished the slave trade? Did they want slavery back?

It was in this atmosphere that the Afro-Shirazi Party (ASP) was created in 1957 out of the merger of the African Association and the Shirazi Association. The organisation was a reaction to the peasant anti-colonial movement; its principal objective was to oppose the struggle for immediate independence. Objectively,

225

therefore, it became aligned to British colonial rule.[9]

The creation of the ASP, however, could not subdue the escalating movement towards independence which was now gaining unprecedented mass support. As a result the British had to concede to the demand for constitutional reform by appointing a Constitutional Commission headed by Sir Hilary Blood which later recommended the introduction of universal adult suffrage and a form of parliamentary system. Even at this stage, in its memorandum to the Commission, the ASP continued to oppose immediate independence, arguing that the country was not yet ready for it.[10]

The response of the ZNP to the position of the ASP also demonstrated its own narrow nationalism. It took Karume to court on the ground that he was not an authentic Zanzibar citizen. This act immediately turned Karume into a martyr in the hands of Arab oppressors, and helped to rally popular support behind him, especially among the people of mainland origin who felt threatened by this new nationalistic zeal.[11] Vast sums of money were collected for his defence at mass meetings intended for the purpose. Either by accident or design, the verdict came just before the election in which Karume was one of the candidates. He won the case and the euphoria that followed carried him to an overwhelming electoral victory which established him as a national leader in spite of his position on the question of independence. His party's slogan during and after the election campaign was *'Uhuru, Zuia'*, – 'Stop the Move to Independence'.[12]

Facing the combined efforts of the colonialists, the insecure mainland mass, and some backward elements among rural peasants, the ZNP lost in the election but gained in political stature. It stood as the only political party to fight for independence single-handedly and fearlessly. Many Zanzibaris who were abroad, angered by the reactionary turn of events, began to return home and engage whole-heartedly in political action. This was 1957, when the entire continent was in one way or another engulfed in the liberation movement inspired by Nkrumah's victory in Ghana and by the Mau Mau movement in Kenya.

To the returnees, the course of action was quite clear. It was to support the ZNP which had identified the crux of the problem, imperialism. To them the struggle against imperialism was paramount; it was *the* antagonistic contradiction. All other contradictions among the people were secondary, non-antagonistic contradictions which would be tackled later.

The returnees immediately introduced into the ZNP all the sophistication of party organisation techniques. They gave the

226

party a consistent anti-colonialist political line and a grassroots organisation of party branches at local levels. They rid the party of the pettiness which had characterised it during its formative phase and linked the movement with the world-wide, especially African, anti-imperialist struggle. To them the ASP would sooner or later become ineffective once its racism became irrelevant and its reactionary stand was thoroughly exposed in the rough and tumble of the liberation struggle.

As a result of this stand the ZNP became one of the best political movements in Africa. It mobilised the whole urban petty bourgeoisie which brought to the movement its energy and its intellectuals. It organised some of the urban workers and salvaged them from the clutches of the International Confederation of Free Trade Unions (ICFTU). The ICFTU-controlled trade unions had been dominated by Tom Mboya and his Kenya Federation of Trades Unions (KFTU), the major influence over the entire trade union movement in East Africa. The ZNP organised rural workers and seafaring workers most of whom were dhow crews. It organised all of their unions under the Federation of Progressive Trade Unions (FPTU) and was affiliated internationally to the now Prague-based World Federation of Trade Unions (WFTU) in opposition to the ICFTU, a cold-war creation which operated to undermine the world-wide anti-imperialist movement. The ZNP also organised primary and secondary school children and most of the urban and rural youth into a separate organisation known as the Youth's Own Union.

Unlike any other political party in East Africa, the ZNP had a clear-cut international stand. It supported the Mau Mau movement in Kenya, TANU in Tanganyika, the struggle against the Central African Federation, the Algerian revolution and organised mass rallies against French torture in Algeria; it supported the anti-apartheid and liberation movements in Southern Africa; and it supported the Palestinian struggle, China's rightful admission to the United Nations, and the unification of Korea and of Vietnam. In short, it was in the vanguard of all liberation struggles in Africa, Asia and Latin America, and it played a prominent role in the Cairo-based Afro-Asian Peoples Solidarity Organisation.

This involvement helped to broaden the political consciousness of the masses of Zanzibar irrespective of their political affiliations. It was a unique experience at that time in East African politics, where the strategy was to concentrate only on narrow and parochial issues of national independence, and on nothing else. The ZNP thus incurred the wrath of the imperialist camp as a whole, and not just of the British colonialists. They first sought to isolate the ZNP from the other East African movements by describing it to them as an 'Arab dominated' organisation; internally, they described it as 'communist dominated' and 'atheist' in order to discredit its most active members. The colonialists adopted particularly repressive measures against the ZNP by obstructing its youth and trade union activities and eventually banning them from politics, while at the same time giving official backing to the rival trade unions as 'registered' unions and flooding them with ICFTU money and blessings. Irving Brown, identified by former CIA officer John Stockwell as 'principal CIA agent for control of the ICFTU', went in and out of the country to 'advise' those trade unions.[13]

But the more repressive the colonialists were against the ZNP, the greater the prestige of the latter among the masses who now saw it as the authentic leader of the liberation struggle. Correspondingly, the ASP was tarnished by its identification with the colonialists. It had no clear-cut policy on any issue; it merely reacted negatively to every political initiative taken by the ZNP. They even opposed ZNP's stand against the establishment of the American so-called 'satellite tracking' station on Zanzibar soil.

The ASP leadership was increasingly becoming isolated nationally and internationally, and in 1958 at the first conference of the Pan-African Freedom Movement of East and Central Africa (PAFMECA) in Mwanza, the ASP became an embarrassment to TANU, its sister party, when it took a pro-imperialist stand. The ZNP attended the conference with a well-defined policy statement covering all aspects of the anti-imperialist struggle in Africa and elsewhere. It laid down a strategy for a common struggle among the liberation movements in East and Central Africa and suggested a clear line of policy to be adopted by these parties at the impending first All-African People's Conference in Accra, Ghana. It proposed that a united front be formed immediately between the ZNP and ASP with a common platform calling for immediate independence of Zanzibar.[14]

All the proposals were accepted by the conference and the ASP reluctantly agreed to form a united front with the ZNP after pressure from TANU leader Julius Nyerere. The two parties went separately to the Accra Conference in December 1958 where further pressures were brought to bear on the ASP to struggle for independence in a united front with the ZNP. Nkrumah and George Padmore, who mounted the pressure, were quite clear about the strategic importance of Zanzibar and its significance to the liberation struggle in East and Central Africa. The ASP then asked for an assurance from the ZNP that in the event of a split within the

ASP as a result of their new political position, the ZNP would not take advantage of it by siding with the splinter group. The assurance was accordingly given and witnessed by Nkrumah, Padmore and Kanyama Chiume of Malawi, among others.

The struggle for independence was now gaining momentum and liberation movements were attracting all sorts of people who had previously been hesitant to stand up and be counted. The petty bourgeoisie, mostly from the civil service, who now saw their future careers in the political movements, began to join whichever party appeared to offer the best prospects in the future. They brought with them their chronic pettiness, especially their petty struggles for better posts in government. They also brought with them their fear of 'communism', implanted by their colonial masters.

As a result of this influx of confused and conflicting influences, the parties began to evolve two wings of left and right, reflecting the long- and short-term interests of groups now defining themselves within the parties. The interest group divisions were naturally more profound in the ZNP than the ASP. The ZNP was a much more thoroughgoing political movement and therefore it attracted people with more or less definite political positions. Moreover, it assumed the leadership of the entire people on the issue of independence. As such, it attracted to its fold people from different classes, and clashes of class interest were therefore inevitable sooner or later. Furthermore, the ZNP was more representative of the people of Zanzibar as a whole; consequently, regional and local differences and jealousies were reflected within the party. Finally, it attracted its intellectuals from the urban petty bourgeoisie who brought to the party their inherent political instability. In short, it was more heterogeneous.

The ASP on the other hand was more homogeneous in that it represented almost the entire community of people of mainland origin in the city. Its support in the rural areas was centred on a few but densely populated areas like Donge and Chaani and could not therefore reflect wide-ranging regional contradictions. It had virtually no support from Pemba Island after the ZPPP split (to be discussed below) except in a small area of Mkoani. The ASP had no intellectuals of its own and derived its inspiration from TANU on the mainland. The problems that faced TANU on the mainland were quite different from those that faced ASP in Zanzibar, and the latter could not therefore evolve a consistent intellectual leadership accurately reflecting and responding to specific Zanzibar problems. A narrowly conceived movement cannot have sharp inner-party conflict and the division between right and left wings, which is essentially the outcome of higher political experience. It was because of its inability to analyse various social forces that the ASP tended to ally itself with the Indian National Association (INA), which largely represented the interests of the most reactionary section of the merchant class and big business. Their common ground was their opposition to independence and their fear of the growing political consciousness of the workers and peasant masses. But because the INA was not represented in the ASP their class interests could not be reflected in the ASP's inner-party conflict.

It is incorrect to say that either one of the two parties *represented* any one particular social class. At this stage they both had the support of the workers and peasants (poor and middle peasants); they both had some property owners, although the ASP also had the support of merchants through the INA. On the other hand, the ZNP had more property owners, large landowners as well as peasants.

In spite of these similarities, however, the two parties differed fundamentally in their respective political positions. Whereas the ASP took a very conservative, narrow-minded and reactionary position, the ZNP took a very radical, progressive and almost revolutionary position on all the major issues, internally and internationally.

This was the state of the two parties when the ASP was forced by Pan-African pressure to form a united front with the ZNP in the aftermath of the Accra Conference. The colonialists who felt threatened by the ASP/ZNP Declaration signed in Accra on joint struggle for independence now reacted harshly at what they considered ASP's betrayal. They knew its strengths and weaknesses and they could exploit them to the detriment of the party.

Objectively, however, the ZNP was in a more vulnerable position in the face of the colonialist provocations and manipulations. Until now the ASP was exclusively fighting the ZNP and their task was therefore less demanding. The ZNP on the other hand, was fighting both the colonialists and the ASP. Its tactics, therefore, had to be constantly reviewed as one or the other of its opponents temporarily changed its position. It had to be constantly on the move, constantly taking the initiative, and constantly assessing the situation anew, otherwise it could find itself cornered by the combined onslaught of its opponents. To this end, it had to have highly committed and politically well-trained cadres, selfless and disciplined, with a mature social consciousness.

Thus when it came to implement the Accra Joint Statement both parties faced serious inner-party difficulties, but with different impacts. For the ZNP, because of the quality of its cadres, the problem was much easier to handle. It had to convince its supporters that the ASP had turned progressive and was actually and sincerely demanding independence. It was at first hard for the rank and file to be persuaded to accept this, but because of party discipline and its grassroots organisation, it was not too difficult to get the members and supporters to accept this new situation.

The ASP leadership, on the other hand, had a much tougher assignment trying to sell the independence idea to its members. Hitherto their case against independence was that if the British left, the Arabs would take over and reinstitute slavery. The members were now asking what had changed this basic hypothesis on which the entire party strategy and politics had been based.[15] This puzzling question brought about serious confusion within the ASP, among both the leaders and the rank and file. This situation had been foreseen by both PAFMECA and the Accra conference mediators; as we have seen, the ASP itself warned of it before they signed the Declaration. It was to counter this eventuality that the Accra Declaration had stipulated two conditions before signing: (1) both parties must support each other in popularising the question of independence without taking any political advantage against the other; and (2) should there be a split in one or the other party as a result of the Declaration, both parties should jointly condemn the splinter group and isolate it politically. It was a solemn undertaking agreed to by both parties.

However, when the split did occur within the ASP only a few weeks after the Declaration, the ZNP leadership could not resist the temptation to take advantage of their opponents' difficulties. This was facilitated by the fact that the Secretary General of the ZNP, who was also the Secretary of the ZNP/ASP united front Freedom Committee, was abroad and could not invoke the Accra undertaking. This act of dishonesty, the second major ZNP error, irreparably injured the party's moral standing; it frustrated all the efforts for national unity, and it was the harbinger of the bloody path that followed the 1961 elections and the 1964 uprising.

This deplorable act of betrayal was due to the fact that the ZNP was undergoing a qualitative change as a result of the large and sudden influx of petty-bourgeois civil servants into the party. The party began to split into a left wing and right wing as the inner-party struggle intensified. The right wing found common cause with the ASP splinter group, especially in their shared fear of the mainlanders.

The split in the ASP naturally strengthened the right wing of the ZNP. Although Mohamed Shamte, the leader of the ASP splinter group, was himself a landlord, it would be incorrect to say it was a 'landlord split'. It was the split of the most reactionary rich peasant

231

elements in the ASP, which largely represented the Pemba faction of the party. The formation of the Zanzibar and Pemba People's Party (ZPPP) from the splinter group robbed the ASP of a large section of its rural intellectuals as well as most of its Pemba rank and file supporters. Most of the ASP rural intellectuals in both Pemba and Unguja resented what they described as mainland domination in the ASP and went along with the ZPPP wholeheartedly in the hope of leading it.

To the left wing of the ZNP, which took a long-term view of the anti-colonial and post-colonial struggle, the split within the ASP was most unfortunate, while the immediate ZNP support of the splinter group was viewed as catastrophic. Apart from the fact that the ZNP action exposed it to the accusation of treachery, the split left the ASP virtually without intellectuals of its own, which rendered it more and more subject to mainland domination. Moreover, the exodus of the intellectuals left the party wholly dependent on a politically weak leadership which made the party aimless, at best, and destructive, at worst. Such an outcome was seen as likely to encourage similar blind forces within the ZNP; reducing the struggle to petty squabbles, it would move it away from liberation.

This loss left a vacuum in the ASP leadership which was immediately filled by the Indian National Association. For instance, I.G. Rawal, one of the richest merchants in the country, became virtually the leader of the ASP in Pemba, with considerable influence in shaping the party's policies. In Unguja, V.S. Patel, the President of the Indian National Association, and his alter ego, Rustam Sidhwa, now asserted considerable influence on the party's policies.

The colonialists of course were jubilant about these developments, and the growing influence of the mainland. TANU's domination of the ASP by proxy was actively encouraged by the colonialists who saw in it a positive anti-communist influence.

Serious disagreements within the ZNP between the left and the right became unavoidable, centred on the party's attitude to the ASP, the whole strategy of the party towards independence now that it was becoming inevitable, and post-independence plans. The left, led by the urban and some rural petty-bourgeois intellectuals, seriously criticised the right on their opportunistic position towards the ASP split. They saw that the struggle against the ASP was not fundamental or antagonistic. It was transient and could be justified only as long as the ASP maintained its anti-independence stand. Once they agreed to participate fully in the liberation struggle through the Freedom Committee set up by PAFMECA and in accordance with the Accra Declaration, the task of the ZNP was to support it and give it the intellectual leadership it lacked after the split.

The left also stressed that it was dangerous to yield to the temptation of exploiting petty party advantages as this was leading the ASP deeper and deeper into the clutches of the merchant class and mainland intellectual domination. If these two situations were left to develop further the whole Zanzibar independence struggle would be in jeopardy. Some on the left even called for immediate breakaway from the ZNP to join the ASP *en bloc*, but the majority felt that the ZNP was in the last analysis their own creation, the result of their untiring labour − accordingly, they should remain within the party and struggle to take over its leadership and put the party back on a proper revolutionary course.

This majority felt that the task for the left was now to step up ideological orientation, as political maturity was reaching a new high. Hitherto, the principal preoccupation of the left was to establish the ZNP as a mass movement and their effort was centred on organising the masses − setting up party branches at all levels, organising women and youth movements, encouraging trade unions, and making the party an efficient electoral machine. To be sure, ideological work had been carried out and a party pamphlet − *Utawala wa Kibeberu* − based on the Leninist thesis of imperialism, was widely studied. Nevertheless, until then there had been little time to set up ideological schools and study circles on a broad basis. The priorities were of course to work for as broad a unity as possible, intensify the anti-colonial struggle and organise for electoral victory, especially in view of the formidable anti-liberation stand of the ASP.

Now, however, the situation had changed. Firstly, the ASP leadership was already, if grudgingly, talking of independence, thanks to PAFMECA and the Accra Declaration. Secondly, the reactionary forces, both in the ZNP and the ASP, had come out into the open and had begun some anti-socialist and anti-progressive campaigning, with the active support of the colonialists. Thirdly, within the ZNP the right had launched a struggle to capture the complete leadership of the party by foul and base means, and backward propaganda. Fourthly, the breakaway ASP faction had now organised itself into a new party, the ZPPP, and its leaders were making tentative approaches to the ZNP right to form a united front, on condition that the ZNP purge its radical and socialist elements. All these developments were unanticipated only a few months earlier and they had become possible only because of the unique situation to which Unguja, but not Pemba, was historically conditioned.

233

This uniqueness was of course due to the large numbers of immigrant workers from the mainland who played an active but often negative role in the internal politics of the country, always in favour of the ASP's stand against independence. For the left, this situation posed a serious and delicate problem which required very careful handling. This was one of the reasons why it was felt that the time was now ripe to launch intensive ideological struggle both within the ZNP and in the country at large, rather than break away from the party.

The majority of the left was influenced by the following analysis of this concrete situation. The mainland urban workers in Zanzibar were not proletarians in the classical sense, but only small property-owning petty bourgeoisie. Almost all of them owned some land back home and they utilised part of their wages in employing farm-hand labour to plant food or even some cash crops on their land. They were not the classical type of poor peasants who had to sell part of their labour in order to make ends meet, in other words, semi-proletarians. They came to work in Zanzibar in order to make extra cash to develop their land at home in order eventually to develop themselves into small-scale farmers.[16] This class of aspiring farmers was extremely unstable and could not be relied upon to develop proletarian class consciousness and class solidarity. Their support of the ASP was primarily for self-preservation and their nationalism was racial rather than political. They were loyal primarily to TANU and only incidentally to the ASP.

It was difficult, for instance, to convince them of their exploitation by the merchant class to which their leaders were attached; they felt this might threaten their jobs. They were so pliant that they often acted as scabs wherever there was a confrontation between the local workers and employers. In dealing with this phenomenon, therefore, the left had to be cautious not to be identified with them wholly, but at the same time try and expose them to the proletarian ideology and working-class inter-nationalism. The left had to show them that the working-class struggle in Zanzibar was the same as on the mainland, but owing to different conditions the struggle in Zanzibar would necessarily assume different manifestations. In other words, to educate them on the theory and practice of class struggle.

Then there was the minority of the indigenous workers. These too, like their mainland counterparts, had some land back home, but these were genuine semi-proletarians. They were driven to the urban centres because they could not make a living off their land and not because they wanted extra cash to pay their employees, as in the former case. They were constantly faced with the threat of mainland workers taking over their jobs and consequently they had an almost pathological abhorrence of them. This antagonism exposed them to the propaganda of the reactionaries and made them responsive to it. To the left this situation posed dual dangers. On the one hand, if the workers were divided on the basis of chauvinism the indigenous workers would be at the mercy of the ZNP/ZPPP reactionary leadership, and this might lead to a dangerous political situation. On the other hand, the immigrant workers would be drawn even closer to the merchant/ASP alliance to the detriment of proletarian leadership. Only intensive ideological popular education would extricate both these groups from the clutches of the above political forces.

Another factor that made the ideological struggle essential and urgent at this particular juncture was the position of the peasant masses who initiated the ZNP and who gave it a solid base. The large majority of them were of course unaware of the gathering clouds of the inner-party storm which also created some problems for the left. To bring the inner-party struggle into the open while the masses were not yet prepared for it would not only confuse the peasants and therefore weaken the very base of ZNP support, but also play into the hands of the colonialists through whose machinations the whole problem was brought to the fore. But, at the same time, to let the peasants remain in the dark about what was brewing was equally wrong not only because it was their right to know what was happening, but also because when the inevitable open struggle occurred it was in the interest of the revolution that the peasants should not be taken by surprise and back off.

While the left was thus bracing itself for massive ideological struggle, their political position within the ZNP was gradually weakening. The general political situation was deteriorating very fast and public exchanges were increasingly taking on an outright racial tone. Politics, with class struggle, ideology, etc. as its raw material, went overboard, and racial animosity took over. This deterioration was the result of the split within the ASP which left the party not only leaderless but also desperate. What was left of the leadership was so shocked and shaken by the split that they lost all sense of direction and consequently had nothing positive to offer to their followers. Desperate and irresponsible elements found their way into positions of influence within the party. Most of these were lumpen proletarians with all their negative attributes, and they led the party to gutter politics in which personal abuse took the place of political polemics.

This provoked a reaction of a similar kind within the ZNP and politics from then on became really 'dirty'. The reactionary elements within the ZNP gained ascendancy by using the fear of racial conflagration (now openly advocated by the new leaders of the ASP) to frighten the rank and file of the party. Racism, as a more deeply felt instinct for survival in the circumstances, became the real issue and those who relegated it to lower priority by advancing class and ideological issues became temporarily irrelevant politically.

This situation not only weakened the left, but also put them in an acutely difficult position. Although they were in sympathy with the ASP as a result of their post-Accra Declaration problems, they could not condone the blatant racial turn which the party was taking. Nor could they condone the reactionary trend within the ZNP. The bloody disturbances of 1961, a direct result of the deteriorating situation, further weakened the position of the left who were now seen as appeasers of the ASP.

The ZPPP, meanwhile, was helping to make the confused situation more confounded. In order to justify their treachery against the ASP, they embarked on anti-mainlander tirades. The January 1961 election stalemate had put them in a decisive position for a coalition of any kind, and when the majority of them opted to side with the ZNP, they felt obliged to project themselves not as anti-African but anti-mainlander. When the right-wing ZNP adopted this ZPPP platform, a very tense confrontation ensued between the mainlanders and the locals, with a corresponding slinging match of invectives.

The alliance between ZNP and ZPPP was a marriage of convenience between two right-wing groupings, each seeking to use the other to gain political dominance. The ZPPP was a creation of the colonialists to weaken the ASP when the latter was forced by the Accra Declaration to accept the independence platform. It was also used, on the other hand, to weaken the ZNP by forming an alliance with its right wing in order to provide it with the muscle to disable the left politically. The purpose of this move by the colonialists was to destroy the only political party in East Africa with any serious international standing which had a clear-cut anti-imperialist position as part of a world-wide alliance of anti-imperialist forces, spearheaded by the socialist countries.

In the circumstances the left decided not to give in but to step up the struggle within the party to save it from destruction. It argued that the party had enjoyed international prestige among progressive people and countries and international political organisations not because of the personalities of its leaders, but because of its anti-imperialist stand. If this position were to be diluted by political compromises that prestige would turn into contempt. Thus the left insisted that while maintaining an electoral alliance with the ZPPP, the party should in principle dissociate itself from ZPPP reactionary positions, especially its rabid anti-mainlander and pro-imperialist postures. Being a senior partner in the electoral alliance the ZNP should insist that its policies were to be paramount.

The left further argued that as independence approached this clear-cut stand would inspire the thousands of militant youths who would rally behind the party to ensure its success and safeguard its gains. As a gesture to revive the old progressive position of the party in the short period that was left before the 1963 pre-independence election, the party should nominate known progressive candidates to stand in safe constituencies to ensure that it enjoyed popular support. In the meantime, the party should publish its election manifesto stating its position unequivocally on all important issues such as the land question, economic priorities of the new government, the role of the working class and its place in the new government, and the party's social philosophy. It should also make a public pledge that as soon as the alliance emerged victorious in the forthcoming election, it would at once invite the ASP to come together with the ZNP/ZPPP to form a national government of anti-imperialist forces as pledged to PAFMECA and in accordance with the Accra Declaration.

This assessment of the situation was disputed by the rightists who rejected the recommendation on the argument that the alliance with the ZPPP was a most significant event in Zanzibar's political history since for the first time it brought together the people of authentic Zanzibari origin. According to this myopic thesis, as soon as the election was over and the ZNP/ZPPP victory assured, the majority of the ASP rank and file, especially genuine Zanzibaris, would go over to the ZNP/ZPPP alliance and this would lead to the disintegration of the ASP.

The rightists' position won the day and the left felt that the party had already gone too far to the right to be retrievable. Their continued association with such a party would only discredit them nationally and internationally. At a pre-election party conference in which the leaders were also to seek a mandate for the forthcoming constitutional talks at Lancaster House in London, the left decided to make a formal announcement that they were quitting the party because they had no longer any effective role to play within it.

The same afternoon the Umma Party was formed and the effect was unprecedented. The youth of all parties who were beginning to be demoralised and disenchanted with the political atmosphere were immediately charged with new enthusiasm. The first mass rally of the new party on the second day of its formation attracted several thousand young people, especially young workers from all political parties. The first week of the party's existence saw the registration of masses of youth as card-carrying members. The three major parties were shaken by the event because they were rapidly losing their youth support to the new party. The situation was charged with anticipation of impending changes of far-reaching consequence.

The Umma Party and the Zanzibar Revolution

After the 1963 general election and the resultant self-government constitution, the ZNP/ZPPP formed the new government which enjoyed most of the state powers short of complete independence. The colonialists still held the key portfolios of defence, foreign affairs and finance, but most of the coercive and repressive powers were in the hands of the new government, a rather shaky government at that. It was this government which had detained and imprisoned many activists and the left, including the General Secretary of the ZNP.

When the country gained its independence, the appetite for more repressive power by the new rulers was correspondingly increasing. The first significant action of the new government was the introduction in parliament of two repressive bills seeking to give itself powers to ban any political party and proscribe any newspaper deemed to be troublesome and dangerous. The obvious target of both these bills was of course the Umma Party and its press.

In order to oppose the bills before they became law the Umma Party entered into a tactical alliance with the ASP, which was the official parliamentary opposition. The party also initiated the formation of the Zanzibar Journalist Union, primarily to mount a vigorous opposition to the bills which would mobilise the masses outside parliament. This brought a close working relation between the party and ASP, especially between the youth sections of the two parties.

However, the government succeeded in pushing both bills through and they became law. As anticipated, on January 6, 1964 the Umma Party was banned. Its daily news bulletin was proscribed and all party assets (typewriters, duplicating machine, etc.) were confiscated by the government. In other words, the ZNP/ZPPP leadership immediately proved itself to be more ruthless than the colonialists it had just replaced, and against whom the people had been fighting so valiantly for so long. The government also proved that it had no intention of restoring justice and bringing about democratic rule, although these were among the primary objectives of the people's anti-colonial struggle. The new government, instead of liberating the people from colonial bondage, had extended its own bondage over the people and strengthened it.

In addition to banning the party, the new government was preparing to bring 'treason' charges against the leaders — a charge which carried a mandatory death penalty. The repressive nature of the new regime immediately exposed itself to the rest of the country, creating widespread insecurity and despondency among the people, especially the followers of the ASP.

In order to appease its anti-mainlander supporters, the government issued instructions to the effect that all police officers of mainland origin were to be identified with a view to retrenching them from the service as soon as possible. This unwarranted move further aggravated the prevailing sense of insecurity, now spreading to the police force on whose loyalty alone the government could survive. The police not only lost confidence in the government but were immediately turned into a potential enemy. This was the third and last major mistake the ZNP made before and after independence, and it proved to be fatal.

No government, especially a newly independent one whose immediate task is to seek to bring about the unity of state and nation, can rule effectively for any length of time if more than half of the people they govern are alienated and opposed to it. It is worse if, instead of looking for ways and means of bringing about post-colonial conditions favourable to national reconciliation, the government is seen to be utilising state power to repress the people rather than to liberate them. The government was seen to be promoting state terror to strengthen its shaky position. Thus, when the government was overthrown only a week after the banning of the Umma Party, many people, including some of its own supporters, thought of it as having 'got what it deserved'. Those who rule by force shall be removed by force, as the old adage tells us.

The Zanzibar uprising of 1964 that overthrew the ZNP/ZPPP government was conceived, planned and implemented entirely by the unemployed, frustrated urban youth of the ASP, who were angered by the weakness of their own party leadership and by what they perceived as an improperly conducted election that had robbed them of their rightful victory. (The ASP had more votes than those of the ruling parties put together, but they had fewer seats in parliament. This was anticipated in advance because the Lancaster House Constitution, which was agreed to by all parties concerned, provided for a system of constituency voting rather than a proportional representation system.)

In other words, the uprising was a lumpen-proletarian affair, with all its limiting and negative aspects. John Okello, the arch-lumpen, led his band of angry, frustrated but daring members of the ASP Youth League, who had originally intended to simply burn down Zanzibar Town in order to create maximum social chaos. However, wise counsel later prevailed and turned the original idea into a political insurrection, with the primary objective of overthrowing the regime. It took them only one day to do the job — so much for the pomposity and arrogance of a government which chose to rely on coercion rather than consensus.

Some members of the Umma Party were aware in advance that 'something' was afoot, as indeed were most of the people including the government's own security system, but others were actually tipped off about the impending event. However, neither the party nor any of its leading cadres had anything to do with the organisation or implementation of the uprising. They intervened in favour of the insurrection in order to save a messy and ugly situation from getting worse.

The Umma Party had the necessary leadership, the skills, the trained 'professional' revolutionaries and the party programme to rise to any occasion of national emergency; and the insurrection was one such situation. The party had trained its cadres to be vigilant and prepared for any eventuality, whether for defence or offence; whether for resistance or attack; but, above all, it was guided by a revolutionary ideology of proletarian world outlook. The party represented the 'broad left' of Zanzibar politics and it enjoyed the confidence of all the oppressed people in the country, including rank and file members of both the ZNP and ZPPP, not to mention the ASP. It was thus regarded as the 'natural leader of the people'; it symbolised the people's own leadership.

Thus when it intervened at the crucial moment of the uprising it immediately transformed the status of what until then was simply a rebellion into a revolutionary insurrection. It broadened the objectives of the uprising from a narrow, lumpen, anti-Arab, anti-privilege, anti-this and anti-that perspective into a serious social revolution with far-reaching political, social and economic objectives. Although these objectives were limited in the short term to a narrow horizon, given the objective conditions of the country at the time, nevertheless the anti-imperialist position that the revolution took after the intervention of the Umma Party opened up a huge vista of revolutionary social change. This intervention of Umma combatants immediately turned the revolution into a popular one, enjoying overwhelming support of the people of all political parties, including ZNP/ZPPP rank and file.

This spontaneous popular support for the uprising helped to

minimise bloodshed by avoiding inter-racial and inter-party violence, the threat of which had been ever-present since the 1962 riots. Any inter-racial war at this critical moment would have had most disastrous consequences, creating permanent racial tension. The party's intervention was instrumental in preventing such a catastrophe from happening. Although the uprising was subjected to massive hostile propaganda from the Western media and Arab kingdoms, claiming a widespread 'massacre of Arabs' — kindled, it is true, by Okello's wild claims on the local radio of thousands of casualties, in the hope of instilling fear in his listeners — the real casualty figure was minimal. There was no violence on Pemba Island. Most of the casualties in Unguja were the result of individuals settling old scores, and the perpetrators when caught received severe punishment from the revolutionary authorities.

The new revolutionary government was immediately formed, comprised of leading members of the ASP and Umma Party. The Revolutionary Council became the leading organ of the state. As the ASP had no economic or political programme of its own, the Council adopted *in toto* the Umma Party's minimum programme. The party's policy on health, education, land reform, social welfare, etc. were immediately implemented and they still remain the most shining and popular aspects of government policies.

Although the intervention of the Umma Party in the uprising had helped to transform it into a social revolution, the objective conditions in the country at the time were not yet mature enough for a serious and viable social revolution. In other words, the material basis for such a revolution was still missing. The revolution itself was naturally chaotic, with no central coordination and no post-revolution objectives. Okello, as a leading member of the Revolutionary Council, 'fell in love' with the radio and was addressing the nation almost hourly, giving conflicting accounts of what the government was doing or planning to do, and making threats of one kind or another which succeeded in creating confusion. The ASP, which had lost confidence in itself and its leadership after the defeat in the election of 1963, now revealed not only a lack of policy and authoritative leadership, but also a serious, divisive, all-absorbing inner-party struggle between the intellectuals and the Karume faction. This left the responsibility for running the affairs of the state, and of preventing the situation from deteriorating into further chaos, entirely in the hands of the Umma Party and its cadres.

The party organised government departments, reassured the frightened bureaucrats, and contacted foreign governments for recognition. Zanzibar was the first government in Africa to accord the German Democratic Republic full ambassadorial status, while the other African governments allowed themselves to be terrorised by the so-called Hallstein Doctrine which was imposed by the West German government. It also recognised North Korea when most other governments were hesitant, thanks to US threats. The party introduced a new trade strategy not only with socialist countries and the so-called non-aligned, but also with the 'traditional' trading partners in the West. The Zanzibar delegation took a leading role in collaborating with Cuba at the first UNCTAD Conference in Geneva in February, 1964, and was instrumental in the formation of 'The Group of 77'.

In domestic policies it reorganised the police force in collaboration with the Tanganyika government; it established a People's Liberation Army and trained new revolutionary recruits. It abolished all privileges at the expense of the state: e.g., no first-class air travel for senior civil servants or ministers; no special status for anyone, however high in authority (even Karume, the President, was driving his own car, with no outriders, no flags, or any of the pompous paraphernalia so common in ex-colonial countries); everybody was equal; everybody was a 'comrade'.

The national radio was eventually 'liberated' from Okello. Umma Party cadres, professionals in radio journalism, took over the political and professional leadership of the department. Umma military cadres patrolled the streets to maintain order; they even fought Okello's armed gangs who looted shops and banks, and those who tried to harass defenceless women and other vulnerable people. Schools were immediately reopened and Umma cadres escorted students who lived too far from their schools.

The radio became the leading organ of public education, especially on questions of civic responsibility and revolutionary maturity; on the question of mass/state relations; on people's own leadership, especially at local levels; on guarding against foreign penetration; and on forming vigilante groupings and people's defence militia. On international questions, the radio took an out-and-out anti-imperialist line: it warned against possible US intervention in collusion with some neighbouring states; it exposed the machinations of the imperialist powers aimed at bringing about distrust, fear and suspicion among East African governments, etc.

The party took the initiative on behalf of the Revolutionary Council to invite legal experts to advise on the proposed new revolutionary constitution; it brought economic experts to advise on immediate and long-term economic strategy, including structural change from a colonial to an independent national economy. It devised a new 'trade strategy' for utilising the country's export and import trade as a means of facilitating the envisaged structural change and of promoting a new pattern of economic development, especially development and expansion of the home market.

The revolutionary government supported the party's 'revolutionary diplomacy' of alliances among progressive countries and isolation of reactionary countries; a fraternal approach towards the socialist countries, on the one hand, and a cautious approach towards the imperialist camp, on the other. It took a definite stand on supporting liberation movements, up to and including military training − not only African movements but all movements fighting for their liberation, e.g., in South Yemen, Dhufar, Vietnam, Palestine and the Arab struggle in general.

Party cadres also undertook almost single-handedly the task of revolutionary struggle for education, mobilising and promoting people's own leadership. It intervened in the ASP inner-party power struggle by trying to minimise inter-personal conflicts and promoting ideological alliances as the most enduring ingredient for revolutionary solidarity. The Revolutionary Council became the leading light in the revolutionary upsurge throughout East and Central Africa, and it was viewed by the reactionary and pro-imperialist leadership in those areas as the 'most dangerous and subversive' influence in the area, while the Umma Party was regarded as the 'evil spirit' behind it all.

The leading role of the Umma Party thus gave the impression to friends and foes that the Zanzibar revolution was a 'socialist' revolution of the same magnitude and importance as the Cuban revolution. Zanzibar was described as the 'Cuba of Africa' and it was to be dealt with accordingly. The imperialist camp was divided in their assessment of the degree of its 'redness'; some described it as 'pro-Peking' and some as 'pro-Moscow'. (Chou en Lai, on a visit to Mogadishu at the time, after his famous Africa-is-ripe-for-revolution speech, said 'China does not want to take the credit for the Zanzibar Revolution.')

Political leaders in East Africa, too, were influenced by this 'communist scare' campaign and most of them actively collaborated with the United States in its attempt to drive a wedge between the ASP and the Umma Party. Karume was singled out as a true and authentic 'African nationalist' and 'non-aligned', although some members of the ASP, led by Abdulla Kassim Hanga, the Vice-President of the party, were regarded as 'pro-Moscow'. East African politicians, influenced by the US, appointed a committee − under the chairmanship of Oginga Odinga, then Kenyan Vice-President, and with Tanganyika's deputy Foreign Minister at the time, Walwa, as its secretary − specifically to retrieve Karume from the assumed clutches of the communists. The committee came out with a most reactionary report designed to divide the ranks of the revolutionary forces.

When the Revolutionary Council sent US Ambassador Pickard packing for interfering in the internal affairs of the country, the entire East African establishment was alarmed and saw this as proof of communist influence in the country. This establishment in large measure collaborated with the US in their 'Zanzibar Action Plan' (ZAP) which was designed to prepare the ground for either British or US military intervention to overthrow the revolutionary government of Zanzibar, in the same fashion that the US, twenty years later, intervened in the overthrow of the government of Grenada in the West Indies with the support of reactionary governments in the area. Secret US documents which recently came to light reveal embarrassingly the extent to which African governments were being manipulated and pressured by the US to take a negative stand against the Zanzibar Revolution.[17]

It was largely this induced fear of communism that led to the secret negotiations between Karume and Nyerere for the surprise formation of the Union of Tanganyika and Zanzibar, behind the backs of the Umma Party and the Revolutionary Council, only one hundred days after the uprising and the formation of the People's Republic of Zanzibar. The hundred days of the People's Republic of Zanzibar, though brief historically, have nevertheless tranformed the politics of the region more profoundly than anything that has happened in the area either before or after its formation. Even the spontaneous army mutinies in Kenya, Uganda and Tanganyika, on January 20, 1964, which entailed bringing back the British army to suppress them, and which were erroneously credited to the Zanzibar Revolution, did not have as much lasting political impact as did the existence of the short-lived People's Republic of Zanzibar.

The Union succeeded, of course, in stemming the tide of the revolution in the region at the time. Most of the active revolutionaries were immediately transferred to the mainland government. Zanzibar, a brilliant revolutionary star of Africa, was henceforth to be reduced to one of the worst bungling and tyrannical petty-bourgeois despotisms in Africa. It ceased to be the vanguard of the African revolution, a leader in economic and social transformation and reconstruction, and it descended into the doldrums of the worst third world political, social and economic malaise with steady decline all round. Corruption, which was once taboo and morally repugnant, became the norm. While the revolution had uprooted the entire structure of privileges, the Union created conditions for the evolution of new structures of privilege and corruption.

To summarise, although the Umma Party did not fire the first shot of the uprising, it nevertheless rose to the occasion with revolutionary zeal and skill. It helped to transform a wholly lumpen — in many ways apolitical — uprising into a popular, anti-imperialist revolution, which, left to its own momentum, and without the external intervention that followed, would undoubtedly have opened up a new path — the road to socialism.

However, from the short-term perspective, the lumpen uprising, which was inevitable at the time given the objective social conditions, aggravated as they were by an inept and vindictive administration, nevertheless did bring about an atmosphere of revolt in which the revolutionary potential of the Zanzibar youth revealed itself with a dramatic impact and showed far-reaching future potential to which the imperialists reacted not only with alarm but also with active preparation to combat it militarily. In that respect, this lumpen uprising was positive.

Although it had occurred at a historically disadvantageous moment when the upsurge of nationalism was still ascending and had not yet reached its peak, the intervention of the socialist forces did create more favourable conditions for revolutionary and indeed socialist prospects throughout the region.

From the long-term perspective, on the other hand, the revolution had the potential of a 'grand rehearsal' for future revolutionary development in the region. The many useful lessons, both positive and negative, that were gained from that experience and most of which have yet to be investigated, analysed and studied more thoroughly, will certainly help to illuminate the path of future revolutions. As new revolutionary experiences continue to unfold in Africa, as the youth of Africa are everywhere increasingly spearheading the current revolutionary struggle against neocolonialism and imperialism with all its agents, the lessons of the Zanzibar Revolution, its ups and downs, its betrayals and heroism, will no doubt contribute enormously towards enriching and strengthening the struggles.

At this crucial historical juncture, anti-colonial nationalism has already exhausted its potential and run out of steam. Its limited objectives have led perilously to the bleak realm of graft, corruption and economic decline. Its former usefulness has actually turned into a negation of all that Africa has stood for and indeed fought for. Only through socialism, whose direction has already been pointed out by the Zanzibar Revolution, can Africa re-emerge from the shackles of neocolonialism and imperialist domination with their legacy of poverty, starvation and disease. Only socialism can put Africa once again on the road to rejuvenation and rekindle that

post-independence mass enthusiasm which has now everywhere
been replaced by cynicism. Only socialism can open the way
towards turning the entire continent into a unified, progressive
Africa, utilising its almost unlimited natural and human resources
for the benefit of its people. Only socialism can turn Africa into a
giant among giants of today. That is the meaning and legacy of the
Zanzibar Revolution.

Notes

1. Former General Secretary of the Zanzibar Nationalist Party and later
   leader of the Umma Party. This is an analysis by a participant and major
   actor in the struggle largely based on his own memory. Notes have
   been provided by the editors.
2. See chapters in this volume by Bowles and Sheriff.
3. Zanzibar Archives, 'General Statistics of Zanzibar Protectorate', p. 197.
4. The coast of Kenya was recognised during the Scramble for Africa as
   part of the territories of the Sultan of Zanzibar, but it was leased to
   Kenya Colony.
5. Even the Afro-Shirazi Party had accepted the Sultan as a constitutional
   monarch. See Zanzibar Protectorate, *Report of the Constitutional
   Commissioner, Zanzibar, 1960*, (Blood Report), Zanzibar, Government
   Printer, 1960, p. 36.
6. For further discussion of the role of Ahmed Lemki, see M. Lofchie,
   Zanzibar: Background to Revolution, Princeton, Princeton University Press,
   1965, pp. 140–147.
7. The assassin, Mohamed Hamoud, apparently died in prison after the
   revolution. His son, Hamoud Mohamed, assassinated Karume on 7
   April 1972.
8. 'The period of party politics': this is the term now commonly used in
   Zanzibar to refer to the period from 1957 to 1964.
9. M. Lofchie, *op. cit.*, p. 158.
10. See Blood Report, *op. cit.*, p. 33.
11. An early ZNP publication admitted this 'mistake'. It accused the
    colonial government of conniving in the registration of non-citizens to
    defeat the ZNP, and insisting that it was the duty of the citizens to lodge
    individual objections. The ZNP was thus forced into this 'trap'. See
    ZNP, *Whither Zanzibar?*, Political Education Series Pamphlet No. 2, Cairo,
    ZNP, 1960, p. 25.
12. The slogan 'zuia' was used during the intense inter-party conflicts after
    the 1957 election which included a boycott of Arab and Asian shops
    and buses, and this was the economic content of the slogan. See
    Lofchie, *op. cit.*, p. 188.
13. 'Irving Brown – European representative of the American Federation
    of Labor and principal CIA agent for control of the International

Confederation of Free Trade Unions' are Philip Agee's words in his autobiography, *Inside the Company: CIA Diary,* New York, Stonehill, 1975, p. 604. See also, Jonathan Kwitney, *Endless Enemies: The Making of an Unfriendly World,* New York, Congdon and Weed, Inc., 1983; Barry Cohen, 'The CIA and African Trade Unions', in Ellen Ray, *et al., Dirty Work 2: The CIA in Africa,* Secaucus, New Jersey, Lyle Stuart Inc., 1979; and Ronald Radosh, *American Labor and United States Foreign Policy,* New York, Vintage, 1969.
14. See Lofchie, *op. cit.,* pp. 189—91.
15. *Ibid.,* pp. 192—6.
16. A large number of the temporary immigrants from the mainland came from Unyamwezi, driven by the same poverty and colonial taxation that sent their colleagues to the sisal plantations and elsewhere. In view of the low and declining wages shown in Chapter 2, it is doubtful they would have earned enough to employ labour on their farms back home. Most were anxious to earn enough to buy a bicycle to take home.
17. See 'The 100 days that made Tanzania,' *Africa Now,* April, 1984, pp. 15—21.

Conclusion

ABDUL SHERIFF

On January 12, 1964, a violent revolution overthrew the system which had emerged at the end of a long political and constitutional process. It has become fashionable to view it as the overthrow of an oppressive racial minority by the downtrodden African majority. That view is simplistic, for social processes on the scale of revolutions are necessarily more complex phenomena. Fundamental differences which have appeared in society through time are revealed in a moment, while opposing forces clash to resolve these contradictions. In this conclusion we will identify contradictions and analyse the class forces that shaped the revolution in Zanzibar.

Class differences developed through the complex history of transition from a slave mode of production that had developed in the shadow of capitalism, to colonial capitalism dominated by imperialism. The old mode was partially dissolved to destroy its independence, while elements of pre-capitalist relations were preserved and articulated with the capitalist mode, but classes in general were prevented from maturing into classical capitalist forms under colonial rule. The exhausted classes of past years, such as the landlords, were neither retired from the stage of history nor transformed into a dynamic class. The peasantry was preserved in its semi-decomposed form as cheap migrant labour, but did not realise its full potential through the maturation of its component strata. The free working class that grew out of slavery was frozen in a semi-proletarian, semi-peasant condition, while the stunting of the industrialisation process in the colonial economy hindered the emergence of a true proletariat.

As a result, the Zanzibari social formation during the colonial period was riddled with unresolved conflicts whose basic class character was camouflaged by ideologies of race and communal identities. The latter differences were secondary at that stage of national liberation from colonial rule, but they were permitted to take precedence over those that were primary. This prevented the emergence of a broad-based national alliance of the colonised to fight against imperialism. Bitter differences between rival wings of the nationalist movement overshadowed the struggle against British colonialism. The Zanzibar Revolution was a direct outcome of this state of affairs: without a class wielding a clear ideology to lead the struggle along a well-defined path, the revolution was a 'lumpen' affair, bloody without being thoroughgoing, settling old scores without opening up new doors of emancipation and democracy.

Classes in transition

The slave mode of production which had developed on the isles during the nineteenth century was itself a contradictory phenomenon. It emerged precisely at a time when its antithesis, the capitalist mode, was becoming a world system. It was integrated into that system from its inception as a producer of commodities for export. Its labour process contained incongruous elements which appear to be concessions to the capitalist mode.[1] Because clove harvesting is highly seasonal and the price of cloves had been in decline since the 1840s, landowners sought to reduce production costs by shifting part of the cost of reproduction of labour to the slaves themselves. They were given two 'free' days to work on subsistence plots; they could sell any surplus in the market. The slave mode was further compromised by the indebtedness of the landowning class to merchant and moneylending capital, thus weakening its domestic power before the imposition of colonial rule.

British policy in the region was not single-minded. While championing the abolitionist movement it emerged as the patron of the Busaidi state. Having pursued a policy of progressively narrowing the arena of the slave trade to East Africa, culminating in the abolition of the slave trade by sea in 1873, London developed cold feet and took a full quarter of a century to abolish slavery itself on Zanzibar. After partitioning the Zanzibari commercial empire and incorporating the islands under its rule in 1890, Britain was less moved by the ideological crusade of the missionaries than by the practical need to establish a colonial state.

At the political level, the new British Agent Gerald Portal carried out in 1891 what has been aptly described as a *coup d'état*, seizing control of the Sultan's finances and appointing European officials to run the administration.[2] The British retained the Sultan, but assumed control over succession to the office, twice blocking independent-minded Khalid b. Bargash, even at the cost of bombarding the palace in 1896, and placing on the throne a series of pliant puppets. Portal even favoured the abolition of the sultanate which he considered to be the 'embodiment of all the worst and most barbaric characteristics of a primitive Arab despotism', but London was not ready for such a dramatic political change at a time when it was trying to put together the apparatus to run the new protectorate. British support for the Sultan from the 1850s had made him increasingly dependent. The origin of the colonial state in Zanzibar lay in an alliance formed by Britain with a particular segment of the old élite, although the ties were generalised to embrace the whole landowning class from 1896.[3] The old ruling class remained a useful junior partner in the British system of indirect rule through a 'hybrid state'.[4]

At the economic level, the British were divided between those who wanted to preserve the plantation system and those who pushed for peasant production. Several colonial officials considered the landlords a spent force in the economy and were prepared for the elimination of the plantation. As early as 1913, one official had declared that 'the question of ownership is in a transition stage pending the formation of a new class of owners from the natives of the islands.'[5] Bearing in mind the various problems that the clove economy had faced since emancipation − indebtedness, labour shortages, and rising costs of production − they argued in favour of peasant producers who, they said, were

> self-supporting as regards labour; ... they are incomparably the cheapest instrument for the production of agricultural produce ... and ... are capable of a rapidity of expansion and a progressive increase of output that beggar every record.[6]

Those who argued for the perpetuation of plantation production completely ignored the strides being made by the peasants, arguing instead that they were an unknown quantity on which to base revenue. This view was sentimental as well as political, for officials spoke of a 'sense of obligation to a race upon whom we have imposed our protection'.[7] They feared that basic economic change might precipitate a social revolution and undermine the system of indirect rule. These arguments ultimately prevailed, as the Arab landowning aristocracy was preserved, although deprived of political power and much of its former economic autonomy.

Having decided to preserve the plantation system, the colonial state tried to transform its relations of production very gradually. Sir John Kirk, an influential advisor to the Foreign Office, wanted to allow the former slaves to work for their ex-masters for as long as possible after emancipation.[8] Continuity of plantation ownership was recognised and former slaves were coerced to remain on the land as squatters. The emancipation process was so cumbersome for slaves, and the condition of freed slaves was so similar, that few bothered to demand their freedom formally. The British attempted to retain the old system under which the slaves had worked a certain number of days for the master and the rest for themselves. While this enticed those now free to hang on to their limited rights to land, shortage of labour after emancipation enabled them to revise the condition of their tenure.

Semi-free squatter labour proved inadequate for the requirements of plantation production. Efforts to import Chinese and Indian coolie labour, and migrant labour from Kenya, proved too expensive. 'Voluntary' labour migration from Tanganyika was later to materialise with the migrants paying the cost of transportation, and it was very useful for general cultivation and weeding. Clove picking, however, required an elastic reservoir of local seasonal labour to harvest a clove crop that fluctuated widely. Until the end of the nineteenth century the peasantry in Zanzibar was largely self-sufficient and autonomous. To extract labour from this peasantry, its self-sufficiency had to be destroyed through forced labour, taxation and legislation. When that was accomplished, economic mechanisms such as 'free passage' to Pemba to pick cloves, loans and clove picking contracts were used to ensure the continued outflow of labour when it was needed. In 1943, nearly half of Unguja's adult male population was available to pick cloves in the plantations.

The colonial state thus solved the immediate labour problem through various categories of semi-proletarianised labourers, each of which had one foot firmly planted in subsistence agriculture and the other in seasonal plantation work. This formula, widespread during the era of imperialism, permitted capital to shift part of the cost of reproducing labour onto the shoulders of the pre-capitalist social formation. By paying only a 'bachelor wage' to seasonal labourers when employed, and casting them back to the rural areas for survival until they were needed again, capital was able to 'super-exploit' them. The semi-proletarianised were conscious of resulting impoverishment and poverty, but class consciousness required for organisation and change was slow to appear.

The same process which created the semi-proletariat also transformed the landowners into heavily-indebted semi-capitalist farmers who were little more than managers working on behalf of the moneylender to produce cloves for the British clove distillation industry and consumers abroad. The inability of landowners to protect their own interests became clear with the imposition of a 25 per cent tax on cloves; previously this class had enjoyed almost total exemption from taxation. Its loss of control over the labour force after emancipation led to cut-throat competition for labour and a rising cost of production. The impact of these unfavourable forces caused the landowners to sink into greater debt. By the late 1920s, some of the contradictions of colonial capitalism had begun to mature and threaten the very basis of colonial production. The British tried with greater vigour to keep the landowners afloat. An attempt was made to reduce production costs by creating the Clove Growers' Association (CGA) with the objective of reducing the cost of labour. These efforts were successful to a considerable extent.[9] A more critical situation arose with the Great Depression. Middle-level merchants and moneylenders, who had been financing and marketing the clove crop, had now become an impediment to production and accumulation in the era of capitalist crisis, and a move was made to cut them out. In 1934, the government declared a moratorium on agricultural debts and gave the CGA a marketing monopoly. However, the merchants in Zanzibar collaborated with their counterparts in India to fight back. The outcome was a compromise: moneylending intermediaries were replaced by a parastatal body which borrowed from British banks to finance the clove crop. The merchants' freedom of action was restricted by the same body which tried to regulate clove prices, but they could not be eliminated because of their key role in the colonial economy. Nevertheless, the events of the 1930s showed that this class could not pretend to be independent.

Colonial intervention had saved the landlords from total demise. Between 1939 and 1963 the class as a whole was partially stabilised by the debt settlement scheme, though the size of the class may have diminished. The tendency towards fragmentation of landed property and peasantisation of landlords reasserted itself. A few big landholders continued to amass property, but the sons of many landlords were forced to seek incomes as salaried petty-bourgeois government officials, teachers, etc. The landlord class had been freed from 'Shylock's embrace' only to fall into the clutches of the CGA which, despite its name, was not a producers' cooperative. It was a highly exploitative commercial arm of the state on which the landowners became dependent.[10]

Although the colonial state propped up the landlord class, the peasantry continued to grow at its expense. During the nineteenth century it had remained aloof from the clove economy, but the shortage of labour after the abolition of the slave trade and slavery improved its bargaining position. Some were initially prepared to pick cloves on a crop-sharing basis and the poor peasantry was later to develop as a reservoir of seasonal labour. The rest, especially in Pemba, were willing to participate in the clove economy as peasants rather than workers: clearing the forest and planting clove trees in return for a share; or planting cloves on their own land; or purchasing small plots from impoverished landlords. They joined the expanding number of Arab landlords who were sinking to peasant status, working smaller *shambas* with family labour. Once the peasants had obtained a toehold in the clove economy, they were able to expand their holdings so that by the 1920s they constituted over 90 per cent of the clove owners and owned more than half of the clove trees. The pattern was even more marked in Pemba.

The last class to appear on the scene was the proletariat, bearing the scars of its semi-peasant migratory character. Grounded in a commercial economy with insignificant industry, its nucleus was in clove and coconut production, processing and export. There was also a large stratum of casual labourers in urban construction, and another of domestic servants dispersed in the numerous homes of landlords, merchants, the petty bourgeoisie and colonial officials. Because industry was discouraged – even domestic clove distillation was blocked for a long time – the industrial labour force was small and appeared late in the colonial era. The most militant members of the working class were the better paid stevedores at the docks who, at times, were bought out with special privileges.

The colonial state worked consistently to control trade unions and channel them to purely economic issues. Though workers succeeded in asserting their autonomy in the late 1940s, and mounted a couple of strikes, their independence was crushed. When trade union activities revived again in the 1950s within the confines of rigid colonial regulations, they fell under the spell of local political parties and the western-dominated ICFTU with its strong CIA connections. As trade unions proliferated in the 1950s, leadership was invariably captured by the educated petty bourgeoisie skilled in managing bureaucratic structures imposed by colonial regulations. Moreover, the workers' movement was split into rival factions – the ZPFL and FPTU – led by political parties; the development muted the vanguard role of the unions in the struggle for national liberation.

Class struggles

These were the primary actors in the political economy of Zanzibar under colonial rule. Like all aspiring performers, they often stuttered and stammered, and occasionally missed their cues. They were classes in various stages of formation and transition, but the processes were halting under the reactionary conditions of imperialism; old classes went senile while nascent ones were frozen in immaturity. Class consciousness was obscured by race, ethnic and communal identities, a development encouraged through colonial recognition of numerous associations and by racial representation in the country's political life. This type of identity obstructed the formation of a broader alliance for independence based on a national consciousness.

In a small protectorate of only a quarter of a million people in the middle decades of colonial rule, three racial groupings were officially recognised. These, in turn, were divided into no less than 23 ethnic or communal associations. The Arabs were split into those who hailed a couple of centuries earlier from Oman and those who had originated in Yemen; the latter were split into those from the coast and those from the interior. The small Asian community was separated into a bewildering number of religious, sectarian, caste and linguistic groups that left even their colonial patrons baffled. Among the Africans were the indigenous Shirazi and the more recent immigrants from the mainland; the latter had their own 'tribal' allegiances.

Most of these associations contained a cross-section of classes dominated by the most powerful interests. Control over ethnic constituencies was exercised through communal activities and clientage relationships which tended to structure consciousness along ethnic lines. For example, long after the majority of the Asians had been reduced to petty-bourgeois clerks and government servants, they were recognised as — and considered themselves — a business community to be represented in official bodies by the most prominent merchants. The same was true of Arab 'landowners', many of whom had long ceased to be such. The élites of these communities emphasised the distinctiveness of their ethnic 'fiefs', maintaining rigid boundaries between the memberships of each, while leaders made alliances across these boundaries to promote their interests through such political groups as the Indian National Association and the Arab Association.

The colonial state recognised these communal associations and often supported their leading factions when challenged from within. It patronised the broader racial federations, using them to represent the diverse economic interests of their clients. When the Protectorate Council was set up in 1914 as a purely advisory body, the British selected four 'leading' Arabs and Asians to represent landowners and merchants respectively. The same practice was

Conclusion

repeated in 1926 when the Legislative Council was established containing unofficial 'representatives' from the two racial communities. It was not until 1946 that the first African 'representative' was appointed to this pseudo-democratic body. Racial representation in this and other official bodies encouraged those dominant groups to portray their interests in racial terms and to mobilise their constituencies in support of ethnic demands.

In the first major case of class conflict in the 1930s, the whole Asian community was targeted by the colonial state as the scapegoat for the economic crisis, although this community consisted of quite diverse strata of merchants, moneylenders, a number of genuine landowners, a large group of petty-bourgeois clerks, semi-proletarianised potters in the south of Unguja, and some extremely poor groups such as washermen. Threatened with continued erosion of their mercantile role − which had, in fact, contributed to the impoverishment of the community as a whole − the leading merchants were able to mobilise the whole community to protect their narrower interests. In the rough and tumble of the clove boycott movement which lasted a couple of years, the interests of different components of the community became distinguished, but were sacrificed one by one to secure those of the big clove traders. The economic activities of the latter, however, were now greatly circumscribed and they had become a spent political force. When political struggles intensified in the 1950s, the Asians no longer stood as a single bloc, but were fractured to some extent along class lines. The comprador big merchants, organised in the Indian Association, sought accommodation as a subordinate but rich racial group with the Afro-Shirazi Party (ASP). Some of the petty-bourgeois Asians tried to organise themselves as a political group under the banner of the Muslim Association; although it won a seat in the 1957 election, it was an irrelevant gesture that evaporated before the next contest. The rest, with deeper roots in Zanzibar and nowhere else to go, embraced the non-racial ideology of the Zanzibar Nationalist Party.

In spite of efforts to keep these communities distinct, the institutions of colonial rule inevitably led to a society in which ethnic and communal boundaries were becoming anachronistic. By the early 1950s, the distant rumble of a Zanzibari national consciousness was heard with the creation of the Zanzibar Association among urban intellectuals, and the formation of the National Party of the Subjects of the Sultan (NPSS) among the impoverished peasants of Kiembe Samaki. By 1958, many Zanzibaris simply refused to be classified into racial categories in the census that year, although this does not mean that a common national consciousness had triumphed unequivocally.

Conclusion

The ideology of Zanzibari nationalism was conceived in the 1950s, but the period of gestation was difficult as reactionary ethnic loyalities and immature class identities battled it out. The first group to articulate nationalist feelings was, not surprisingly, a more radical faction within the Arab Association, still smarting from the loss of political power more than half a century earlier. However, these sentiments − initially expressed against colonial manoeuvres to use Asians to counterbalance Arabs in politics − were rapidly jettisoned when it received the support of the Shirazi Association, resulting in a multi-racial call by Zanzibaris for a greater say in the affairs of their country. The colonial state reacted against this strongly nationalist stance by the association's weekly, *Al Falaq*, and charged the whole executive committee with sedition. This radicalised its previously conservative membership which then adopted *in toto* the political programme of the young radicals.

The cornerstone of this programme was the rejection of ethnic representation and an unequivocal demand for a common roll election open to all Zanzibaris leading to eventual independence. It has become fashionable, following Lofchie's analysis, to interpret this call by a formerly privileged minority as a clever manoeuvre to capture the leadership of the whole nationalist movement before the Africans became conscious of their interests and organised.[11] This is a cynical and racist view of the history of Zanzibar under colonial rule, during which many race distinctions had begun to seem quaint and irrelevant. It was certainly a gamble that the young Arab radicals were taking to test whether the Zanzibaris had transcended their parochial ethnic loyalties, a gamble that nearly failed in the 1957 election. Later events were to prove that the nationalist tree had taken root.

While the urban intellectuals were expressing nationalist demands, the peasants of Kiembe Samaki were hit hard by colonial authorities, forcing them to discover through bitter struggle that the solution lay with a nationalist rather than a parochial ideology. Land alienation to build and expand the airport had begun to destabilise the peasant economy in the area in the 1940s. When the colonial state tried to enforce the inoculation of cattle against anthrax − a procedure which seemed to kill as much as cure − the peasants rose in defiance and forcibly freed their leaders from prison. The revolt was violently crushed, but from its ashes arose the first explicitly nationalist party, formed by farmers and cattle herders. Calling for a non-racial struggle against colonialism, they named their movement the National Party of the Subjects of the Sultan of Zanzibar, highlighting its national character and rejecting petty ethnic loyalties, which was progressive indeed for a small rural initiative.

Conclusion

The Kiembe Samaki peasants and the young Arab radicals started their nationalist activities in very different circumstances and by contrasting means: in the former case it was a violent struggle in a rural setting; while the latter developed in the urban milieu in a constitutional manner. But the colonial experience unified them around a common programme of anti-British nationalism and the rejection of racialism. The NPSS provided a more appropriate organisation because it was national and anti-colonial from its inception, and the young urban intellectuals began to join it in large numbers. In the dynamic process it was inevitable that the NPSS would change its character from a small peasant movement into a broad-based nationalist party, renamed the Zanzibar Nationalist Party. The urban intellectuals developed its ideology, giving it a more consistent and internationalist stance, and they also built up an effective organisational structure covering the whole country. The ZNP thus continued to attract support from a section of the working class, the petty bourgeoisie and, most importantly, the peasants in north Unguja and Pemba where eventually it was to win most of its support.

In contrast, the ASP derived its initial impetus from the town and from ethnic associations, the African Association and the Unguja section of the Shirazi Association. The former consisted of Africans hailing from the mainland, many of whom did not share a common religion with the Muslim majority in Zanzibar. Added to the resulting sense of insecurity was the loss of its intellectual leadership when colonial regulations prohibited educated civil servants from joining political parties. Its organisational structure was thus weak and its ideology wallowed in the shallow waters of racialism. It had little understanding and sympathy for the rural peasantry, especially in Pemba where it hardly had a foothold.

The Unguja section of the Shirazi Association derived much of its support from the semi-proletarianised peasants in the central and southern parts of the island. They were in close touch with the urban Africans in Zanzibar Town and had had a bitter experience of seasonal clove picking on the large plantations in Unguja and Pemba. There was thus some common ground between these two sections of the population, but it required the active intervention of Julius Nyerere of TANU on the mainland to bring about a union on the eve of the 1957 election. The attempt to extend this alliance to the Shirazi peasants of Pemba failed, based as it was on the threadbare ideology of a common racial identity and the absence of a clear-cut nationalist programme. The Shirazi Association candidates in Pemba stood as independents in the 1957 election and joined the fragile ASP only on a conditional basis, an arrangement that soon broke down.

Conclusion

It was on the rock of peasant politics that the ASP assumption of African racial unity — and the racial theories of some social scientists — floundered. The peasantry constituted a vast and contradictory mass which had begun to differentiate during the colonial period; it did not display uniform political behaviour. The semi-proletarianised peasantry of central and southern Unguja discussed above, behaved differently from the poor peasantry of Tumbatu and the northern tip of Unguja; the latter, although poor, were independent fishermen. Pemba was a peasant region *par excellence*. The majority were still fairly stable, property-owning, middle and rich peasants who found little in the ASP programme that reflected their interests. The ASP's intense anti-Arabism was meaningless to a population that shared a common condition of life with Arab peasants with whom they lived cheek-by-jowl. The catastrophic decline in the price of their cloves after the post-Korean boom — which provides the economic backdrop for the *zama za siasa*, or 'period of politics', of the late 1950s — affected both sections of clove producers, so the cause of their misery was not seen as local but rather external, caused by the CGA and foreign market forces against which the colonial state had failed to protect them. The Pemba peasantry was therefore much more responsive to the non-racial nationalist programme of the ZNP and later the Zanzibar and Pemba People's Party (ZPPP) which was formed when the Pemba section broke away from the ASP.

The breakaway of the ZPPP was to precipitate a fundamental realignment of political forces in Zanzibar during the struggle for independence. The loss of the peasant base in Pemba, except for a small area around Mkoani, rendered hollow the ASP claim to represent the whole African population. On the other hand, the alliance between the property-owning peasantry in the ZPPP and the landowning section in the ZNP began to tilt the balance within the ZNP towards the right. This alienated the left wing which was associated with the small proletarian section and the youth. On the eve of independence, the left found its position in the party no longer tenable, and it quit to form the Umma Party.

This second split completed the polarisation of Zanzibar politics, making things extremely volatile as the country approached independence. In the last election under colonialism, the ASP won just over half the total number of votes but failed to win a majority of the parliamentary seats. The ZNP/ZPPP alliance won a majority of the seats with somewhat less than half the votes. Zanzibar was thus split right down the middle. Reactionary racial ideologies and immature class distinctions prevented the rival nationalist movements from realising the supreme need to resolve what was the fundamental contradiction at that moment, namely, the necessity to carry through a national democratic revolution to end imperialist domination. In this situation, a group with virtually no social base in Zanzibar provided the spark that ignited a violent convulsion. The focus of the struggle was suddenly shifted from the immediate task of national liberation towards a different goal of resolving other contradictions among the people. The two stages could not be combined because the 'Hundred Day Revolution'[12] lacked a mature class base to carry them through.

The left in the Umma Party and in the ASP tried to guide the revolution along classical socialist lines by snatching power from lumpen elements, but within a matter of months the left was outmanoeuvred, dispersed and eliminated. The Umma Party, which saw itself as a vanguard socialist party, had superb organisational skills but lacked a mass base, so it tried to use ASP's popular support to establish itself as a leading political force. However, leadership in the Umma Party was soon at daggers drawn: those who felt that the revolution had accomplished all of the primary objectives – they became part and parcel of the new regime – were opposed by those who thought the uprising of January 12 was only a beginning. Inexplicably for a revolutionary socialist party, the whole leadership allowed itself to be persuaded to dissolve the party and merge with the unreformed ASP which they had previously criticised so bitterly. It tried to combine with the left wing of the ASP, centred around Vice-President Kassim Hanga, to corner the demoralised and ideologically confused petty-bourgeois leadership of the party and force it to adopt a series of spectacular measures to give the regime a pronounced radical posture. Zanzibar was declared a one-party state and the other parties were suppressed. Diplomatic relations with the socialist countries were established and the American ambassador was sent packing. From afar, Zanzibar appeared for a time to be on a revolutionary path.

Although the petty-bourgeois leadership was cornered, it still had the support of the ASP masses and it was able to regroup under the protection of a contingent of Tanganyikan police that was sent to the islands. Taking advantage of the absence of the Umma Party leader, Abdulrehman Babu, Zanzibar President Karume and Tanganyika President Nyerere rushed through a union between their two countries with little prior consultation. This consolidated the position of Karume and his supporters and cut the ground from under the feet of the leftists who were then sent outside Zanzibar, dispersed to ministerial positions on the mainland and diplomatic posts overseas. Those who challenged the supremacy of the now dominant faction in Zanzibar were systematically eliminated, whether they were of the left or the right. As the regime secured its hold, it moved to eliminate other organs of potential opposition. The rival trade union federations of the pre-1963 period which had been merged to form the Federation of Revolutionary Trade Unions, as well as the ASP Youth League and the Women's Union, were dissolved. Nothing was left to stand in the way of the populist autocracy.

Notes

1. See Chapter 4.
2. J.E. Flint, 'Zanzibar, 1890—1950', in V. Harlow and E.H. Chilver, eds, *History of East Africa*, Vol. 2, Oxford, Clarendon Press, 1965, pp. 542—3.
3. F.J. Cooper, *From Slaves to Squatters: Plantation Labor and Agriculture in Zanzibar and Coastal Kenya, 1890—1925*, New Haven, Yale University Press, 1980, p. 57.
4. See Chapter 1.
5. Flint, *op. cit.*, p. 655.
6. G.D. Kirsopp, *Memorandum on Certain Aspects of the Zanzibar Clove Industry*, London, Waterlow & Sons Ltd., 1926, p. 32.
7. *Ibid.*, p. 7.
8. Cooper, *op,. cit.*, p. 42.
9. B.H. Binder, *Report on the Zanzibar Clove Industry*, Zanzibar, Government Printer, 1936, pp. 31—2.
10. See Chapter 3.
11. M.F. Lofchie, *Zanzibar: Background to Revolution*, Princeton, Princeton University Press, 1965, *passim*.
12. So termed by A.M. Babu, 'Whither the Revolution?', *Africa Events*, March/ April 1988.

Bibliography

Archival sources
Zanzibar Archives

1. Residency
Files B 41 & 48; CC 1; E 1; F 8; G 3, 8 & 13

2. Secretariat
Files 10,543; 10,680; 10,770; 11,456; 12,413; 13,454; 13,831; 14,348; 14,354; 14,470; 14,732; 16,217

3. Inward and Outward Miscellaneous Dispatches

4. Clove Growers' Association
General Files
Clove Bonus Scheme Registers
General Statistics of Zanzibar Protectorate and Clove Growers' Association

5. Monthly and Annual Reports
Annual Report, Mkoani, 1933
Annual Reports, Pemba District, 1926, 1934, 1937–1945
Annual Report, Rural District of Zanzibar, 1950
Annual Reports, Zanzibar District, 1926, 1931–1943, 1946
Annual Report, Zanzibar Province, 1931
Monthly Reports, Zanzibar District, 1936–1944, 1950–1951

6. Other Reports
Addis, W., 'Review on the System of Land Tenure in the Island of Pemba', Zanzibar, 1934
McCarthy, D.D., 'Report of the Zanzibar Research Unit, June 1934 – September 1937', 1941
Wilson, F.B., 'Notes on Peasant Agriculture and Industries in Zanzibar Island', 1939

Bibliography

Zanzibar Ministry of Agriculture

1. Department of Agriculture
File: 'Coconut Industry — General'
File: 'Coir Fibre'
File: 'Pottery Industry'
General File No. 143

2. Land Distribution Section
File No. 2, 1973

Public Record Office (Kew, Surrey, U.K.)

1. Colonial Office
CO 618 (Zanzibar)
CO 648
CO 689 (Government Gazette)

2. Foreign Office
FO 84 (Slave Trade)

Archives Nationales: Section Outre-Mer (Aix-en-Provence, France)

'Ocean Indien': File 2/10 'Pemba'

Unpublished sources

Akinola, G.A., 'The Sultanate of Zanzibar, 1870–1890', Ph.D. dissertation, University of London, 1973

Batson, E., 'The Social Survey of Zanzibar', 21 volumes, (for the years 1957–1961), Department of Social Studies, University of Cape Town

Bernstein, H., 'Capital and Peasantry in the Epoch of Imperialism', Economic Research Bureau Seminar Paper, University of Dar es Salaam, November 1976

Bernstein, H., and J. Depelchin, 'A Materialist History', History Seminar Paper, University of Dar es Salaam, 1977

Cooper, F., 'Plantation Slavery on the East Coast of Africa in the 19th Century', Ph.D. dissertation, Yale University, 1974

Jabir, M.H., 'The Plantation Economy During the Protectorate Period in Zanzibar', a dissertation submitted in partial fulfillment of the requirements of the degree of Master of Arts in the University of Dar es Salaam, 1977

Mose, A., 'Die herrschende Feudalklasse Sanzibars und die kapitalistischen Kolonial machte', Dissertation zur Promotion A,

Bibliography

Karl Marx Universität, Leipzig, 1974

Nabudere, D.W., 'Imperialism, the National Question and the Politics of Class Formation in Uganda: a critical review of M. Mamdani's *Politics and Class Formation in Uganda*', mimeo, University of Dar es Salaam, January 31, 1977

Sakkarai, L., 'Indian Merchants in East Africa', mimeograph, 1976

Sheriff, A.M.H., 'The Rise of a Commercial Empire: An Aspect of the Economic History of Zanzibar, 1770–1873', Ph.D. dissertation, University of London, 1971

Official publications

Afro-Shirazi Party, *Afro-Shirazi Party: A Liberation Movement,* Zanzibar, Printing Press Corporation, 1973

— *The Afro-Shirazi Party Revolution, 1964–1974,* Zanzibar, Afro-Shirazi Party, 1974

Bartlett, C.A., *Statistics of the Zanzibar Protectorate, 1895-1935,* Zanzibar, Government Printer, 1936

Bartlett, C.A., and J.S. Last, *Report on the Indebtedness of the Agricultural Classes, 1933,* Zanzibar, Government Printer, 1934

Batson, E., *Report on Proposals for a Social Survey of Zanzibar, 1946,* Zanzibar, Government Printer, 1948

Binder, B.H., *Report on the Zanzibar Clove Industry,* Zanzibar, Government Printer, 1936

Bonde, C. von, *Report on a Preliminary Survey of the Marine Fisheries of the Zanzibar Protectorate,* Zanzibar, Government Printer, 1929

Clove Growers' Association, *Annual Report of the Clove Growers' Association,* (for the years 1956–1958), Zanzibar, Government Printer

Crofts, R.A., *The Zanzibar Clove Industry: Statement of Government Policy and a Report,* Zanzibar, Government Printer, 1959

Dawson, E.M., *A Note on Agricultural Indebtedness in the Zanzibar Protectorate,* Zanzibar, Government Printer, 1936

Economic Advisory Council, Committee on Nutrition in the Colonial Empire, *First Report — Part 1 — Nutrition in the Colonial Empire,* (Presented to Parliament by Command, July 1939, CMD 6050), London, HMSO, 1939

Gray, J.M., *Report of the Arbitrator to Enquire into a Trade Dispute at the Wharf Area at Zanzibar,* Zanzibar, Government Printer, 1958

— *Report on the Inquiry into Claims to Certain Land at or near Ngezi, Vitongoji, in the Mudiria of Chake Chake, Pemba,* Zanzibar, Government Printer, 1956

Great Britain, Colonial Office, *Annual Report on Zanzibar Protectorate,* (for the years 1908–1912, 1915–1938, 1946–1960), London, HMSO

Bibliography

— *The Colonial Empire (1939—1947), presented by the Secretary of State for the Colonies to Parliament, July 1947*, London, HMSO, 1947

Great Britain, Diplomatic and Consular Reports, *Report of the Trade and Commerce of Zanzibar*, (for the years 1900—1912), London, HMSO

Kerr, A.J., *Report on an Investigation into the Possibilities of Cooperative Development in the Zanzibar Protectorate and Ancillary Subjects*, Zanzibar, Government Printer, 1950

Kirkham, V.H., *Memorandum on the Functions of a Department of Agriculture with Special Reference to Zanzibar*, Zanzibar, Government Printer, 1931

Kirsopp, G.D., *Memorandum on Certain Aspects of the Zanzibar Clove Industry*, London, Waterlow & Sons Ltd., 1926

Last, J.S., *The Economic Fisheries of Zanzibar, 1928*, Zanzibar, Government Printer, 1929

McGeagh W.R., and W. Addis, *A Review of the System of Land Tenure in the Islands of Zanzibar and Pemba*, Zanzibar, Government Printer, 1945

Middleton, J., *Land Tenure in Zanzibar*, Colonial Research Studies No. 33, London, HMSO, 1961

Pakenham, R.H.W., *Land Tenure Among the Wahadimu at Chwaka, Zanzibar Island*, Zanzibar, Government Printer, 1947

Pim, A., *Report of the Commission Appointed by the Secretary of State for the Colonies to Consider and Report on the Financial Position and Policy of the Zanzibar Government in Relation to its Economic Resources*, London, HMSO, 1932

Sinclair, J.H., *Report on the Zanzibar Protectorate from 1910 to 1923*, Zanzibar, Government Printer, 1923

Strickland, C.F., *Report on Cooperation and Certain Aspects of the Economic Condition of Agriculture in Zanzibar*, London, Crown Agents for the Colonies, 1932

Strickland, C.F., and A. Pim, *Zanzibar, the Land and its Mortgage Debt*, London, Dunstable and Watford, 1932

Troup, R.S., *Report on Clove Cultivation in the Zanzibar Protectorate, 1931*, Zanzibar, Government Printer, 1932

Williams, R.O., *Useful and Ornamental Plants of Zanzibar and Pemba*, Zanzibar, Government Printer, 1949

Zanzibar Government, *Fruits of the Zanzibar Revolution*, Zanzibar, 1965

Zanzibar Protectorate, *A Statement by the British Resident on Constitutional Development in Zanzibar, October 3, 1955*, Zanzibar, Government Printer, 1955

— *Agricultural Production Programme, 1962*, Zanzibar, Government Printer, 1962

— *Annual Report by the Financial Member of the Council*, Zanzibar, Government Printer, 1911

— *Annual Report of the Department of Agriculture*, (for the years 1897—1901, 1921—1960) Zanzibar, Government Printer

Bibliography

- *Annual Report of the Provincial Administration*, (for the years 1937–1960), Zanzibar, Government Printer
- *Annual Report of the Zanzibar Police*, (for the years 1948, 1958), Zanzibar, Government Printer
- *Annual Trade Report of the Zanzibar Protectorate*, (for the years 1925, 1940, 1945, 1948, 1963), Zanzibar, Government Printer
- *Blue Book*, (for the years 1914–1946), Zanzibar, Government Printer
- *Debates of the Legislative Council*, (for the years 1945–1958), Zanzibar, Government Printer
- *Labour Report*, (for the years 1946–1960), Zanzibar, Government Printer
- *Nutritional Review of the Natives of Zanzibar*, Zanzibar, Government Printer, 1937
- *Report of the Commission on Agricultural Indebtedness and Memorandum Thereon*, Zanzibar, Government Printer, 1935
- *Report of the Commission on Agriculture, 1923*, Zanzibar, Government Printer, 1924
- *Report of the Constitutional Commissioner, Zanzibar, 1960*, (Sir Hilary Blood), Zanzibar, Government Printer, 1960
- *Report of the Labour Conciliation Committee appointed on September 2, 1948*, Zanzibar, Government Printer, 1948
- *Report of the Supervisor of Elections on the Elections in Zanzibar, 1957*, Zanzibar, Government Printer, 1958
- *Report of the Supervisor of Elections on the Registration of Voters and the Elections held in January, 1961*, Zanzibar, Government Printer, 1961
- *Report on the Action which is being taken on the First Report – part 1 – of the Committee on Nutrition in the Colonial Empire*, (Cmnd 6050), Zanzibar, Government Printer, 1940
- *Report on the Action which is being taken on Nutrition*, Zanzibar, Government Printer, 1949
- *Report on the Civil Disturbances in Zanzibar on July 30, 1951*, Zanzibar, Government Printer, 1952
- *Report on the Native Census, 1924*, Zanzibar, Government Printer, 1924

Other published sources

Abdurahman, M., 'Anthropological Notes from the Zanzibar Protectorate', *Tanganyika Notes and Records*, 8 (1939)
Agee, P., *Inside the Company: CIA Diary*, New York, Stonehill Publishing Company, 1975
Alpers, E.A., *Ivory and Slaves in East Central Africa: Changing Patterns of International Trade to the later Nineteenth Century*, London, Heinemann, 1975

266

Bibliography

— *East African Slave Trade*, Historical Association of Tanzania Paper No. 3, Nairobi, East African Publishing House, 1967

Amin, S., *Accumulation on a World Scale*, Volume 1, New York, Monthly Review Press, 1974

Anon., 'The 100 days that made Tanzania', *Africa Now*, April, 1984

Babu, A.M., 'Whither the Revolution', *Africa Events*, March/April 1988

Braunthal, J., and A.J. Forrest, eds., *Yearbook of the International Free Trade Union Movement, Vol 2, 1961–1962*, Lincolns–Prager International Yearbook (under the auspices of the ICFTU), 1963

Buell, R.L., *The Native Problem in Africa*, New York, The Macmillan Company, 1928

Burton, R.F., *Zanzibar; City, Island, and Coast*, 2 Vols, London, Tinsley Brothers, 1872, (Johnson Reprint Corporation, 1967)

Clayton, A., *The 1948 Zanzibar General Strike*, Research Report no. 32, Scandinavian Institute of African Studies, Uppsala, 1976

—'The General Strike in Zanzibar, 1948', *Journal of African History*, XVII, 3 (1976)

Cohen, B., 'The CIA and African Trade Unions', in E. Ray, *et. al.*, *Dirty Work 2: The CIA in Africa*, Secaucus, New Jersey, Lyle Stuart Inc., 1979

Cooper, F., *From Slaves to Squatters: Plantation Labor and Agriculture in Zanzibar and Coastal Kenya, 1890–1925*, New Haven, Yale University Press, 1980

Coupland, R., *East Africa and Its Invaders: From the Earliest Times to the Death of Seyyid Said in 1856*, Oxford, Clarendon Press, 1938

—*The Exploitation of East Africa, 1856–1890: The Slave Trade and the Scramble*, London, Faber and Faber, 1939

Craster, J.E.E., *Pemba, the Spice Island of Zanzibar*, London, T. Fisher Unwin, 1913

Crofton, R.H., *A Pageant of the Spice Islands,*, London, John Bale Sons & Danielsson, 1936 ,

Davies, I., *African Trade Unions*, Harmondsworth, Penguin, 1966

Documents relatifs à la répression de la traite des esclaves publiés en exécution des articles LXXXI et suivants de l'Acte général de Bruxelles, (for the years 1895–1901), Bruxelles

Emmanuel, A., *Unequal Exchange*, New York, Monthly Review Press, 1972

Engels, F., 'The peasant question in France and Germany', in K. Marx and F. Engels, *Selected Works*, Vol. III, Moscow, 1973

Farrant, L., *Tippu Tip and the East African Slave Trade*, London, Hamish Hamilton, 1975

Flint, J.E., 'The wider background to partition and colonial occupation', in R. Oliver and G. Mathew, eds., *History of East Africa*,

Vol. 1. Oxford, Clarendon Press, 1963

— 'Zanzibar, 1890–1950', in V. Harlow and E.M. Chilver, eds., *History of East Africa*, Vol. 2, Oxford, Clarendon Press, 1965

Gray, J.M., *History of Zanzibar from the Middle Ages to 1856*, London, Oxford University Press, 1962

Gray, R., and D. Birmingham, *Pre-Colonial African Trade: Essays on Trade in Central and Eastern Africa before 1900*, London, Oxford University Press, 1970

Grazebrook, W., *The Clove of Commerce*, London, Commercial Calculating Company, 1925

Gregory, R.G., *India and East Africa: A History of Race Relations within the British Empire, 1890–1939*, Oxford, Clarendon Press, 1971

Hindess, B., and P. Q. Hirst, *Pre-Capitalist Modes of Production*, London, Routledge & Kegan Paul, 1975

Hollingsworth, L.W., *Zanzibar Under the Foreign Office, 1890-1913*, London, Macmillan and Co., 1953

Iliffe, J. 'The creation of group consciousness among the dock-workers of Dar es Salaam 1929–1950', in R. Sandbrook and R. Cohen, eds., *The Development of an African Working Class*, London, Longman, 1975

Ingrams, W.H., *Zanzibar: Its History and Its People*, London, H.F. & G. Witherby, 1931

Jivanjee, Y.E., *Memorandum on the Report of the Commissioner on Agriculture, 1923*, Poona, Aryabhushan Press, 1924

Kaniki, M.H.Y., ed., *Tanzania Under Colonial Rule*, London, Longman, 1980

Kay, G., *Development and Underdevelopment, a Marxist Analysis*, London, Macmillan, 1975

Kwitney, J., *Endless Enemies: The Making of an Unfriendly World*, New York, Congdon and Weed, Inc., 1983

Lenin, V.I., *The Development of Capitalism in Russia*, Collected Works, Vol. 3, Moscow, Foreign Languages Publishing House, 1956

— *Imperialism, The Highest Stage of Capitalism*, Collected Works, Vol. 22, Moscow, Progress Publishers, 1974

Lofchie, M., *Zanzibar: Background to Revolution*, Princeton NJ Princeton University Press, 1965

Lugard, F.D., *The Rise of Our East African Empire*, Edinburgh and London, Blackwood & Sons, 1893

Luthy, H., 'India and East Africa: Imperial partnership at the end of the First World War', *Journal of Contemporary History*, Vol. 6, No. 2, 1971

Mangat, J.S., *A History of the Asians in East Africa, c 1886 to 1945*, Oxford, Clarendon Press, 1969

Mao Tse-tung, *On Contradictions*, Foreign Languages Press, Peking, 1964

Bibliography

Marx, K., *Capital*, Vol. 1, New York, Vintage Books, 1977
— *Capital*, Vol. III, Moscow, Progress Publishers, 1974
— 'The Class Struggles', in K. Marx and F. Engels, *Selected Works*, Vol. I, Moscow, 1973
— 'The eighteenth Brumaire of Louis Bonaparte', in K. Marx and F. Engels, *Selected Works*, Vol. 1, Moscow, 1973
— *Grundrisse*, Harmondsworth, Penguin Books in association with New Left Review, 1975
Meynaud, J., and Anisse Salah Bey, *Trade Unionism in Africa: a Study of its Growth and Orientation*, London, Methuen, 1967
Moore, E.D., *Ivory: Scourge of Africa*, N.Y., Harper & Brothers, 1931
Nabudere, D.W., *The Political Economy of Imperialism*, Dar es Salaam, Tanzania Publishing House, 1977
Nicholls, C.S., *The Swahili Coast: Politics, Diplomacy and Trade on the East African Littoral, 1798—1856*, London, George Allen & Unwin, 1971
Onimode, B., *An Introduction to Marxist Political Economy*, London, Zed Books, Ltd., 1985
Orde Browne, G. St. J., *The African Labourer*, New York, Barnes & Noble, Inc., 1967 (reprint of 1933 edition)
Pearce, F.B., *Zanzibar, The Island Metropolis of Eastern Africa*, London, T. Fisher Unwin, 1920
Petras, J., and H. Zemelman Merino, *Peasants in Revolt; A Chilean Case Study, 1965—1971*, Austin, University of Texas, 1972
Prins, A.H.J., *The Swahili-Speaking Peoples of Zanzibar and the East African Coast*, London, International African Institute, 1961
Radosh, R., *American Labor and United States Foreign Policy*, New York, Vintage, 1969
Rolleston, I.H.O., 'The Watumbatu of Zanzibar', *Tanganyika Notes and Records*, 8, 1939
Selsam, H., *et al.*, eds, *Dynamics of Social Change: A Reader in Marxist Social Science*, New York, International Publishers, 1970
Sheriff, A., *Slaves, Spices and Ivory in Zanzibar: Economic Integration of East Africa into the World Economy*, London, James Currey, 1987
Shivji, I.G., 'Working class struggles and organisation in Tanzania, 1939—1975', *Mawazo*, Vol. 5, No. 2, December 1983
Singh, M., *History of Kenya's Trade Union Movement to 1952*, Nairobi, East African Publishing House, 1969
Standard Bank Review, August 1958
Stichter, S., 'Trade unionism in Kenya, 1947—1952: the militant phase', in P.C.W. Gutkind, R. Cohen, and J. Copans, eds., *African Labour History*, Beverly Hills, Sage, 1978
Tidbury, G.E., *The Clove Tree*, London, Lockwood & Son, 1949
United States Department of Labor, Bureau of Labor Statistics, *Directory of Labor Organizations: Africa*, Washington DC, US

Bibliography

Government Printing Office, 1962

Ward, B.E., 'Cash or credit crops? An examination of some implications of peasant commercial production with special reference to the multiplicity of traders and middlemen', in J.M. Potter, *et. al.*, eds, *Peasant Society; A Reader*, Boston, Little Brown, 1967

Woddis, J., *Africa, The Lion Awakes*, London, Lawrence & Wishart, 1961

World Marxist Review, Vol. 20, No. 8, August 1977

Zanzibar Nationalist Party, *Whither Zanzibar? The Growth and Policy of Zanzibar Nationalism*, Political Education Pamphlet No. 2, Cairo, ZNP, 1960.

Index

Abbas, Maalim Zam-Ali, 224
Accra Conference (*see* All-African People's Conference)
Accra Joint Statement, 230-1
adoption, 194-5
Adulteration of Produce Decree, 181
Africa, Southern, 227
African Association, 93, 100, 134; formation of Afro-Shirazi Party, 225, 258
African Trade Union Conference, 209
African Wharfage Company, 91, 191, 202
Africans, mainland, 92, 93, 255; and Afro--Shirazi Party, 100, 101; and overthrow of government, 104; description of 192-4; plantation workers, 30, 40; relations with indigenous workers, 92; slaves, 12; small-holders, 155
Afro-Asian People's Solidarity Organisation, 227
Afro-Shirazi Party, alliance with Umma Party, 197; and African Association, 225, 258; and Indian National Association, 230, 232, 256; and mainland Africans, 100, 101; and overthrow of government, 104; and racialism, 236; and Shirazi Association, 225, 258; and TANU, 228, 229, 232, 234, 258; and trade unions, 205-6, 210; and Umma Party, 238, 241; and Zanzibar Nationalist Party, 226; formation of, 101, 135, 204, 205, 225-6; left wing of, 260; on food production, 90; organisation of, 258; Pemba, 229, 259; racialism, 259; reactionary nature of, 227, 228; role in 1964 revolution, 239-40; social composition of, 100-101, 229, 230; split in, 231-2, 235; support among squatters, 99; Unguja, 259; united front with Zanzibar Nationalist Party, 228-9, 230-1; Youth League, 240, 261
Agricultural and Allied Workers' Union, 206
Agricultural Produce Export Decree, 181
Agricultural Workers' Union, 206
Airport extension, 94, 135, 257
Akinola, G. A., 12
Algeria, 227
Alidina Visram, 174
Alienation of Land (Restriction and Evidence) Decree (1934), 69, 133, 158, 180
All-African People's Conference, 228-9, 230
All-African Trade Union Federation, 209

All-Zanzibar Journalist Organisation, 210
Americans (*see* United States of America)
Anthrax, 95, 221
Anthrax Revolt (1951) (*see* riots)
Arab Agricultural Advisory Committee, 132
Arab Association, 255; and Legislative Council, 101, 103, 223; and nationalism, 101, 135, 223-4, 257; Arabs, 224; Copra Board boycott, 87
Arabs, *149* ; and 1964 revolution, 241, 243; and Zanzibar Nationalist Party, 99; Arab Association, 224; boycott, 100; British support of, 143-4, 151, 153, 154-60; capitalism, 30; colonisation of Zanzibar, 142-3, 145-6; formation of clove trade, 146; land ownership, 30-2, 86, 129-30, 151-2, 172; nationalism, 92, 101, 223-4, 257, 258; penetration of East Africa, 151; planters, 12, 13, 30-2; racial factors, 255; radicals, 225, 257, 258; rule over Zanzibar, 143-4, 153; slavery, 12, 13, 14-15, 19-20, 25, 143, 146, 150
Asians, 118, 255, 256

Babu, Abdulrehman, 6-7, 260
Babu, Mohammed, 98, 104
Bargash, Khalid b., 251
Bartlett, C. A., 158
Bazaars, *177*
Bei khiyar sales, 130-1
Beit al-Hukm palace, *16, 17*
Beit al-Sahil palace, *16*
Bey, Salah, 198
Biashara (food vendors), 23
Binder, H. H., 159
Blacksmithing, 114
Blood, Sir Hilary, 210, 226
Boat Builders' Union, 206
boatmen, 191
Bombay, as mercantile centre, 164; Government, 165; High Court, 174
borrowing system (*see Kopa* system)
Boustead Brothers, 16
boycotts, 207; Arab, 100; clove trade, 6, 69, 69, 84, 133, 159, 182
British (*see* Great Britain)
British Agency, 165
British Resident, and strikes, 92; announces self-government, 103; licensing authority, 159, 181; salary, 64

271

Index

Brown, Irving, 228
Bububu, 63, 124
Building and Construction Workers' Union, 206
building industry (see construction industry)
Burre system (free land), 118
Busaidi Sultanate, and British imperialism, 6; and free labourers, 188; and Great Britain, 170-1, 250-1; and Indian merchants, 164-5; and Mwinyi Mkuu, 117; and taxation, 165; Egyptian invasion threat, 170; succession crisis (1859), 168; support by British, 168 (see also Sultans)
buses, 124
Bushland (see Uwanda)

cacao (see cocoa)
Cameron, Donald, 162n
capitalism, and abolition of slavery, 143; and clove trade, 150; and peasantry, 109-11, 123; and pre-capitalism, 142; and racism, 145; Arabs, 30; colonial, 4, 12, 36-78, 171; dominance in production, 19-20; expansion of surplus value, 44-5; labour as a commodity, 44; merchant capital, 163-87; reinvestment of profits, 68
caravan trade, 27, 40, 164
cassava, as replacement for rice, 71-2, 90-1; subsistence on, 125
cattle, 93-5
Cattle Riot (1951) (see Riots)
Central African Federation, 227
Chaani, 229
Chepe (foreman), 190
China, 208, 227, 243
Chiume, Kanyama, 229
Chou en Lai, 243
Chukuzi (Customs coolies), 23
CIA (see United States of America)
civil servants, 64, 65
classes, social, 2, 249-50; and colonial state, 4-5; and labour, 234; and nationalism, 205; and race, 7, 12-13, 132, 144-5; class struggle, 197, 254-61; transitional phase. 250-4
Clove Bonus Registers, 139n
Clove Bonus Scheme, and Clove Growers' Association, 132; and moneylenders, 179; and smallholders, 129; institution of (1922), 128, 157-8
Clove Exporters Decree (1934), 69, 133, 159, 181
Clove Growers' Association, 253; and Clove Bonus Scheme, 132; and Shirazi Association, 134; exploitative role of, 4; export strategy, 97; formation of, 132, 158, 179; monopoly of, 84-5, 159, 181; pricing control, 183; role as moneylender, 96; role in stimulating consumption, 175; transport of cloves, 123-4
Clove Growers Association Decree (1934) 69, 133, 181
Clove Purchasing and Exportation Decree (1937), 69, 159
clove trade, 190; accidents, 81-2; and

capitalism, 150; and underdevelopment, 89-91; and World War II, 183; basis of Zanzibar economy, 4; boycotts, 6, 69, 84, 133, 159, 182; colonial policy, 251; compared with ivory trade, 150; Depression, 50, 253; division of labour, 57-9; dominance of, 79-80; export licences, 181; exports, 38-9, 41-4, 52, 96, 133, 181, 183, 221; fall in demand, 96-7; formation of, 146; freelance workers, 121; grading, 69, 181; half-and-half system, 128; imported labour, 172, industrial cloves, 43; introduction of, 14, 18, 112, 185n; Kopa system, 121; labour contract system, 91, 120-1; labour force, 52-3, 81, 250, 252, 253; landowners, 80-1; 252-3; Mahonda, 129; marketing, 158-9, 181-2; merchants, 175, 179-80; migrant labour system, 80; Mpemba, 129; peasant labour, 252, 253-4; Pemba, 133, 254; picking, 29, 47-8, 50-2, 57, 80, 81-3, 121-2, 147; piece-work system, 4, 27, 47-55, 82-3, 121; plantation ownership pattern, 80-1, 130; production (post-1897), 38-40; replanting scheme, 39; role of Clove Growers' Association, 96; role of Indian merchants, 179-80; sharecropping, 119; slaves, 117-18, 148, 152, 251-2; smallholdings, 68-9, 127-31, 155, 159; squatters, 36, 39-40, 98-9, 118, 192, 252; state intervention, 83-4; state marketing monopoly, 135-6; state revenues from, 62-4, stemming, 148, taxation, 20, 32, 35n, 60, 84, 172, 173, 253; transportation, 123-4; wage differentials, 53, 57-9; wages, 47-59, 82-3, 97-8, 132; weeding, 48-50, 57, 80; weighing, 148; workers' living conditions, 82; working conditions, 29 (see also peasantry, smallholdings)
coal trade, 23
cocoa growing, 79, 84
coconut oil manufacturing, 196
coconuts, 4, 28, 125, 149 (see also coir rope industry; copra trade)
coffee growing, 87
coir rope industry, 126
Colonial Development and Welfare Act (1940), 199
Colonial Labour Advisory Committee, 200
Colonial Office (see Great Britain)
colonialism, and capitalism, 4, 12, 36-78; and class oppression, 67; and Sultans, 166; and trade unions, 197; and Zanzibar Nationalist Party, 236; dissolution-conservation theory, 141-2 (see also Great Britain)
Commission on Agricultural Indebtedness, 158
Commission on Agriculture, 39, 68, 154-5
commodities, consumption, domestic, 60-1; definition of, 2-3, 44
Concubines (see Masuria)
Congress Working Committee (see India)
Constitution, Lancaster House, 237, 239; revolutionary, 242

Index

Index

Index

Labour Officer, 201-2, 204
Labour Reports, (1946), 201; (1948), 194; (1954), 204; (1955), 189; (1957), 207; (1958), 195
labourers, day (*see vibarua*)
Lancaster House, 237, 239
land, airport extension, 94, 135, 257; Arab ownership, 151-2, 172; bushland (*see Uwanda*); control of by Indians, 173; coral country (*see Uwanda*); family building site (*see kiambo*), fertility, 80; free land system (*see Burre* system), grazing, 93-4; reform, 135; state acquisition of, 94; state limits on transfer of, 69; transfer, 131-2, 133, 158, 180
Land Alienation Board, 134
Land Alienation Decree (1939), 69
Land Protection (Debt Settlement) Decree (1938), 69
landlord class, 141-4, 160; and colonial policy, 5, 17, 143-4, 157-60, 253; decline of, 152-4, 249; origin of, 145-52; role in colonial era, 5
Landowners, 126-7; clove trade, 80-1, 252-3; competition with merchants, 86-7; indebtedness, 126-7, 128, 154-7, 172, 252-3
Last, J. S., 158
Legislative Council, 82, 182, 256; and Arab Association, 101, 103, 223; and copra trade, 86-7
Lemky, Ahmed, 223
Lenin, V. I., 110, 142
lime (building material) industry, 126
Lofchie, M. F., 257
lorries, *65*
Lyne, R. N., 47

Madagascar, 160, 183
Mahonda plantation, 129
mainland Africans (*see* Africans, mainland)
Makunduchi, 126
makuti huts, *113*
Malawi, 229
Malindi harbour, *65*
Malindi, 33n
malnutrition (*see* nutrition)
'Manga' shopkeepers, 101
Mangrove poles, 125
manufacturing industry, 195-6
Manyema dance, *194*
Maritime and Allied Workers' Union, 206
markets, *176*
Marx, Karl, on commodity, 2-3; on history, 11; on merchant capital, 163; on piece-work, 46; on proletarianisation of peasants, 46; on slavery and free labour, 37; on West Indian slavery, 21
Masheha (headmen), 119, 120
Masters and Servants Decree (1925), 41, 121
Masuria (concubines), 24, 195
Mathews, General, 151
Mathews, Sir Lloyd, 25, 47, 211n
Mau Mau, 226
Mazizini, 94
Mboya, Tom, 209, 227
Memorandum on Certain Aspects of the Zanzibar Clove Industry (Kirsopp), 40
merchants, 256; and British, 164, 165-72, 174; and colonial state, 4; and slave owners, 68; as agents of industrial capital, 6; capital repatriation, 169; clove trade, 175, 179-80; competition with landowners, 86-7; control of commerce, 164-5; domestic servants, 195; Indians, 12, 13, *13*, 30, 86, 164-5, 168, 170, 178-80; influence on peasantry, 123; involvement in slave trade, 170; loss of power, 165-8; re-exports, 60, 61; re-investment of profits, 68; source of profits, 172; state limitations on economic power, 69-70
Merikani (*see* cotton trade)
Merino, H. Z., 135
Meynaud, Jean, 198
Micheweni, 125
Ministry of Food (*see* Great Britain)
Mkoani, 131, 259
Mnazi Mmoja grounds, *94*
Mohammed bin Sayed (*see* Tippu Tip)
Mombasa, 33n
Moneylenders Decree (1934), 133
moneylending, 83, 130-1; and Arab landlords, 30, 31, 143, 144, 152; and Clove Bonus Scheme, 179; Clove Growers Association, 96; Indians, 30, 31, 143, 152, 158, 159, 173; state intervention, 183, 253
Moresby Treaty (1822), 184n
Morogoro, 2
Mose, A., 20
Mozambique, 184n, 192
Mpemba, 129
Msewe dance, *193*
Muhsin, Ali, 225
Muscat and Oman, 14, 142-3, 164, 223
Muslim Association, 256
Mvyale, 116
Mwinyi Mkuu, 116-17, 146
Mzanzibari, 224

Nabudare, D., 12
Nasib, Jamal Ramadhani, 206-7
National Assembly, *103*
National Labour Committee, 210
National Party of the Subjects of the Sultan of Zanzibar, 95; 222-3, 256, 257; organisation of, 258 (*see also* Zanzibar Nationalist Movement)
National Unity Movement, 222
nationalism, and social class, 205; and trade unions, 205; and Zanzibar Nationalist Party, 99-100; Arab Association, 101, 135, 223-4, 257; Arabs, 92, 101, 223-4, 257, 258; beginnings of, 224; landlords, 144; mainland Africa, 203-4; suppression of, 101
Native Labour Control Decree, 40
Ngalawas (outriggers), 114, *115*
Ngambo, 81, 88-9, 93, *191*
Nkrumah, Kwame, 226, 228, 229
Nungwi, 126
nutrition, 70-2, 125; during Depression, 70-1, 72; peasantry, 70-2; (*see also* food)
Nutritional Review of the Natives of Zanzibar (1937), 70-1

275

Index

Index

Sheriff, Adbul M. H., 146

Shimba, 27

shipbuilding, 114

Shirazi, 11, 134, 255

Shirazi Association, 257; and contract system, 121; conflict with African Association, 100; connection with Iran, 93; formation of, 134; formation of Afro-Shirazi Party, 225, 258; Unguja, 135

shopkeeping, 175 (see also 'Manga' shopkeepers

Sidhwa, Rustam, 232

'Siku Kuu' (Eid) fair, 94

slave trade, abolition of (1873), 3, 13, 15, 17, 117, 185n, 250; Arabs, 12, 13, 14-15, 19-20, 25, 143, 146, 150; British toleration of, 167; export of slaves, 166-7; involvement of merchants in, 170; Select Committee on the Slave Trade (1871), 170

slavery, abolition of (1897), 4, 15, 17, 21-4, 117, 153-4, 250; abolition and the labour supply, 21, 24-8, 160, 188-9, 253; and Islam, 19, 33n; closure of slave market, 169; clove trade, 117-18, 148, 152, 251-2; East Africa compared with USA, 19; four-three system, 28-9; growth of subsistence system, 118; Indian, 34n; mainland Africans, 12; Pemba, 25; slave categories, 23-4; slave owners and merchants, 68; transition to capitalism, 3-4; transition to free labour, 21, 22-8, 37-8

smallholdings, 31 (see also clove trade; peasantry, Africans, mainland)

Smee, Captain Thomas, 164, 184n

Smith Mackenzie & Co., 16, 178

soap manufacture, 196

socialism, 245-6

Socotra, 184n

Sofala, 184n

South Yemen, 243

Soviet Union, 208

Special Branch, 103

Special Constabulary, 95

squatters (see clove trade; labour)

Stanley, H. M., 27

Sterling, exchange value of, 85 (see also currency standardisation)

stevedores, 191, 254

Stichter, Sharon, 201

Strickland, C. F., 156

strikes, 197, 199; dhow workers, 209; dockworkers, 6, 199; general, 4, 91-2, 95, 202-3; wachukuzi, 200, 201, 203

sultans, amity and commerce treaties, 15, 150; British military assistance, 151; cooperation with colonialism, 166; erosion of power of, 16-17, introduction of Indian rupee, 37; move to Zanzibar, 146, 165; peasants' support of, 223; salary, 64 (see also Busaidi Sultanate)

surplus value, concept of, 44-5, 55-7, 59-60, 62-3

Swahili, 1, 164, 193

sweet potatoes, 125

Tanganyika, 227; army mutiny, 244; as German Protectorate, 171; dockworkers, 196; general strike, 202; immigrant labour from, 88-9, 192, 252; police 95-6, 242, 260; trade unions, 206, 209; union with Zanzibar, 244, 260 (see also Tanzania)

Tanganyika Federation of Labour, 206

tannin industry, 125-6

TANU, 227; and Afro-Shirazi Party, 228, 229, 232, 234, 258; formation of, 206

Tanzania, 2 (see also Tanganyika)

taxation, 120; Busaidi Sultanate, 165; clove trade, 20, 32, 35n, 60, 84, 172, 173, 253; exports 20, 60, 84; hut tax, 40, 120, 128; imports, 180, 183; jizia rent, 192; poll tax, 117; reimposition of import levies, 180 (see also customs revenue)

Tippu Tip, 169

tobacco growing, 84

Topan, Tharia, 169, 170, 178

Trade Union Decrees (1931), 198, 199, 200; (1941), 199; (1958), 210

trade unions, 97, 98, 197; and nationalisation, 205; and political parties, 205-6, 210; and World War II, 197, 208; casual labourers, 189; colonial policy towards, 6, 198-200, 201-2, 204, 207, 254; evolution of, 205-10; federation, 209-10; Kenya, 209, 227; legislation, 197-9, 200, 201-2; list of independent unions, 219; list of registered unions, 215-17; Tanganyika, 206, 209; Uganda, 209; Wachukuzi, 201

Trades Union Council, 200, 207

Transport and Allied Workers' Union, 206

transportation system, 123-5, 189-90

Travancore, 71-2

Tsetse fly, 94, 95

Tumbatu, inter-island transport, 123; peasants, 98; sheha, 116; wages, 98

ubani (incense), 113

Uganda, army mutiny, 244; immigrant labour from, 192; trade unions, 209

Umba district, 27

Umma Party, 6, 104; and Afro-Shirazi Party, 238, 241; and 1964 revolution, 238-46; foreign relations, 241-2, 243; formation of, 197, 210, 237-8, 259; left wing of, 260; proscription of, 238

UNCTAD Conference (1964), 242

Unguja Island, 1; and Afro-Shirazi Party, 259; and Legislative Council, 86; clove pickers, 81; geographical zones, 112; Hadimu (see Hadimu); land fertility, 80; lime (building material), industry, 126; peasant riots, 93-6; peasant smallholdings, 129; peasants, 80; political organisation, 134-5, 233-4; schools, 87; Shirazi Association, 135; squatters, 98-9; Tumbatu (see Tumbatu); villages, 113

Unguja & Pemba Transport Workers' Union, 206

Union of Tanganyika and Zanzibar, 244, 260

unions (see trade unions)

United Agriculturalists' Organisation, 202

United States of America, CIA, 208, 209, 228;

277

Index